EAVAN BOLAND
INSIDE HISTORY

Eavan Boland, 1980s
(Arlen House Archive)

Siobhan Campbell and Nessa O'Mahony
Editors

EAVAN BOLAND
INSIDE HISTORY

ARLEN
HOUSE

EAVAN BOLAND: INSIDE HISTORY

is published in 2017 by
ARLEN HOUSE
42 Grange Abbey Road
Baldoyle
Dublin 13
Ireland
Phone: +353 86 8207617
Email: arlenhouse@gmail.com

978–1–85132–140–7, paperback
978–1–85132–150–6, hardback

International distribution by
SYRACUSE UNIVERSITY PRESS
621 Skytop Road, Suite 110
Syracuse, New York
USA 13244–5290
Phone: 315–443–5534/Fax: 315–443–5545
Email: supress@syr.edu
www.syracuseuniversitypress.syr.edu

Typesetting by Arlen House

Cover Artwork: 'Fake New World' by Diana Copperwhite
oil on canvas, 100 x 100 cm, 2015
Photograph by Gillian Buckley
Image courtesy of the artist and Kevin Kavanagh Gallery

Eavan Boland: Inside History has
received financial assistance from
the Arts Council under the
Publications/Title by Title Scheme

CONTENTS

EAVAN BOLAND
INSIDE HISTORY

FOREWORD

Mary Robinson

I am honoured to provide the foreword to this book, *Eavan Boland: Inside History*. I won't, however, attempt to add to the assessments of Eavan's poetry. Her work has been richly covered and commented on in this book. Instead, I would like to reflect briefly on the extraordinary friendship Eavan and I have shared, and the influence it has had on me in my own work.

I use the term 'extraordinary' because the friendship is very deep, and even though we don't meet for months – or sometimes even years – we resume our warm conversation as though we had been parted only for a day. At this stage we usually swap photos of grandchildren, but we also find ways to convey how much we have thought about the other in the interim.

Eavan and I met as students in Trinity in the 1960s. There was an immediate connection and we began meeting for endless cups of coffee in Trinity itself or on Grafton Street. Eavan had already had her first poems published, and was aware that she would be a writer. I was as eager to hear her talk about poetry as she was to understand my interest in law.

Sometime later, when I was practicing as a barrister in Dublin, serving in the Irish Senate and teaching Law in Trinity, Eavan called to tell me she was on her way to a meeting of the Irish Women's Liberation Movement. She needed me to give her 'seven laws that discriminate against women'.

'Why seven?' I asked. 'I could give you more'.

'Seven is a good number and about all I would be able to remember!' she replied.

At a more profound level, I realised that Eavan was instilling in me a deep belief in the need for us to look at civic life and an imaginative life as inseparable. I had seen enough in my own work and study to know how deprived law or language, indeed life itself, could be if it was cut off from imagination.

When I became President some of my best days happened as I visited small towns, as I was privileged to look closely at projects a community had spent a great deal of time on. Maybe it was the opening of a new hall or the launch of a small business initiative or an arts centre. Whatever it was, I knew those events had happened not just because of a community project, but because those involved honoured the imagination they all shared – and needed to share – to bring their task to fruition.

Eavan and I shared that sense of the importance of imagination from the very beginning of our friendship. Decades after our first meeting in the coffee shop in Trinity, when my inauguration was being planned I chose a line from her poem, 'The Singers', to quote in my inaugural speech. It is about the sean-nós singers of the west of Ireland. The poem tells us they live on 'an unrelenting coast'. Nevertheless the very dangers and challenges they face are inseparable from the music they make. And so they are strengthened by a 'true measure of rejoicing' – and the last line was the one I chose to insert as follows:

> As a woman, I want women who have felt themselves outside history to be written back into history, in the words of Eavan Boland 'finding a voice where they found a vision'.

In Ireland we're fortunate to live in a country where voice and vision so often come together. It so happens that I have had a poet as a close friend since we were very young. But as a people, in a broader sense, we also have had a strong friendship with poetry, and as a nation our poets have looked to public service as an integral part of our identity. These are connections I treasure. And they are connections we need to cherish so as to hand them on to be part of our future, just as they are part of our past.

INTRODUCTION

Siobhan Campbell and Nessa O'Mahony

Eavan Boland's presence as poet, critic and teacher has been of major importance for generations of writers and the occasion of her seventieth birthday in 2014 prompted a surge of interest in the work of this leading Irish poet. Symposiums and public discussions were held and a number of celebratory and critical publications appeared with the aim of bringing a new focus to the writer and her work. No reading of contemporary poetry in English would be complete without taking full account of Boland's oeuvre and this collection is intended to offer a reappraisal of Boland's influence as a poet and critic in the twenty-first century. This book seeks to critically re-encounter the work, offering essays, interviews and creative responses. To do so it brings together writers and thinkers from Ireland and the UK, from Europe and the USA to address the tropes, themes and craft of Boland's work in varied and surprising ways. The thrust of this volume is to read the poetry of Boland anew. The book thus attempts to reposition Boland scholarship, offering new ways forward with a focus on the most important aspect: the poems themselves.

Eavan Boland is always considered an Irish poet, though she has made much of her professional and poetic career in the US. Boland's work is characterised by the art of making the personal understood as political. She is known for a distinctive expression of the realities of family life as well as for subverting ideas of nationhood and of the place of the poet in relation to tradition. Re-readings of history and mythology are animated by a keen awareness of the dangers of inherited myth and stereotype while her explorations of married love are paired with a fierce critique of the idea of 'love poetry' in the canon.

Boland is the recipient of the Lannan Award for Poetry and an American-Ireland Fund Literary Award. She is represented in the major anthologies of poetry from both sides of the Atlantic including *The Norton Anthology of Poetry* (Norton, 1998), *Americans' Favorite Poems* (Norton, 1999), *The Norton Anthology of English Literature* (Norton 1999), *The Body Electric: America's Best Poetry from the American Poetry Review* (Norton, 2000), *The Longman Anthology of British Literature: The Twentieth Century* (2002) as well as in *The Faber Anthology of Irish Verse, The Penguin Anthology of Irish Verse* and the *Pan Anthology of Irish Verse.*

Boland has taught or been a visiting professor at Trinity College, Dublin; the School of Irish Studies, Dublin; University College, Dublin; Bowdoin College, Maine and the University of Utah. Currently she holds the Bella Mabury and Eloise Mabury Knapp Professorship in Humanities and is Director of the Creative Writing Program at Stanford University, California where she previously held the Melvin and Bill Lane chair. She has also been Hurst Professor at Washington University and Regent's Lecturer at the University of Santa Barbara. She has served on the board of the Irish Arts Council and was also a member of the Irish Academy of Letters. She is also a member of the advisory board of the International Writers Centre at Washington University.

The daughter of Frederick Boland, a diplomat, and Frances Kelly, a noted artist, Eavan Boland was born in Dublin in 1944. She spent part of her childhood in London and in New York, later studying at Trinity College, Dublin. Her first two collections, *23 Poems* (1962) and *Autumn Essay* (1963) were published before she was twenty years of age. Even as a young poet, Boland was acutely aware that the act of writing takes place within a constructed and possibly constrictive environment. In *Object Lessons*, she writes, 'I began to write in an enclosed self-confident literary culture'.[1] It would become part of her life's work to open up that literary culture, sifting it with feminist ideas as well as with her revision of the 'proper' subjects of the poem and consequently rendering it less enclosed and more aware of its own contingencies.

A strong supporter of how the poetry workshop can democratise literary access, Boland is known for her encouragement of early-stage poets and for her generosity as a teacher. Her essay 'In Defence of Workshops'[2] defends the creative writing workshop as a place which could subvert the literary establishment's refusal to give 'societal permission to be a poet'. Her work to almost single-handedly open up possibilities for poets in terms of subject matter and approach is noted by many critics including Fiona Sampson in a review of *Domestic Violence*: 'her highly-articulated *ars poetica* has already remapped the territory of contemporary poetry'.[3]

Throughout her career, Boland has articulated her own project in individual essays and prose collections. Jody Allen Randolph, a contributor to this volume, has written of these works: 'Boland makes a complex ethical argument about the history of a set of image systems in poetry'.[4] Boland herself states:

> The poet's vocation – or, more precisely the historical construction put upon it – is one of the single, most problematic areas for any woman who comes to the craft. Not only has it been defined by a tradition which could never foresee her, but it is constructed by men, about men in ways which are poignant, compelling and exclusive.[5]

In 1995, *Collected Poems* appeared from Carcanet, allowing readers access to the early collections, including work originally published by Arlen House in the 1980s as well as the Carcanet volumes. Seen in total, it was clear that a systematic experimentation with form, theme and language was well underway.

The exploration of cultural identities continues in *The Lost Land* (1998) while the interrogation of the poetic tradition is a key focus of *Against Love Poetry* (2001) published as *Code* in the UK. Reviewing in *Times Literary Supplement*, Clair Wills noted that:

> Boland is a master at reading history in the configurations of landscape, at seeing space as the registration of time. If only we know how to look, there are means of deciphering the hidden, fragmentary messages from the past, of recovering lives from history's enigmatic scramblings.[6]

The New Yorker had been publishing the work of Boland under the poetry editor Alice Quinn for fourteen years by 2001. In an interview on the publication of *Against Love Poetry*, Boland and Quinn discuss the poems as written against the tradition of love poetry in the poetic canon. Boland says:

> Love poetry from the troubadours on is traditionally about that romantic lyric moment. There's little about the ordinariness of love, the dailiness of love, or the steadfastness of love. John Donne is, to my mind, the most beautiful poet of marriage and the stoicisms of love but he is rare.[7]

This interview also gives a sense of how the dual traditions of Irish and American poetry have intertwined for Boland as she says:

> I have always loved American poetry, and I think it's very coherent and consistent for an Irish poet to love it. First of all, there is a much higher level of experiment in American poetry. I really do believe you could not have had an Irish Wallace Stevens. That powerful interior world that manages to speak to everybody by just speaking deeply privately seems to me the great treasure of American poetry, whereas you know Irish poetry has had a very strong and fractious struggle with the public voice and the demands of it.[8]

The publication of *New Collected Poems* (2005 in the UK, 2008 in the US) was an opportunity to view the Boland oeuvre anew. Adding one hundred pages to the previous volume of collected work, this book includes selections from the early volumes as well as an excerpt from an unpublished verse play entitled 'Femininity and Freedom'. Elaine Feinstein writing in *Poetry Review* noted that:

> Boland is one of the finest and boldest poets of the last half century ... Looking back from *New Collected Poems*, it becomes clear that the originality lies in her control of language and tone.[9]

Publishers Weekly added, 'Here is the poet who learned from Adrienne Rich, among others, how to tackle big topics of loyalty, rebellion, descent and dissent'.[10] Anne Fogarty, writing in *The Irish Book Review*, agrees that 'Boland's recent volumes have become increasingly spare and honed'. She places Boland at the fulcrum of contemporary poetic endeavour saying:

> *New Collected Poems* acts as a timely reminder of the significance and innovatory force of Boland's achievement ... More vitally, it underscores the vibrancy of her ongoing project as a poet.[11]

In her review of *Domestic Violence*, Boland's tenth full collection published in 2007, Fiona Sampson says:

> She is our pre-eminent poet of experience, evoking that strange nexus where thought, feeling and sense all struggle to contain both the everyday and its extraordinary connotations ... she shows us once again the rare contingency of our world and all that we invest in it.[12]

Boland's next book of prose essays in 2011, *A Journey with Two Maps: Becoming a Woman Poet*, contains a clear critique of the contemporary aesthetic dilemma in poetry which she characterises in the section 'Letter to a Young Woman Poet'. In describing what she calls a 'technical widening and ethical narrowing' Boland laments poetry which has 'shrugged off links with the community' asking 'why should a poet try to reflect in a dislocated language instead of finding a plain and luminous one ...?'[13] As the essays in this volume explore, her attention has always been to continue to develop a poetics to match her deepest intention. As the *Boston Review* says, 'She's a poet of both painterly and worldly engagements, equally attentive to the dance of the intellect and the testimony of the senses'.[14]

This book endeavours to consider the several layered engagements present in Boland's work. Much of her oeuvre is covered, with both Jody Allen Randolph and Patricia Boyle Haberstroh including Boland's latest volume, *A Woman Without a Country* (Carcanet, 2014), a book in which the poems are perhaps seen as acts of preservation in themselves.

The editors hope that this volume will challenge as well as expand upon the existing readings of Boland's work. We are delighted that the book concludes with the conversation that took place between Eavan Boland and Paula Meehan on the stage of the Peacock Theatre, Dublin, on 15 June 2013, and which first appeared in the publication *Eavan Boland: A Poet's Dublin*. Special thanks are extended to Michael Schmidt of Carcanet Press for his support. The themes of identity, geography and tradition raised in that conversation are an appropriately neat synthesis of the various threads raised in earlier essays. Interspersed between the essays are a series of poems selected by the poets because of associations with Eavan Boland. Thomas Kinsella, Medbh McGuckian, Michael Longley, Paula Meehan, Sinead Morrissey, Éilean Ní Chuilleanain, Moya Cannon, Katie Donovan, Dermot Bolger, Nuala Ní Dhomhnaill, Paul Muldoon, John Montague, Jean O'Brien and Nessa O'Mahony have each selected a poem written for Boland, or which resonated with themes to be found in her work.

As editors, we've been delighted to be part of the conversation that this volume continues. It has been a privilege and an honour to work on this collection particularly as we both feel poetically in Eavan Boland's debt, as do many contemporary writers. We want to thank contributors for their swift and generous response to our requests for work and for their graciousness through the editorial process that followed.

We believe that the studies here will set the terms of debate on the work of Eavan Boland for many years to come.

NOTES

1   *Object Lessons: The Life of the Woman and the Poet in Our Time* (Manchester, Carcanet, 1995), p. ix.
2   Paddy Hickson and Jessie Lendennie (eds), *The Salmon Guide to Creative Writing in Ireland* (Galway, Salmon Publishing, 1991).
3   *The Irish Times*, 24 March 2007.
4   *PN Review* 106, Vol. 22, No. 2, Nov-Dec 1995.
5   *Object Lessons*, p. 80.
6   *TLS*, 1 February 2002.
7   *The New Yorker*, 29 October 2001.
8   *Ibid*.
9   *Poetry Review*, 96, 3, 2006.

10   *Publishers Weekly*, 21 Jan 2008.
11   *The Irish Book Review*, 1 March 2005.
12   24 March 2007.
13   from the essay 'Letter to a Young Woman Poet', p. 261.
14   Oct/Nov 1994.

Eileán Ní Chuilleanáin

A SLOW MARCH

Lento, as a threshold wearing down,
as the hesitant writer's hand,
the man with the trombone
stands waiting for the moment, for
the horn solo to finish, for the pause
until he lifts the long slider.

No other tone brings the body
so close, and how does it speak
about distance too? shaping the presence
of a breathing body, the note steady
as the lungs are slowly pushing out air
and the sound travels for miles,

while the girl with the piccolo goes on
waiting her turn, for her five bars,
watching while he plays, her stance
as stiff as the pins holding her hair
flattened in place, gripping it down
– one eye on the score, counting the repeats

– and what harm if these characters
were to wear down to a trace and be lost
like the bump of an old defensive wall?
It would still take longer than
the notes of the trombone
and the piccolo too, fading away.

EAVAN BOLAND:
A HISTORY OF THE POET IN FIVE OBJECTS

Lucy Collins

Eavan Boland's interrogation of Irish national identity and
its problematic intersection with women's lived experience
has been a formative aspect of her work since the
publication of her 1986 collection *The Journey and Other
Poems*. Both in her poetry and her prose writings, Boland
positions the woman poet in Ireland as 'outside history',
struggling to find space within the national tradition for
her historical role and her creative expression. In many of
Boland's poems the representation of the past is mediated
by material objects, emphasising a world of consumption
and exchange into which women must enter. Yet these
objects can be symbolic too; they express the power of the
created object to carry personal and cultural meaning. In
this essay I will explore five objects that feature in Boland's
poetry and consider how these illuminate her thinking on
the relationship between memory and art.

The material past has become an important focus for memory studies, with what Paul Connerton has called 'cultural salvage' a significant dimension of our current engagement with history.[1] These acts of reclamation acknowledge the significance of objects as expressive of dynamics of power and suggest the ways in which specific social patterns may be reflected in material culture. Boland's approach to the past shows an awareness of nuances of class and gender, set within a complex and fluid political landscape. She often reflects on the relationship between luxury and everyday items and between objects from the distant and recent past. In the seventeenth and eighteenth centuries the growing importance of objects as signifiers of status and identity was compounded in the Irish case by the relationship between resources, craft and consumption, which saw the native Irish as among the preponderance of makers, rather than consumers, of this material. Luxury items were purchased by the middle and upper classes but many were exported, emphasising Ireland in a worldwide culture of commodity exchange. Within the country the proximity of native Irish, old English and new English led to complex relationships materially too: 'exquisite refinement lived side by side with rough-hewn rusticity, urban squalor and not-infrequent brutality'.[2] In this way, the objects that have come down to us offer very different readings of the lived past.

These contradictions are an important part of history, which we approach at least partly through material culture. For Boland, objects bear meanings that are at once personal and political, expressive of both the detail of lived experience and larger patterns of social development. They thus have the power to communicate aspects of individual and collective identity that might otherwise elude the grand narrative of history. In her desire to address these excluded or marginalised perspectives, Boland often turns to personal possessions or domestic objects as a way of understanding the past. Yet she notes too that these are rarely seen as fitting material for poetry:

> An undue emphasis on the domestic ... was criticized as having shadows of the small, the reduced ... For me, that all made up a series of prejudices and assumptions which were both academic and out of touch. For hundreds of years in painting, [domestic objects] have been rendered with a lot of care. If you look at a painting by Chardin or Morisot, you can see that a cup or a dish has been painted as the messenger of someone's life ... You can see those images have a charged place in the larger history.[3]

Objects express history in a complex way, disturbing established narratives and offering new perspectives on past events; yet there is much that remains hidden. The world of objects both supports Boland's desire to confront the reality of the past directly, yet also allows her to reflect on what it cannot tell us.

There is an important dynamic in Boland's poetry between the narrative of history and its marginalised or excluded subjects. In order to reclaim the past, and to open it to fresh scrutiny, Boland often turns her attention to material culture as a means to access the lost lives of women. Daniel Miller argues that we possess a 'depth ontology', a tendency to assume that the truth of our own subjectivity is located within us, rather than on the surface, rendering our interior lives more important than material objects.[4] Boland's art offers a clear refutation of this assumption; it projects a subjectivity that is intimately connected with the objects that we encounter in daily life. The particularity of the objects that Boland chooses is significant. Paintings feature frequently in her poems, as do prints and engravings; silver and glassware deepen her engagement with the labour of craft and the privilege of ownership. More intimate objects are particularly significant, however: clothing, jewellery and domestic possessions articulate the place of women socially but also shed light on their personal relationships. In these cases, it is the lost lives of individual women that are important to Boland since, as Jane Schneider has noted, the significance of objects is deepened by their encoding of the 'names, biographies, memories and histories' of those with whom they were associated in the past.[5]

The economic significance of the circulation of commodities is of concern to anthropologists and sociologists alike. Arjun Appadurai argues that, in order to understand the human transactions and motivations that govern them, we must 'follow the things themselves, for their meanings are inscribed in their forms, their uses, their trajectories'.[6] This mobility of the object is an important facet of Boland's engagement with material culture. Not only does the encounter with the object invoke a past relationship, it also acknowledges how the object can be loosened from this context and accumulate new meanings. Christopher Steiner has argued for the full recognition of human agency in the study of material culture:

> many authors have attributed too much power to the 'things' themselves, and in so doing have diminished the significance of human agency and the role of individuals and systems that construct and imbue material goods with value, significance and meaning.[7]

In this sense the object becomes a part of Boland's own creative development and is remembered as much for its role in her earlier thinking, as it is for being an object in its own right. Her first collection, *New Territory* (1967) featured 'From the Painting *Back from Market* by Chardin'. This poem is the first of a number by Boland on specific works of art. Here the focus is 'Chardin's peasant woman' yet the real subject is the problem of representation itself, 'what great art removes:/Hazard and death, the future and the past'.[8] Dwelling on the momentary quality of the painted scene, and its incapacity to present either the real conditions or the flow of life, Boland begins to reflect on the relationship between art and subjectivity, returning to Chardin's painting again years later in 'Self-Portrait on a Summer Evening' where, once again 'the ordinary life/is being glazed over'.[9] Yet here no specific painting is named and the focus has shifted away from the object and towards the objectification of women.

It is in the volume *Outside History* (1990) that the importance of the material past exerts a persistent presence in Boland's work. The opening section constitutes a direct meditation on the material world: it is dominated by a series of objects of the representational or decorative arts that draw attention to the important interaction between the lived past and its objects. Here the chief reflection is on forms of relationship and the objects function to advance these dynamics. There are gifts (Audubon's *Birds of America*) and legacies (the 'Bright-Cut Irish Silver' which is 'passed on from father to son').[10] Yet the presence of these objects speaks of absence, of the damage that living creatures inflict on one another and on their environment. The title poem of the sequence is itself an allegory of broken form. Two scenes are depicted: the first a genre scene that appears on a decorative mug: 'Dogs. Hawking. Silk./Linen spread out in a meadow'.[11] As in so many of Boland's poems, the description is precise, yet exceeds its role: it tells us more than the object itself can, and it is here that it connects to the larger scene of the poem – the depiction of a house move and the intimacy of a newly-shared space. Though the lengthening and contracting lines mimic the curve of the mug, language reveals the scene as a metaphor for crisis, envisaged here as 'the way land looks before disaster'.[12] Time is held in suspension: the intimacy of shared domestic life is set against the knowledge of its brevity. The broken mug at once expresses this misfortune, this violent severance of ordered lives, but also stops time, fixing the speaker and her husband in this between space of tension. In many of Boland's poems the object captures a process of connection or interaction either just before, or just after, it has happened. Even the most lasting objects can evoke a world in flux.

Such poems are indicative of the relationship between metaphor and materiality in Boland's work as a whole, and disclose the fragility of objects that disappear or break, or reveal themselves to be resistant to interpretation. In spite – or perhaps because – of their tenuous nature, these objects provide a fulcrum for Boland's investigation of personal responsibility to the past. Sherry Turkle posits a close connection between emotional and intellectual responses to the material world:

> We find it familiar to consider objects as useful or aesthetic, as necessities or vain indulgences. We are on less familiar ground when we consider objects as companions to our emotional lives or as provocations to thought. The notion of evocative objects brings together these two less familiar ideas, underscoring the inseparability of thought and feeling in our relationship to things. We think with the objects we love. We love the objects we think with.[13]

This unfamiliar ground is the very practice that Boland has made her own: her objects are always provocations to thought. If the subject-object relationship has been a vexed one for women artists and writers, then the resituating of the female experience by means of its relationship to the material world productively complicates this dynamic. The making of objects is an important concern for Boland, drawing attention to the role of the artist herself, to the dynamics of creation and reception. All objects, from a piece of glassware to a poem, act upon the world and thus affect those who engage with them. While her language may seem simple, Boland's poems resist complete understanding and thus their agency extends to readers who have not yet encountered her work. In this Boland's poems not only represent the object but also embody its power to captivate the witness. This interweaving of aesthetic and social elements is at the centre of her oeuvre.

II

Throughout Boland's career her engagement with the visual arts has been a striking dimension of her aesthetic development. From her early preoccupation with Chardin, to work inspired by Degas, Canaletto and Morisot, she often identifies specific artworks that prompt an interrogation of the creative process itself. Equally important, however, are Boland's explorations of genre painting where convention, rather than the unique artistic vision, is paramount. In these instances she interrogates the process by which the everyday becomes a subject of art. The first object, 'Fruit on a Straight-Sided Tray', appears in the sequence 'Domestic Interiors', from the collection *Night Feed* (1982). Hinting at still life, its modernist elements open the image to wider interpretation, emphasising the process of arrangement that is integral to the creation of art here. Yet Boland identifies the 'true subject' of the painter not as the objects themselves but rather the spaces between them, shifting our attention from the particularity of the fruit to its aesthetic qualities, its varied shapes and textures. In doing so, Boland alerts us to the relational dimension of her own art of objects and, since this poem is part of a sequence, to the dynamics of part and whole. Though the artistic impression is cumulative, it is in the separateness of object, and of poem, that both meaning and aesthetic pleasure can be discerned. Yet there is something unnatural about the representation here: the blue and purple shades are 'gross' – repugnant rather than refined – and a 'shadow of bloom' can be detected on the skin of the fruit, combining hints of flourishing and degeneration.

> The afternoon sun
> brings light but not heat and no distraction from
>
> the study of absences, the science of relationships
> in which the abstraction is made actual[14]

The mood of the poem is detached, and its stimulus limited, so that the scene seems at first to be characterized by lack of feeling. The 'assembly of possibilities' serves to defer actuation, yet it cannot hold back the passage of time. Though this still life is defiantly ordinary – 'a homely arrangement' – it models an issue of existential proportions, which is only directly expressed in the final two lines of the poem. Human experience is fundamentally singular: even the closest of human bonds, that between mother and child, will gradually loosen. The shape of the poem reveals how the expectations of aesthetic order, confirmed by the tercets with their tight alliterative frame, must in the end be broken to permit the emotional response to the object and its meanings to be recorded. By exploring the relationship between the abstract and the actual, Boland deepens her interrogation of the dynamics of art and everyday life.

'The Black Lace Fan My Mother Gave Me' is an important text for any consideration of how the past can be recalled and represented through the agency of the object. As the opening poem of the 'Object Lessons' sequence in *Outside History*, it signals how the created object can not only act as a catalyst for memory but also provoke awareness of the limitations of this process. Immediately, the mobility of the object is made clear: the speaker has been given the fan by her mother, who had received it as a gift from the speaker's father before they married. The power of the object to represent a relationship – between mother and daughter and between lover and beloved – is the starting point of this poem. As Marcel Mauss has argued, gifts retain something of their givers, expressing their place in a network of social relations.[15] So this gift is closely linked to its context, to the exoticism of pre-war Paris with its stifling heat and premonitions of coming conflict. The temporal preoccupations of the volume as a whole are condensed here: the fan, as a 'first gift', is both the beginning of a newly-significant relationship and evidence of its duration, allowing time to contract and enlarge within the scope of the single poem.

Some important details are clearly carried in the memory of the mother, for whom the patterns of their early relationship – her punctuality, his lateness – resonate much later in life. Yet from the beginning the poem interweaves remembered facts ('It was the first gift he ever gave her') with a lyrical interpretation of the scene ('A starless drought made the nights stormy').[16] The speaker clearly moves beyond the information she has gleaned to enter the mind of her mother and record her thoughts. This identification with the female perspective is an important dimension of Boland's representation of the fan in this poem, and contributes to her sense of the emotional resonance of the object, which has been kept and passed on. Yet the fan is also part of a larger network of meaning. It is an aesthetic object and the exact detail of its production is situated at the very centre of the poem:

> These are wild roses, appliqued on silk by hand,
> darkly picked, stitched boldly, quickly.
> The rest is tortoiseshell and has the reticent,
> clear patience of its element. It is
>
> a worn-out, underwater bullion and it keeps,
> even now, an inference of its violation.[17]

The dynamics of making are clearly rendered here: the rhythms of decorative stitching are contrasted to the structure that the tortoiseshell frame provides. Yet it too expresses the circumstances of its transformation into this decorative object – the hawksbill turtle from which it is derived is now an endangered species.

Temporally, then, the poem points in two directions: backwards towards the past it seeks to recall and to make sense of, and forward to prompt our consideration of an object from the past with a new eye to the significance of its making. The poet confronts the spectre of a past at once full of story and memory, yet also 'empty' of certain meaning: 'no way now to know what happened then – /none at all – unless, of course, you improvise'.[18] The gap in the story invites an imaginative intervention, yet this returns us to the beginning of the poem, and to the premise that the entire text is not based on memory but instead on invention. In the final image of the blackbird the speaker brings us back to the living present and suggests that this observation may be the moment of inspiration from which the entire poem is derived. This analogy is, of course, itself a form of improvisation, yet it is also a reminder of the dynamic nature of the past. Catherine Kilcoyne links this poem to others by Boland in their mixed feelings concerning the representation of the past:

> Her memory poems both show frustration at the failure that is always behind any reconstruction of the past and at the same time revel in the playfulness of memory's openness to textual creation.[19]

This relationship between material circumstances and the emotional response to them will become more complex as Boland's career develops.

Ten years later, 'Lava Cameo' takes the idea of the object as expressive of relationship further. This poem touches directly on the circumstances of Boland's grandmother's life yet acknowledges that the story that has come down to the poet may be closer to 'folk memory' than actual narrative. Again Boland draws us into the story before casting doubt on its authenticity. She asks us to recognise the ways in which language opens imaginative possibilities, forms of interpretation that exceed the actual detail of experience. Here she reflects on the choices inherent in her own act of writing: 'If I say wool and lace for her skirt/and crepe for her blouse…//If I make her pace the Cork docks, stopping/to take down her parasol as a gust catches/the silk tassels of it'.[20] Yet in spite of the provisional nature of these lines, their images remain in the text and in the mind of the reader:

there is a way of making free with the past,
a pastiche of what is
real and what is
not, which can only be
justified if you think of it

not as sculpture but syntax:

a structure extrinsic to meaning which uncovers
the inner secret of it.[21]

This act of 'making free' with the past requires moral consideration, yet it also draws attention to the difference between monumental forms of art and those more responsive to the human moment. The line-breaks carry this contingency ('what is/… what is/… can only be') so that the stanza expresses, both directly and indirectly, how a poem's form and language may reach more deeply into its subject.[22] By juxtaposing sculpture and syntax, Boland posits a way of engaging with the past that is continuous rather than fixed, suggesting not only the enduring power of memory but also the self-reflexive nature of its representation in poetry. Her repeated return to episodes from her own family history not only keeps this material in the minds of readers but returns to her earlier texts, creating a cyclical act of reading where meanings accumulate in the spaces between these poems. The brooch around which this text forms offers the perfect juxtaposition of destruction and creation that Boland seeks to investigate here. Depicting the profile of a human face on volcanic rock, this object carries not only the experiences of its wearer but also the idea of endurance itself. It expresses how the imagined past emerges from its bare facts and the necessity of this emergence as a means to bear witness to earlier lives. In this the lava cameo itself occupies an ambiguous position: unlike the black lace fan we cannot be sure that it exists in the present, that the object itself is not part of the created past. This ambiguity marks Boland's deepening engagement with material memory in her work.

In a Time of Violence (1994) marks an intensification in Boland's interest in the craft of making, so that material culture becomes more closely linked with aesthetic concerns in her work at this time. 'At the Glass Factory in Cavan Town' is a long poem that at once tells the story of how decorative glass is made and draws attention to the stages of creative process and their relationship to ideas of transformation. Here the poet locates us firmly in space and time, both through the title of the poem and its first word, 'Today'.[23] The poem, like the process of modern glassmaking, begins with the issue of consumption: swans are 'in demand'; myth and nature are to be put to the service of profit. Here Boland creates a dialogue with W.B. Yeats, in particular with his poem 'The Wild Swans at Coole', a text in which presence and absence are held in delicate balance.[24] If Yeats seeks allegories in nature for human isolation, Boland finds them in the difficult transition from nature to art. At first an apparently passive presence in the poem, soon the workings of the speaker's mind become evident, as she notes the elemental stone and fire, the glimpsed image of her daughters in the mirror. The figures in this scene move as though in myth: the pole through which the crystal is blown comes 'from the earth's //core: the earth's core/is remembered in/the molten globe at/the end of it'.[25] The slow revolution of these lines mimics both the process and the earth, and brings to mind Yeats's 'deep heart's core' and its fundamental attachments.[26] The rhythm of the poem itself is attuned to this process – 'It is red. It is/ruddy and cooler./It is cool now' – half-lines marking the stages from molten to solid form.[27] We see Boland's own art working similarly – a strongly felt emotion becoming gradually subject to measured syntax. Here the cooling glass bears within it the spirit of place, the landscape that surrounds them – a landscape that is at once the stuff of myth and of contemporary witness. The living swans seen there are re-created twice in the poem – first in glass, then in language. Yet it is this convergence of imagery that gives rise to the poem in the first place. This realization finds its parallel in the reflection of the speaker's daughters in the mirror, at once marking their proximity and their separateness from her:

… … Here, now –
  and knowing that

the mirror still holds
  my actual flesh –
I could say to them:
  reflection is the first

myth of loss, but
  they floated away and
away from me …[28]

Reflection creates an image that is at once the same as, and other to, the self; an image that is shattered by the ever-changing nature of the living subject. The speaker knows that her daughters, like the swans, will 'float away' and, specifically, away from her – an awareness that draws attention to the singularity of the poet's position. The swans appear directly in this poem yet they also elude representation. They turn away from their own image, creating a bifurcation of life and art, becoming 'a substance of [their] own future form', in another Yeatsian echo.[29] Yet they are both free of, and implicated in, their transformation into art – they float away 'as if/no one would ever blow//false airs on them'.[30] It is significant that the glass images of these creatures are both multiple and objects in process, not finished forms expressive of a particular human context, but rather ones that contain the potential for such life. By merging object and life form at the close of the poem, Boland prompts us to think again about the character of materiality and the interwoven nature of the given and the made.

The fifth object draws us deeper into the relationship between materiality and representation. In 'Emigrant Letters', from *Code* (2001), the focus is on ideas of mobility and specifically on the role of the object in negotiating transnational experiences. The poem begins in motion, its layered syntax expressing the endless transitions that modern air travel presents: 'That morning in Detroit at the airport,/after check-in, heading for the concourse'.[31] Observation is delayed by process here but we reach it at stanza end: the overheard Irish voice that 'syllables/from somewhere else had nearly smoothed out'.[32] The subject matter here – emigration – is already familiar from Boland's earlier work but in this poem transformation is envisaged both temporally and spatially: movement detaches the accent from its place of origin while prolonged time abroad opens the individual to new sounds and, by inference, to new versions of the self. The poet reflects on this issue as she flies over the Michigan landscape: again we see her creative process described for us from the moment of inspiration to the ostensible subject of the poem, which is also, of course, that creative process itself. The poet tries to think of loss but instead of this abstraction the vivid reality of emigrant experience emerges and their letters, not as concepts but as physical objects, enter the poem. They are evidence of the need to capture fleeting experiences in material form, and of the personal significance of this materiality:

> Each page six crisp inches of New England snow.
> And at the end a name: half-signature, half salt.
>
> How their readers stood in cold kitchens
> heads bent, until the time came to begin again
> folding over those chambers of light:[33]

These cherished objects are expressive of the new lives of their creators, embodying the landscape and weather of their American existence. This environment begins to take over their subjectivity, as their own signatures become submerged in the new ground, both actual and textual. For their readers these letters are transfiguring, arresting them in a heightened state of awareness. They are a manifestation of the power of language but also of the importance of the text as an object that speaks of the contexts of both writing and reading. Here the letters 'become' the new landscapes they describe, offering a way for the recipients to store these details for later reflection. Steven Connor has described the form of the newspaper as the 'subordination of writing to time' – these emigrant letters represent the antithesis of this process; they speak of immediate experiences but the significance of their writing and reception renders the objects themselves, paper and ink, still meaningful.[34] The final image of the poem, the cupboard that won't close 'informed as it was/ by those distant seasons. And warped by its own' brings both sides of the correspondence together, revealing the material world to be shaped by spoken and unspoken experiences.[35]

This conclusion helps us to understand Boland's persistent engagement with material culture in her work, conscious that though it communicates past lives in powerful ways, it also expresses the limitations of our access to the past. Through objects she re-negotiates the representation of subjectivity, exploring dynamics of fixedness and fluency, of endurance and fragility across all her writing. In the words of Bethany Bear:

> Boland ... [suggests] that for poetry to sanctify an object means not to make it an ideal or an emblem but to affirm its ambiguous, complex reality by placing it within a space that is both poetic and sacred.[36]

It is this co-existence of the extraordinary and the ordinary that allows Boland's engagement with material culture to open such fruitful lines of investigation in her creative life.

NOTES

1   Paul Connerton, 'Cultural Memory' in Chris Tilley *et al.* (eds), *Handbook of Material Culture* (London, 2006), p. 316.

2   William Laffan, 'Colonial Ireland: Artistic Crossroads' in William Laffan and Christopher Monkhouse (eds), *Ireland: Crossroads of Art and Design, 1690–1840* (Chicago, 2015), p. 20.

3   Jody Allen Randolph, 'Eavan Boland' in Jody Allen Randolph (ed.), *Close to the Next Moment* (Manchester, 2010), p. 240.

4   Daniel Miller, *Stuff* (London, 2010), p. 16.

5   Jane Schneider, 'Cloth and Clothing' in Tilley *et al.* (eds), *Handbook of Material Culture*, p. 204.

6   Arjun Appadurai, 'Introduction: commodities and the politics of value' in Arjun Appadurai (ed.), *The Social Life of Things: Commodities in Cultural Perspective* (Cambridge, 1986), loc. 196.

7   Christopher Steiner, 'Rights of passage: on the liminal identity of art in the border zone' in Fred R. Myers (ed.), *The Empire of Things: Regimes of Value and Material Culture* (Santa Fe, NM, 2001), p. 210.

8   Eavan Boland, *Collected Poems* (Manchester, 1995), p. 4.

9   Boland, *Collected Poems*, p. 103.

10   Boland, *Collected Poems*, p. 140; p. 145.

11   Boland, *Collected Poems*, pp 139–140.

12   Boland, *Collected Poems*, pp 139–140.
13   Sherry Turkle (ed.), *Evocative Objects: Things We Think With* (Cambridge MA, 2007) loc. 59.
14   Boland, *Collected Poems*, p. 97.
15   Marcel Mauss, *The Gift* (London, 1954).
16   Boland, *Collected Poems*, p. 137.
17   Boland, *Collected Poems*, p. 137.
18   Boland, *Collected Poems*, p. 137.
19   Catherine Kilcoyne, 'Eavan Boland and Strategic Memory', *Nordic Irish Studies*, 6 (2007), p. 91.
20   Boland, *Collected Poems*, p. 195.
21   Boland, *Collected Poems*, p. 189.
22   Boland, *Collected Poems*, p. 189.
23   Boland, *Collected Poems*, p. 185.
24   W.B. Yeats, 'The Wild Swans at Coole' in Richard J. Finneran (ed.), *The Collected Poems of W.B. Yeats* (London, 1989), pp 131–32.
25   Boland, *Collected Poems*, p. 185.
26   W.B. Yeats, 'I hear it in the deep heart's core' from 'The Lake Isle of Innisfree', *Collected Poems*, p. 39.
27   Boland, *Collected Poems*, p. 186.
28   Boland, *Collected Poems*, p. 187.
29   W.B. Yeats, 'Which of her forms has shown her substance right?' from 'A bronze head', *Collected Poems*, p. 340.
30   Boland, *Collected Poems*, p. 187, my italics.
31   Eavan Boland, *Code* (Manchester, 2001), p. 36.
32   Boland, *Code*, p. 36.
33   Boland, *Code*, p. 36.
34   Steven Connor reflects on the meaning of newspapers: 'what matters about the paper is precisely not its matter, but the signs, the news, it carries'. Steven Connor, *Paraphernalia: The Curious Lives of Magical Things* (London, 2013), p. 120.
35   Boland, *Code*, p. 36.
36   Bethany Bear, 'Writing within a zone of grace: Eavan Boland, sacred space and the redemption of representation', *Contemporary Literature*, 54:1 (Spring 2013), p. 90.

BIBLIOGRAPHY
Allen Randolph, Jody, 'Eavan Boland', *Close to the Next Moment* (Manchester, 2010), pp 233–44.

Appadurai, Arjun, 'Introduction: commodities and the politics of value' in Arjun Appadurai (ed.), *The Social Life of Things: Commodities in Cultural perspective* (Cambridge, 1986), loc. 157–1400 [Kindle edition].

Bear, Bethany, 'Writing within a zone of grace: Eavan Boland, sacred space and the redemption of representation', *Contemporary Literature*, 54:1 (Spring 2013), pp 77–108.

Boland, Eavan, *Code* (Manchester, 2001).

Collected Poems (Manchester, 1995).

Connor, Steven, *Paraphernalia: The Curious Lives of Magical Things* (London, 2013).

Kilcoyne, Catherine, 'Eavan Boland and strategic memory', *Nordic Irish Studies*, 6 (2007), pp 89–102.

Laffan, William, 'Colonial Ireland: artistic crossroads' in William Laffan and Christopher Monkhouse (eds), *Ireland: Crossroads of Art and Design, 1690–1840* (Chicago, 2015), pp 19–35.

Mauss, Marcel, *The Gift* (London, 1954).

Miller, Daniel, *Stuff* (London, 2010).

Schneider, Jane, 'Cloth and Clothing' in Tilley, *Material Culture*, pp 203–20.

Steiner, Christopher, 'Rights of passage: on the liminal identity of art in the border zone' in Fred R. Myers (ed.), *The Empire of Things: Regimes of Value and Material Culture* (Santa Fe, NM, 2001), pp 207–31.

Tilley, Christopher *et al.* (eds), *Handbook of Material Culture* (London, 2006).

Turkle, Sherry, *Evocative Objects: Things We Think With* (Cambridge MA, 2007).

Yeats, W.B., *The Collected Poems of W.B. Yeats*, edited by Richard Finneran (London, 1989).

Paul Muldoon

PUTSCH

Though we've scoured the realm
of oak and elm
for their bright dyestuffs,

on the first of May
it's a leg of grey
our Queen has birled.

Battleship grey, to be precise.
In mothballs, on ice,
we huff and puff

as we dance on the spot
while more pot-shots
are fired, more insults hurled.

For in Belfast we found the will
to remain at a standstill
when General Gruff

instituted his shoot to kill
policy in the Antrim hills.
The wind-drums whirled. The wind-pipes skirled.

In Sharon Springs,
meanwhile, I sight a king
only in the bronze cloak and neck ruff

of a wild turkey and his mate
as they rotate
the planet with their unfurled

claws ... Having lost her crown
to the browns,
the black and tans, the buffs,

a humming bird
has this morning set her little outboard
motor to the world.

MYTH AND EXPERIENCE:
THE POETRY OF EAVAN BOLAND[1]

Colm Tóibín

What are we going to do with experience? In some poems,
the very experience of making the poem itself is conveyed,
as though the technical impulse, the urge to find the right
words, sound patterns and rhythmical system might be
enough to satisfy some need within the poet's nervous
system. It matters then what the poem mysteriously does
as the poem becomes close to a musical performance. It
matters less what the poem says, or what it is about.

There is a beautiful moment in the ancient Irish
narrative *Tóraíocht Dhiarmada agus Gráinne* in which the
king, now an old man, has wished to marry the young and
beautiful Gráinne, who in turn has convinced Diarmaid,
one of the king's handsome warriors, to run away with
her. As they are pursued across Ireland, Diarmaid, out of
loyalty to the king, is unwilling to make love with Gráinne.
She taunts him as they cross a stream, telling him that the

water that has splashed her thigh is braver than he is. And thus they become lovers.

Eavan Boland's version of the story, called 'Song', appears in her 1975 collection, *The War Horse*. The first of four six-line stanzas has twenty-seven words, a comma, a semi-colon and a full-stop. Twenty-four of the words have only one syllable. The other three need more time; they take time; they are almost the key words – 'outsleep'; 'water'; 'afraid'. The beat is iambic trimeter, with a variation in the fourth line 'Too fast, too fast' which matches the meaning, catches the speed, not only the speed of the water, but the speed of the voice itself, with the comma denoting a hesitation in the first person singular voice which will declare itself in the last line:

> Where in blind files
> Bats outsleep the frost
> Water slips through stones
> Too fast, too fast
> For ice; afraid he'd slip
> By me I asked him first.[2]

The stanza depends on its rhythm, the single-syllable words suggesting fear, flight, urgency. Although the stanza does not rhyme, there are many repeating sounds, the 'i' sound in 'blind' coming fast in 'file' and again in 'ice'. And then there are the half-rhymes of 'frost', 'fast' and 'first' at the end of the second, fourth and sixth lines; there is the waking echo of 'outsleep' in 'slip'; and the waking echo too of 'bats' in the repeated word 'fast'.

The last two stanzas of the poem tell the story of the water hitting Gráinne's thigh and her taunting Diarmaid, and then his giving in. The third stanza reads:

> My skirt in my hand,
> Lifting the hem high
> I forded the river there.
> Drops splashed my thigh.

Ahead of me at last
He turned at my cry:[3]

Of the nouns and verbs in this stanza, there is only one which has an obvious Latin root and that is the last word 'cry'. This mirrors the first stanza, where there are no words with a Latin root, and the other two stanzas where the two words with a Latin root stand out – 'venom' in the second stanza and 'attempt' in the last stanza.

This story of female transgression is not, in Eavan Boland's version, a translation, but rather an effort to find a mode in English which will match not only the sense of risk and movement of the text it is based on, but also which will suggest, using words of Anglo-Saxon origin, a pre-modern time. The song of the title has a prose origin; it manages with concise skill and precision to tell a story in a poem, a story which has its original form in prose narrative.

What does this have to do with experience? For those of us brought up in Ireland with parents or grandparents who belonged to the revolutionary generation, these ancient stories had a special power. Indeed, the act of translation itself into a vernacular by figures such as Douglas Hyde and Lady Gregory at the end of the nineteenth and beginning of the twentieth century gave an impetus to the movement for Irish independence more powerful than, say, any set of economic arguments. Suggesting that these texts belonged to Ireland and, in Lady Gregory's phrase, added dignity to the country, stirred up a set of strong emotions in what was a sort of political vacuum after the fall of Parnell in 1890.

Some of the ancient stories remained controversial even then, however, because of their portraits of a female sexuality which could not be easily ignored. This was apparent not only in the story of Gráinne, but also in the depiction of Queen Maeve in *The Táin*, the epic translated by Lady Gregory in 1902. Lady Gregory, more interested in the heroic elements in *The Táin*, was uneasy about the frank depiction of sexuality in the text and made some cuts. But when the text was again translated in 1969 by the poet Thomas Kinsella, he was unembarrassed by the sexual content.

Eavan Boland's 'Song', then, followed in a tradition begun with Douglas Hyde's *Love Songs of Connacht* (1893) in attempting to find a form and tone for Irish mythology or Irish language texts which was not itself archaic, which used a diction that was not openly or obviously contemporary but rather was part of a living speech or tone of voice which suggested something composed now more than translated from then. Also, as a poem about a woman who leads rather than follows, as a poem written by a woman, it matched earlier translations of Irish texts in responding to contemporary and pressing concerns; it allowed the present in from the shadows to make the translation or the re-telling more part of both an exquisite technical experience of making a poem in this form and a personal experience of making a poem which has contemporary resonance.

Experience, of course, shifts and changes, will not stay in place, will not stay still. The distance between Eavan Boland's volume *The War Horse* and her volume *In a Time of Violence* is nineteen years, the distance, in a woman's life, between thirty-one and fifty. Light years. And in a poet's life, more than that. All we have to do is think of the distance between the W.B. Yeats of *The Wind Among the Reeds*, published when he was thirty-four, and the poet of twenty years later, or the distance in the sensibility of T.S. Eliot over the twenty years between *The Waste Land* and 'Little Gidding'. This is not about growing older, but about an enrichment and refinement which comes from reading the self, re-creating the self, re-imagining the self, finding dictions to match discoveries.

Eavan Boland's poem 'Love' from the volume *In a Time of Violence* both uses and creates myth; it allows, as the poem's second line suggests, myths to collide. The poet herself is a sort of Orpheus in the poem, charming a loved one with her lines. She invokes Aeneas in the underworld, and Icarus's dangerous flight over the world above, and also Ceres and Persephone, as she remembers a child who recovered from illness. But, to match this, or set against it, she finds a plain-spoken tone that belongs to now; she heightens this tone and makes it taut, but it remains the voice of a woman speaking. History is now and it is in the words she writes. The opening of the poem is in Iowa City, a real place in a real time: 'Dark falls on this mid-western town'.[4]

The bridge over the river is seen in dusk, and the dusk 'slides and deepens' to a remembered mythology – 'the water/the hero crossed on his way to hell'. But she wants this myth to collide with the facts of things 'a kitchen and an Amish table' in 'our old apartment'. And then she invokes the eponymous word – love – and then love becomes mythologised, a thing 'with the feather and muscle of wings'. And then there is a stanza about the child spared, and once more a mythology is evoked, as the hero 'hailed by his comrades in hell' is brought into service, given his due in the poem, only to be tossed aside since the poem wants to swim out to calmer waters. There have been two six-line stanzas and one seven-line stanza. The metrical system is uneven but led by a spondaic sound which lends itself to statement more than song.

And now, Eavan Boland is prepared to make a statement, clear, eschewing myth, or maybe proposing an anti-myth, since the Greek root for the word 'myth' suggests the closing of the eyes or the mouth. To be mute. These next five lines will speak with clear-eyed truth. The first line cannot be read as having two iambic beats, but rather four clear rings:

> I am your wife.
> It was years ago.
> Our child is healed. We love each other still.
> Across our day-to-day and ordinary distances
> we speak plainly. We hear each other clearly.[5]

These are six sentences. The first four of them admit no word with a Latin root, as though plain speaking requires an earlier tone. There are no flourishes. The plain tone, because of the references to myth in the previous four stanzas, brings with it a sense of casting off one tone to create another one, a tone more urgent, more exact, a tone caught in a strange grip between clarity and cry, between simple statement and a tense undertone filled with the sheer need to make this statement finally.

What to do now? The poem has four stanzas left. Since the tone has become more urgent, the number of lines in each stanza will shorten. Three stanzas of four lines, and one last stanza of two lines. The first of these stanzas is perhaps the most beautiful in all of Eavan Boland's work in its calm eloquence, its discovery of the resonant power of the image, the simple power of the thing. The statement emerges as though from an urgent impulse to state, to say, the poetry surviving in the space between sudden flashing diction and something chiselled from experience, written to be remembered, a sort of monument:

> And yet I want to return to you
> on the bridge of the Iowa river as you were,
> with snow on the shoulders of your coat
> and a car passing with its headlights on:[6]

It would be easy now to stop the poem here, to let the minor key of the snow on the shoulders of the coat and the car passing with its headlights on create a set of plain single notes for the poem to end on. But just as the poem has earned the right to speak in this tone, it has also earned the right to move the music of the poem into a higher register, to use two exalted words that the poem, even with its delving into what Philip Larkin called the 'myth-kitty', would have earlier resisted. These two words, which belong to mythology and to religion, are 'epic' and 'ascension':

> I see you as a hero in a text –
> the images blazing and the edges gilded –
> and I long to cry out the epic question
> my dear companion:
>
> Will we ever live so intensely again?
> Will love come to us again and be
> so formidable at rest it offered us ascension
> even to look at him?[7]

In these two stanzas, instead of allowing two tones to collide, she has found a match for them. She creates an iambic pentameter line – 'I see you as a hero in a text' – to set a tone, filled now with a comfort and ease as the voice stretches itself from the simple business of asking a fundamental question – 'Will love come to us again' – but insisting also on the right to let the voice soar and the question become more transcendental as the sights rise too, rise to the possible experience of 'ascension', the rising up out of the earth towards the sky, or out of the self towards something that two selves might become.

Once more, it might have been easy to end here, with the daring question, and the sense that even having to ask such a thing implies a knowledge that the answer will never be clear and might indeed be dark. But there are two more lines. These come as a way of invoking the image in mythology of Orpheus walking ahead in a place of shadows with Eurydice behind, Eurydice in this version being the one who sings. But she cannot be heard now in this place where words are shadows. The poem is resigned now to the way things are and will be. The lines follow both the terms of a myth and the tone of a voice as though finally there were no distinction between the two:

> But the words are shadows and you cannot hear me.
> You walk away and I cannot follow.[8]

In looking then at the way in which Eavan Boland plays the mythic against the ordinary, the small, personal experience against the large questions of destiny, it is useful to study two of her recent poems which are among the best poems anyone has made in the twenty-first century. They come from a lifetime's conjuring with tone, conjuring with the pull between plain statement and pure soaring possibility, with the tension between the minutely personal and the effort to find a myth or a governing sense of shared experience. One is called 'And Soul'; the other is 'The Lost Art of Letter Writing'. They both appeared in the *New Yorker* magazine, the first in April 2006, the second in August 2014. 'And Soul' was included in Eavan Boland's volume *Domestic Violence*, published in 2008.

In an interview about the poem 'And Soul', Boland makes clear that the title implies a word that is missing, the word 'body', which comes before soul in the phrase 'Body and Soul'. Since the poem deals with the body, the ailing body of the poet's mother and the body of the city itself, the body of its weather, then the title allows us to consider the poem's aftermath, or its implication as an active force in the poem. It also encourages us to notice the elements in the poem, including indeed its very tone, as having moments which reach beyond the physical towards some other space. It is hard also not to connect the title with the final stanza of the patriotic English poem 'I vow to thee my country' which invokes 'another country' where the dead go. The final two lines refer to the growing number of the living who arrive in the new territory:

> And soul by soul and silently her shining bounds increase
> And her ways are ways of gentleness, and all her paths are
> peace.

Boland's poem begins plainly, factually:

> My mother died one summer –
> the wettest in the records of the state.[9]

This brings with it echoes of both Patrick Kavanagh's 'In Memory of my Mother', which begins: 'I do not think of you lying in the wet clay/Of a Monaghan graveyard'[10] and W.H. Auden's 'In Memory of W.B. Yeats', whose first stanza ends: 'What instruments we have agree/The day of his death was a dark cold day'.[11] The next three lines, as they describe the passive, known world going about its business beyond the subject of the poem, also echo Auden. Boland's lines read:

> Crops rotted in the west.
> Checked tableclothes dissolved in back gardens.
> Empty deckchairs collected rain.[12]

Auden's lines are:

> The brooks were frozen, the airports almost deserted
> And snow disfigured the public statues.
> The mercury sank in the mouth of the dying day.[13]

While the first five lines of 'And Soul' contain four sentences, the rest of the poem – thirty-four lines – is one long sentence. In this sentence there is a battle going on to contain feeling, to stick to the facts, to say something about the city and the body and weather and speech. There is also in the rhythm a sense of someone driving a car, looking out, stopping, moving forward, turning, remaining in control. The poem enacts the drama of someone trying to be all body and mind, trying to drive and think and keep feeling at bay. Feeling is left to the space between the words and to a melody that gathers and is channelled underneath the rhythm as rainwater itself in a city gathers and is channelled.

The poem is concerned to do everything to suggest panic and fear, including an attempt to leave them unmentioned. Thus in the second five lines there are keywords – 'traffic', 'houses', 'curbsides' – which are hard and factual and neither contain nor conceal emotion. But then there is an image of 'lilacs dripping blackly' and the stark phrase 'the last tribute of a daughter' which is both distant, abstract (the word 'tribute') and deeply personal and concrete (the word 'daughter').

The next ten lines have a sort of catch in their diction which suggests a catch in the throat or the voice. The direct statements of the opening lines, the stark facts starkly described, move now into a set of stops and starts and qualifications. The certainty has been replaced by something less sure, but care is still being taken not to use words of easy feeling. Thus the word 'elements', a scientific word, maintains the tone of emotional control, but it also, of course, includes within its fold the word 'lament', a word that will not be used in this poem of lament which enacts as it proceeds some of lament's procedures, the not being able to face loss, the effort to think of other things as a way of not confronting loss.

These 'elements' mentioned in the poem are the city's weather. The weather is filled with rain, and:

> every single day the elements begin
> a journey towards each other that will never,
> given our weather,
> fail –[14]

Notice the soft iambic beat that continues until the first syllable of 'never' and that lets the second syllable die off as though such a confident sound is no longer possible. Then the next line begins with a trochee to match 'never' ('given') and allows in another ('weather'). The trochee sounds do what the poem itself does, begin as though certain and then continue with a softer, less sure beat. And then the next line of the poem has just a single hard sound and a dash, as though there was something more that might have been said but cannot be said.

Since the body, as the poem states, 'is or is/said to be, almost all/water', then the body too is an element beginning a journey, a journey that, given our weather, or given our fate on the earth, will never 'fail': it will move towards death as river water moves towards sea water. The lines enact the slow realisation of that as certainty and then allow in something, or someone, less ready to be certain, almost wanting to turn the metre back and then stop.

In the next eight lines the poem moves between the world itself, the city and the body as they each dissolve and flow, as though each are involved in the same inevitability. The poem plays not only with a tone which is distancing and attempting still to contain feeling, but it also conjures with voice itself, the voice noticing, remembering, but also the voice speaking, as ordinary phrases from the speech of the city appear in the poem, as in 'given our weather' and 'as if that wasn't enough'.

Just as in Yeats's poem 'In Memory of Major Robert Gregory' when the dead man is not evoked until the sixth line of the sixth stanza, as if the poem had been enacting an avoidance of the fact of his death, the first use of the word 'mother' in 'And Soul' is used without any aura of emotion. It is in the first line – 'My mother died one summer –' and offered as stark fact. When it comes again in the twenty-ninth line, it comes at the end of a list in italics, but at the opening of a line. Because the other words in the list are not personal words – 'coast canal ocean river stream' – and each have a hard sound in them, then the words 'mother', with its softer sound and its trochee beat, comes as a shock, lets in a level of emotion which the poem, as though it were a dam or a channel, has been trying to block or conceal or contain and is now forced to release.

There are ten more lines in the poem. After the word 'mother' comes the phrase 'and I drove on' which suggests that the emotion released is now being held again for a line or two, but then the thought comes in the poem, a thought that has been wrapped up in the poem's own shifting between the city and the body, and is suddenly unwrapped as the idea emerges that those impersonal words listed – words for things with water in them – and the word 'mother' could 'be shades of each other', as the mother herself moves towards becoming a shade, with echoes of the moment towards the end of Joyce's 'The Dead', with its own images of Irish weather – 'One by one they were all becoming shades'.

In the last seven lines, the poem allows a catch in its voice again after the word 'shades', as if, having faced the fact of the body as element moving towards soul, it cannot easily proceed. When it does, it seems prepared to allow itself to soar, as fog moves into mist and then 'mist into sea spray' and then we are allowed to feel, since the poem is called 'And Soul', that the sea spray will move into some transcendent form, or at least lead us to a consoling image, but instead, the poem looks at what is hard and visible; it looks closely and sees 'the oily glaze/that lay on the railings' as an image of the mere fact of things and then in the last two lines it lets those real, stark things that do not themselves dissolve take us down into the real city, the real body before it becomes soul. They are the railings 'of the house she was dying in/as I went inside'.[15]

One of the subjects which has nourished Eavan Boland's work from the beginning is the question of form and rhetoric and structure in poetry. At its most simple, this question comes to her as a sort of suspicion. She has been suspicious of her own skill at making a poem and has sought then to find strategies in her work to push through the sort of impersonal skill and eloquence we find in

'Song' towards a poetry of raw statement which attends to lived experience. As a poet, she cannot avoid hearing the long tide of the entire poetic tradition, but she waits for the urgent wave that tells what it has been like for her to be alive in the world.

She has also been concerned with history itself, and the lives and voices that history cast aside. History for her is a set of erasures; poetry then can trace the marks left, or attempt to imagine what has been made shadowy and give it substance. The public poem for her has been as essential as the private one because she has come to see little difference between the two, as the public for her became a lost voice, the name that left no trace, the echo her poem can hear that did not seem to be registered first as sound. While the public poem becomes a way to recuperate, compensate, recover, reinstate, it has also been for her, because of the fragility and tentative nature of what is outside history, as much in need of delicate treatment as her poems which are personal and come from the self, such as 'Love' or 'And Soul'.

Of all her public poems 'The Lost Art of Letter Writing' is perhaps the finest, the poem which seems most to resolve battles which were being waged within her own conscience as a poet, battles about her own eloquence versus her need to be true to lived experience, battles between the hushed tone of concealed and coiled emotion that we get in 'And Soul' and the rhetorical skill that we find in 'Song', battles between her concern with what has been silenced by the loud voice of history and the need to imagine plaintive but perfectly-pitched sound for the poem that redeems the silence.

The poem, written in twelve three-line stanzas, begins with a set of statements which are both complex and simple. The first line of the second stanza reads: 'The hand was fire and the page tinder'. Tinder is the dry flammable material which helps light a fire so, for a second, the reader stops and thinks that, no, the hand is the tinder which helps light the fire of the page. What this line proposes, on the other hand, is that the hand, led by the mind and the will, is the active, burning thing; the page merely enables it. In the next lines, the act of writing itself is indeed a willed, deliberate act:

> Everything burned away except the one
> Place they singled out between fingers
>
> Held over a letter pad they set aside
> For the long evenings of their leave-takings
> Always asking after what they kept losing.

The metre here is interesting, especially the way in which the stress falls on the first syllable of each of these five lines, suggesting decision, deliberation, the mind concentrating, suggesting disruption rather than the ordinary flow of things. It is clear by now that the letters are those written home to Ireland by emigrants. Slowly it will emerge that these letters are acts of imagination and memory as much as acts of communication, that the words written on the page move inward and matter to the writer as much or more than they might to those who will receive the letter. They will invoke places lost, small images, ordinary things. The mere business of 'asking after' things will allow the mind's eye to see, to recover for a brief time the past, as the past moves in one startling stanza of the poem into a future that the letter-writers will never share, never see. Instead they will see:

> a road leading
>
> To another road, then another one, widening
> To a motorway with four lanes, ending in
> A new town on the edge of a city
>
> They will never see.

In the thirty-one words quoted here, twenty-three have only one syllable and only four have their roots in Latin. But this system has no connection, or almost none, with the system of one-syllable words and words with an Anglo-Saxon root in 'Song'. Instead of the gnarled and brilliant rhetoric of 'Song' there is now some of the plain, hushed statement we find in 'Love'. The three-line stanza quoted above is written almost in technical language all the more to offer the soft-edged phrase 'they will never see', like a phrase from a ballad, a haunting emotion, a moment of pure feeling that is hard-won because of the space around it.

What happens in the next lines is that Boland not only suspends her suspicion of her own eloquence but she uses it for all that it is worth to say something now that matters, which is both pressingly private and public. The lines read:

> And if we say
> An art is lost when it no longer knows
> How to teach a sorrow to speak

This is, of course, the art of poetry on which the poet has been engaged for half a century as much as the art of letter writing. It allows in the word 'sorrow', which invokes W.B. Yeats's poem 'The Sorrow of Love' but also his line 'And loved the sorrows of your changing face' from 'When You Are Old and Grey' and also lines from the song 'She Moved Through the Fair':

> The people were saying
> No two e'er were wed
> But one had a sorrow
> That never was said.

The sorrow in 'The Lost Art of Letter Writing' is the sorrow of emigration, the sorrow of long years away. The letters were written in sorrow and the art was lost because the letters, on receipt, were stacked away, not attended to. Those who read the letters did not pay enough attention to know that, by remembering, the emigrant could make the fields stir 'at night as they became/Memory and in the morning as they became/Ink'.

Memory and Ink. Both words are used here to begin lines, to stop the easy flow of complex thinking about loss and the simpler starker feeling about what that loss implies which was coiled around the thinking. It is as if the things that melt into each other in this poem – road into another road, fields into memory, memory into ink – also suggest how thinking itself, or writing, melts into feeling.

The poem is both public and hushed, both private and filled with a sense of shared historical experience. The hand with pen and paper is both individual and communal. By holding the tone of the poem in some carefully modulated minor key in which the 'they' are both individuals with a strange privacy and also whole generations of people, the poem allows itself to have major resonance. Thus the last four words of the poem, which appear in italics – *is it still there?* – have a sense of pure, still voice, a single asking and also a question that was asked by many and belongs to their dreams and now to an art that has been lost, the art of letter writing, and also to an art that has, in full conscience, attempted to redress that loss, the art of poetry.

NOTES
1   An earlier version of this essay first appeared in *The PN Review*, 220, Vol 41, No. 2 (Nov-Dec 2014).
2   Eavan Boland, 'Song', *New Collected Poems* (Manchester, Carcanet, 2005), p. 44.
3   Boland, 2005, p. 45.
4   Boland, 2005, p. 213.
5   Boland, 2005, p. 214.
6   Boland, 2005, p. 214.
7   Boland, 2005, p. 214.
8   Boland, 2005, p. 214.

9   Paula Meehan and Jody Allen Randolph (eds), *Eavan Boland: A Poet's Dublin* (Manchester, Carcanet, 2014), p. 59.

10   Patrick Kavanagh, *The Complete Poems* (Newbridge, The Goldsmith Press, 1972), p. 160.

11   W.H. Auden, 'In Memory of W.B. Yeats' in M.H. Abrams and Stephen Greenblatt (eds), *The Norton Anthology of English Literature* (New York, 2000), p. 2506.

12   Meehan and Allen Randolph, 2014, p. 59.

13   Abrams and Greenblatt, 2000, p. 2506.

14   Meehan and Allen Randolph, 2014, p. 59.

15   Meehan and Allen Randolph, 2014, p. 59.

Moya Cannon

FINGER-FLUTING IN MOON-MILK

We are told that usually, not always,
a woman's index finger
is longer than her ring-finger,
that, in men, it is usually the opposite,
that the moon-milk in this cave
retains the finger prints and flutings
of over forty children, women and men
who lived in the late Palaeolithic.

Here, in the river-polished Dordogne,
as the last ice-sheets started to retreat
northwards from the Pyrenees
in a cave which is painted with gentle-faced
horses and long files of mammoths,
a woman, it seems, with a baby on her hip
trailed her fingers down through
the soft, white substance
extruded by limestone cave-walls
and the child copied her.

Today, the finger flutings remain clear;
the moon-milk remains soft.
As we trundle through the cave's maze
in our open-topped toy train
we are forbidden to touch it.

With no gauge to measure sensibility
we cannot know what portion
of our humanity we share
with someone who showed a child

how to sign itself in moon-milk
one day, late in the Old Stone Age.

Rouffignac, 2010

EAVAN BOLAND:
THE POET IN THE MUSEUM

Patricia Boyle Haberstroh

Anyone who reads Eavan Boland's poetry will quickly
recognise her interest in the visual arts. Over and over again
she alludes to images, forms, strategies and terminology
from the worlds of art. Images of artists, paintings,
drawings, photography, engraving and sculpture appear
often in her work. Most obvious are the allusions to artists
and specific paintings or drawings, often as these reflect
representations of women as imaginative fictions; but there
are other ways in which the visual arts have played an
important role in her work. Boland uses this material in
different ways: to illustrate the issues of representation and
identity; to suggest that while art preserves the past in one
sense, it limits our understanding of it in another; to
examine how certain 'objects' embody 'lessons', a variant on
the concept of sign or symbol. As her work developed,
Boland also made many connections between works of art

and social and historical issues, especially those involving Irish history and culture.

Boland views visual art in a very comprehensive way, including artifact and craft within a wider definition, partially because this allows for a recognition of works beyond museum art and art canons and downplays the traditional distinctions between high and low art. Her wish to acknowledge as art the often-unrecognised women's crafts of weaving or patchwork, or objects like a lava cameo or a black appliquéd lace fan,[1] evolves from Boland's commitment to ordinary and domestic objects which can reveal as much about a culture as works of 'high art'. Bethany J. Smith's work,[2] which focuses on both empathy and ethics in what she sees as Boland's elegiac poems, covers much of this important issue; however, for the purposes of this essay, I will limit my discussions primarily to Boland's poems on museum pieces and her allusions to techniques and types of visual art like portrait, still life and sculpture.

Boland's introduction to the visual arts began early. Her mother, Frances Kelly, was an Irish painter of murals, portraits and still lifes, whose works are exhibited in museums.[3] Born in 1908, Kelly was orphaned early, her mother dying in a fever ward at 31, her father drowning in the Bay of Biscay. A promising artist, Kelly attended the Metropolitan School of Art in Dublin and in 1932 won the Henry Higgins Travelling Fellowship for three years of study in Paris where she was a student of the Cubist painter, Leopold Survage. Although Kelly was not attracted to Cubism, Survage's influence can be seen in the dynamic colours, lines and movement in some of her works, especially her still lifes. Years later, Boland discovered that a painting of her mother's had been signed by Survage in the bottom right corner where her mother's signature usually appeared; it was selling in a gallery in

Dublin for a high price under his name. As Boland notes in 'A Journey with Two Maps': 'His signature. Her painting. Her vision. His price'.[4]

Kelly married Frederick Boland (she was also known as Judy Boland), a diplomat who served as Irish Ambassador to Great Britain and later to the United Nations. As a result, Eavan, one of five children, spent some of her childhood in London. In 'I Remember',[6] Boland describes the effect of one of her mother's evolving portraits on her as a child, emphasising the mystery of the artistic process. The poem's title, recalling a line from a Thomas Hood poem, 'I remember, I remember/The house where I was born',[5] recounts her response to the portrait:

> the spines of my mother's portrait brushes
> spiked from the dirty turpentine and the face
> on the canvas was the scattered fractions
>
> of the face which had come up the stairs
> that morning and had taken up position in
> the big drawing-room and had been still
> and was now gone; and I remember, I remember
>
> I was the interloper who knows both love and fear,
> who comes near and draws back, who feels nothing
> beyond the need to touch, to handle, to dismantle it,
> the mystery; [...]

The 'interloper' who invades the painter's space and the need to 'dismantle' the 'mystery' depict a young observer beginning to understand the artistic process as an almost miraculous integration of 'scattered fractions' waiting to be composed.

In a work like this, Boland draws on the classical rhetorical convention of ekphrasis, where poems focus on works of art and she shares a common trait with other poets who have employed this convention. The poet Alfred Corn, in his essay 'Notes on Ekphrasis', explains its current use:

Perhaps the most effective contemporary poems dealing with visual art are those where the authors include themselves in the poem, recounting the background circumstances that led to a viewing of the painting or sculpture in question; or what memories or associations or emotions it stirs in them; or how they might wish the work to be different from what it is. The center of attention in this kind of poem isn't solely the pre-existing work but instead is *dual*, sharing the autobiographical focus found in the majority of contemporary lyric poems written in English.[7]

Boland, much of whose writing, like 'I Remember', has an autobiographical foundation, provides specific settings, and her speaking 'I' in these poems can often be clearly identified with the poet. What Corn defines as the 'memories' and 'association or emotions' embodied in ekphrastic poems, Boland's poems clearly illustrate. Boland herself gives us a clue to her approach when she says in 'A Journey with Two Maps':

A painting lives in space. The frame encloses it. But when the canvas is stretched and nailed, when the frame shuts around it, the life inside continues. I knew that from my mother.[8]

Boland engages with that life inside the frame, commenting on the subject of the work, sometimes as it relates to her personal life. Throughout her prose, Boland speaks of dialogues, questions or conversations a reader or observer can have with literature or art, explaining that for her 'an apparently monolithic poetic past was transformed into a conversation I could join and change'. To view her ekphrastic poems as conversations gives us a way to approach them; as she suggests, 'how we see a painting, read a poem or write one can't simply be the outcome of a single fixed viewpoint'.[9]

Echoing 'I Remember', which highlights her mother's painting, some of Boland's other poems imagine artists at work on a particular piece. In 'Degas's Laundresses',[10]

Boland describes the artist as he creates the women in his drawing. The speaker imagines the scene as Degas begins:

> See he takes his ease
> staking his easel so,
> slowly sharpening charcoal,
> closing his eyes just so,
> slowly smiling as if
> so slowly he is
> unbandaging his mind.

The later part of the poem suggests a downside of this process: the necessary 'unbandaging' of the artist's mind becomes a 'winding sheet', as the actual women are transformed in the artist's vision and drawing. The speaker's question, 'Why is he watching you?' and the poem's use of such words as 'staking', 'sharpening' and the 'twists', 'white turns' and 'blind designs' of Degas' mind, describe his need for subjects to remain still and silent as he translates them from actual persons to his own image. 'Whatever you do don't turn', the speaker warns the laundresses, as this will undermine the moment the artist is trying to preserve, a stillness within the flux of the laundresses' life.[11] The poem becomes both a description of Degas' control of the laundresses' image, and a comment on the artistic process of converting life into art. In an interview with Pilar Villar, Boland explains:

> The poem is about the painter watching the toil of these two laundresses. And how much control – almost predatory control – is needed to turn these living, shiftless, struggling women into fixed images.[12]

In writing such a poem about a drawing, Boland tries on one level to mitigate the loss of the living women by reanimating them, by imagining the textures, smells, sounds and movement within the actual scene, details added to Degas' drawing which the visual arts cannot always convey as well as poetry can. In Boland's poem, we smell a 'camisole brine', the 'whiff [...] of fields' where the laundry 'bleached and stiffened', and feel 'a linen pit of stitches'. In her dialogue with this work, Boland also suggests what the laundresses might be thinking or saying: 'You seam dreams in the folds/of wash [...] Your chat's sabbatical:/brides, wedding outfits,//a pleasure of leisure women/are sweated into the folds,/the neat heaps of linen.'

One advantage of poetry is to enhance the sensory with what Corn calls:

> the overall resources of verbality, with descriptions developed through surprising metaphors, apt commentary cast in lines with unusual diction and crisp rhythm – perhaps even calling on the techniques of traditional prosody.[13]

In this poem, Boland encases her words in sestets, dramatising the climactic and last line of the last sestet ('it's your winding sheet') by setting it apart from the five lines before it. The intermingling of repetitive sound patterns like alliteration, assonance and consonance in such lines as 'See he takes his ease/staking his easel so,/slowly sharpening charcoal,/closing his eyes just so' illustrates the use of traditional prosody that Corn sees as enhancing the poet's description of the work of art.

In another poem, the sonnet 'On Renoir's *The Grape Pickers*',[14] Boland presents a similar scenario, but this poem places more emphasis on the artist's use of line, light and composition: 'a fuss of shines', 'the ovals of their elbows', a 'round vintage/of circles', a 'work of pure spheres' where 'Flesh and shadow mesh inside each other.' Zeroing in on a detail of the work, however, an observer notices an individual much like the laundresses Boland imagines dreaming in Degas' work: 'Her eyes are closed. Her hands are loosening./Her ears are fisted in a dozed listening./She dreams of stoves, raked leaves, plums.'

One of the themes running through these poems is the posed subject, a consequence of the artist's vision. In other poems, especially those describing formal portraits, Boland also examines how the subjects may agree to present themselves. In 'Woman Posing',[15] Boland turns to Ingres and his portrait of an English woman, Mrs Badham. The poem suggests that this portrait might not accurately portray the sitter. In Ingres' image, Mrs Badham poses in a chair dressed for a formal portrait, with fancy bonnet and elegant dress, holding a book in her hands. Over her right shoulder, harking back to one of the conventions of Renaissance art which influenced Ingres' work, we see a view of Rome, including the Villa Medici and the obelisk at the top of the Spanish Steps.

Boland's poem highlights the sitter's pose and the way in which a woman done up for a portrait can conceal the ordinary details of another life. According to the poem, Mrs Badham is presented here as 'tidied', 'emptied', 'frilled and pat'; her 'shawl […] upholsters her'. As she did in 'Degas's Laundresses', Boland also reads something more into Ingres' image – what the sitter might be thinking: 'She smirks uneasily at what she's shirking – /sitting on this chair in silly clothes,/posing in a truancy of frills.' One could argue here that a smirk was not what Ingres intended an observer to see when he drew Mrs Badham's mouth, but for Boland that would probably be the point. Mrs Charles Badham was the wife of a prominent English doctor (at one point he was physician to the Duke of Sussex) and the couple, on a continental tour, spent time in Rome when Ingres lived there and produced this portrait.

As much as anything, however, the poem addresses the traditions of neoclassical posing and portrait painting where the stated value of what the poem calls 'common sense' gave way to conventional poses and the exaggerations of eighteenth-century manners and dress. The potential difference between the external posing and this woman's other life is highlighted in the last line, 'She holds the open book like pantry keys.' Her domestic life (and her English life) is not reflected in Ingres' representation, as the speaker sees her against a Roman background in 'a truancy of frills.' In an ironic twist, 'Woman Posing' is a version of an English sonnet, Shakespeare's more typical three quatrains and a couplet varied in Boland's poem to couplet, sestet, tercet, tercet. Adopting the sonnet links form with theme as Boland presents a variation not only of Ingres' image of Mrs Badham, but also of the sonnet form. As Ingres borrows the conventions of Renaissance art, Boland writes her poem in a form developed in the Renaissance.

As these poems show, the value of art in capturing an action, a scene, a person is a two-edged sword; it preserves an image but that representation is always limited. Boland pinpointed this very early in her career, in the poem 'From the Painting *Back from Market* by Chardin'.[16] The poem reflects its theme in the speaker's reaction to Chardin's image: a peasant woman, heading home from a dawn market with a loaf of bread under her arm. Noting that Chardin has 'fixed/Her limbs in colour, and her heart in line', Boland also stresses what the visual artist's colour and line might leave out. The poem elaborates on the details in the image, from a foreground where the hindlegs of a hare 'peep from a cloth sack' to the background where 'through the door/Another woman moves/In painted daylight; nothing in this bare/Closet has been lost/Or changed.'

The fact that nothing has been lost or changed, that the subject's limbs are 'fixed', is both an advantage as the artist preserves this woman at a specific moment in time, and a disadvantage, as the multiple dimensions of the woman's life have been lost. The speaker's reflections make this clear: 'I think of what great art removes:/Hazard and death, the future and the past,/This woman's secret history and her loves –'. As she did with the women portrayed in 'Degas's Laundresses' and 'Woman Posing', Boland hints at another life, one in actual, not 'painted daylight'. Though we see in the artist's technique the colour of her limbs and the lines of her heart, we can never know the woman's 'secret history and her loves –'. As Boland says:

> It's an odd paradox of art that it can only work by fixing the moment – whether it's painting or poetry or fiction – and yet once the moment gets fixed, everything in expression restricts it and limits it [....] For me, the limits are the strengths.[17]

Those limits, as Boland suggests, allow the possibility of a continuing dialogue between artist and observer.

We should not see this poem, or many of Boland's other poems on works of art, as a criticism of the artist's work; as Medbh McGuckian maintains, 'From the Painting *Back from Market* by Chardin' is an 'unrebellious reading'.[18] To the contrary, Boland places Chardin in a revolutionary light for the value of his genre painting, whose aesthetic differed from the neoclassical values of a painter like Ingres:

> Chardin's paintings were ordinary in the accepted sense of the word. They were unglamorous, workday, authentic. Yet in his work these objects were not merely described; they were revealed. The hare in its muslin bag, the crusty loaf, the woman fixed between menial tasks and human dreams – these stood out, a commanding text. And I was drawn to that text.[19]

If we think of Boland as engaged in a conversation with a work of art, a later poem, 'Self-Portrait on a Summer Evening',[20] complements Chardin's image of the woman coming from the market, one which fits into Boland's evolving aesthetic about the importance of ordinary life, especially of a woman, as the subject matter for poetry. 'Self-Portrait on a Summer Evening' emphasises how the 'ordinary life/is being glazed over' as the speaker imagines Chardin's attempts to paint a woman: 'All summer long/he has been slighting her/in botched blues, tints/half-tones, rinsed neutrals.' Fulfilling the promise of the title, the speaker here creates an alternative image: her self-portrait. An ordinary woman, in simple clothes, describes the details of her day in the last summer light, surveying her garden and watching her children in the distance. In this poem Chardin's attempts to paint the woman are counterpointed by the poem's self-portrait: 'I am Chardin's woman', the speaker asserts, presenting herself as both subject and artist. In painter's language, she describes herself as: 'edged in reflected light,/hardened by/the need to be ordinary.' Jody Allen Randolph claims that in a poem like this Boland is 'using artists to make a visionary claim for the domestic'.[21]

The poems described above have as their foundation the need to look beyond surfaces, beyond clothes, poses and the artist's difficulties in capturing the ordinary lives of women, especially their domestic lives. Boland uses her own experience as woman, mother, poet to create speakers and self-portraits that fill a gap between some images from literature, myth and the visual arts and her own life as a woman. This is a complicated strategy as each Boland poem is itself capturing a moment in time and thus limited to a single perspective in the same way as any artist's is. However, over a period of years, as her poems repeated and accumulated images and themes, they became both an autobiographical and an imagistic series of changing self-portraits, calling to mind the work of Rembrandt or Käthe Kollwitz whose self-portraits reflected the flux, the changes and especially the effects of aging on their lives. Boland has done something similar in poetry, the later poems focussed often on time passing, recurring memories of what has been lost and changes in her life, an infant in the early poems in *Night Feed*, for example, becoming a married daughter in the later 'Wedding Poem'.[22]

'Domestic Interior',[23] the first poem in *Night Feed*, where Boland's domestic and maternal life provide the setting and subject for several poems, illustrates this process by alluding to Van Eyck's *Arnolfini Wedding Portrait*, one of the most well-known paintings of the Northern Renaissance. Illustrating the precise details, colours and luminosity of the Northern painters, Van Eyck's portrait depicts a man and woman standing in a bedchamber on their wedding day, her hand resting in his. Behind the couple, a convex mirror reflects other figures witnessing the marriage pair, among them Van Eyck's self-portrait. His name also appears on the wall, with the date 1434. Written before 'Self-Portrait on a Summer Evening', 'Domestic Interior' likewise introduces us to a woman who compares herself to the subject of a painting.

In the poem, the observer sees Van Eyck's figure 'by whose edict she will stay/burnished, fertile,/on her wedding day'. In claiming that Van Eyck has paradoxically 'interred' her in joy, Boland links this artist to Degas, who we are told, created the laundresses' 'winding sheet'. In both cases, the artists' images have lost something of the actual women, most importantly that they will never change. Reflecting on Van Eyck's image, the speaker turns to her partner who, she says, sees her in the convex mirror of his eye, not as unchanging, but 'in her varnishes', an actual woman 'who won't improve in the light.' Referring to the varnishes, cracked light, worm of permanence and convex mirror in Van Eyck's work, the speaker takes some compensation from a 'way of life/that is its own witness', the ordinary life of her domestic interior, with her partner, sleeping child and 'the sort of light/jugs and kettles/grow important by.' While the woman in Van Eyck's painting is ageless, the speaker in 'Domestic Interior' knows that time will not stand still for her.

Boland returns to this theme and imagery more than thirty years later in her 2014 volume, *A Woman Without a Country*, in the poem, 'Mirror. Memory'[24] where the subject is again a Flemish painting. The speaker, in a gallery before a formal portrait of a man and woman, observes:

> pride in their eyes, rendered with animal glues,
> in the elaborate loops of their collars,
> even pride in the painter
>
> who only yesterday applied gesso
> and tacked the canvas to make them ready for
> a future of perpetual intrusion –

The observer here participates in that 'perpetual intrusion', one of those to view a painting in the years, even centuries, after it is completed. However, we find this speaker interrogating the image of the formally-posed couple, and imagining instead more ordinary people: 'winter provincials listening for infant cries,/boiling a kettle in the pre-dawn'. Boland chooses again to counterpoint the posed couple 'born to the high summer of Flemish pride' with the ordinary details of the life she describes in 'Domestic Interior', with people who, rather than 'pride', have 'sleep in their eyes'. Repeating the images of mirror, partner, infant and kettle of 'Domestic Interior', this poem with its title 'Mirror. Memory', returns, as Boland so often does, to themes and images in her earlier work, again relating the work of art to her own life.[25] The poems discussed above demonstrate Boland's desire to reflect everyday life in works of art, in her own case to portray her role as a woman poet, married and raising children in a suburb, outside the mainstream of Dublin literary culture and a predominately male literary tradition. In 'Fruit on a Straight-Sided Tray',[26] Boland imagines a mother-daughter relationship as a still life painting, beginning with a description of the artist's technique:

When the painter takes the straight-sided tray
and arranges late melons with grapes and lemons,
the true subject is the space between them:
in which repose the pleasure of these ovals
is seen to be an assembly of possibilities;
a deliberate collection of cross purposes.

The language of the poem is that of the painter: blues, purples, yellows, line, space, light, study, abstraction. The point of the poem is much more complex, however, as Boland transforms this still life into a poem about relationships between mother and child, a 'homely arrangement', like the fruit on the tray. The artist's composition becomes a metaphor: the 'physical tryst/between substances, disguising for a while the equation/that kills'. As inseparable as the mother and infant are at the moment, the speaker realises that this is bound to change: 'you are my child and between us are/ spaces. Distances. Growing to infinities'. Like the still life arrangement where 'the true subject is the space between' the objects on the tray, the space between mother and child will grow as the child ages. Andrew J. Auge explains:

> As a still life, the painting renders the flux of existence static, and thereby, preserves its subjects in their familiar forms. But the speaker [...] realises the distortion inherent in this pictorial representation.[27]

Like 'Domestic Interior', 'Fruit on a Straight-Sided Tray' stresses time's passage, and the child's inevitable move away from the mother becomes, what another poem, 'Before Spring',[28] calls 'a melancholy/in the undersong'.

The artistic term 'still life' works in different ways for Boland. In a later poem, 'Still Life',[29] the title suggests multiple meanings as Boland describes a painting *The Old Violin* by the nineteenth-century *trompe l'oeil* painter William Harnett, a native of Clonakilty in Cork who emigrated to Philadelphia. Noting that Harnett painted household objects and musical instruments in a most realistic way, creating his own version of still life paintings, Boland contrasts his work to an etching in the *Illustrated London News* of a woman holding a baby on one arm and a small dish in the other hand, with the caption 'Woman Begging at Clonakilty'. Margaret Crawford explains that the series of famine images in the *Illustrated London News* in the 1840s varied in how accurately they depicted the Irish famines. Of this engraving, she writes: 'The artist makes some effort to show distress: the woman's eyes seem swollen, her cloak is torn, her baby is a tiny bundle, but she herself is not emaciated'.[30]

Admiring Harnett's realistic depiction, with its torn sheet music and scratched violin hung on a door with rusty hinges, Boland highlights the limitations of the newspaper engraving, telling us in a parenthetical last line, '(The child, of course, was dead.)', which the newspaper caption failed to convey. The dead baby, the 'still life' in the Clonakilty mother's arms, becomes a tragic representation of the effects of the famine while the painting *The Old Violin* is a testament to the success of a realist painter who was able to escape from Clonakilty. In the final lines, the speaker describes another kind of still life experienced on a ride through contemporary Clonakilty: 'I looked back at fields, at the air extracting/the essence of stillness from the afternoon', a still place where the famine's effects are no longer seen.

As her work developed, Boland began to broaden her scope, particularly towards poems that might reflect Irish history and the often unacknowledged suffering of its people. In these poems also, the visual arts often provide the central image. 'In a Bad Light',[31] in the sequence 'Writing in a Time of Violence', develops the title's image to suggest what cannot be clearly seen, what larger cultural values potentially lurk in the background of any work of art. The speaker in 'In a Bad Light' stands in a museum in

St Louis, Missouri, where a figure in a glass case 'represents a woman in a dress,/with crêpe sleeves and a satin apron./And feet laced neatly into suede.' This elegantly dressed woman is depicted as travelling to New Orleans in 1860 in a replica of a cabin on a steamboat. Observing this image, the speaker speculates that the seamstresses who made the woman's elegant clothes would be Irish.

The museum display becomes what the poem calls a 'sign' for those invisible Irish women bent over in a bad light, 'sewing a last/sight of shore', [...] 'coffin ships./And the salt of exile.' Movement from the observer's individual 'I' to a collective 'we' brings the seamstresses out of silence to tell of their own dreams:

> We dream a woman on a steamboat
> parading in sunshine in a dress we know
> we made. She laughs off rumours of war.
> She turns and traps light on the skirt.
> It is, for that moment, beautiful.

Expanding the collective voice, the poem suggests that this museum piece is, in one sense, also a dream, as it fails to reflect the hardships behind the pleasurable steamboat travel, a failure defined as 'history's abandonment'. The poem undercuts the scenario depicted in the glass case as a deeper truth emerges: the difference between the privileged woman on the steamboat and the seamstresses toiling away in bad light, sewing in 'oil-lit parlours' and 'gas-lit backrooms'. Boland's light imagery has numerous implications: the scene in the museum is set in autumn (where light outside is 'clear') but the 'plastic' image casts the museum image in a 'bad light' which does not reflect or acknowledge the seamstresses' difficult work.

Linking her images, Boland connects the backgrounds of the two countries mentioned in the poem. The steamboat scenario is set in the shadow of the American Civil War, the years following the Irish famines, years of exile which brought many of these seamstresses to the United States. 'There is always a nightmare', the poem says, but a notice in the museum ignores all of this as it describes the life of a woman of privilege. As Catriona Clutterbuck says, 'the poverty-stricken Irish immigrant seamstresses speak back to the culture of Southern plantation privilege which existed just prior to the American Civil War', adding that this display is 'dangerous to an audience that will not interrogate it thoroughly'.[32] Developing the idea of nightmare even further, the poem is included in the volume, *In a Time of Violence*, which was published in 1994, when the various warring factions in Ireland mirrored the violence of the earlier nightmares of civil wars and famine.

Boland turns to a more specific event in Irish history in another poem, 'The Death of Reason'.[33] In this instance, her subject is the large issue of the English-Irish conflict. 'The Death of Reason' again depicts a woman sitting for a portrait, but here she is presented as a 'Nameless composite. Anonymous beauty-bait for the painter./Rustling gun-coloured silks. To set a seal on Augustan London.' The gun-coloured silk develops the pattern of war imagery in the poem, which begins with a description of the Peep-O-Day Boys, a group of Protestants in Ulster in the late 1700s who attacked and set fire to the homes of their Catholic neighbours. At the same time, the poem says, 'the art of portrait-painting reached its height/across the water', suggesting that the posing and neoclassical value of 'reasonable' art were dominant in England while the nightmare of conflict raged in the Irish countryside.

Linking the portrait of the woman to the wars, the poem pictures the raging flames set by the Peep-O-Day Boys in images of a painter's colours of 'alizerine crimson with a mite of yellow'. The fires eventually reach the imagined canvas and the woman's image burns, like the homes destroyed by the Peep-O-Day boys:

the eighteenth century ends here
as her hem scorches and the satin
decoration catches fire. She is burning down.
As a house might. As a candle will.
She is ash and tallow. It is over.

This portrait and sitter become symbols for the end of the age of reason, highlighting the distinction between the 'elegance' portrayed on canvas (in an image like Ingres' Mrs Badham) and the bloody battles going on in Ireland. The woman posing in 'The Death of Reason', the poem says, represents not only herself but 'the age [which] is ready to resemble her'.

The images of neoclassical art in Boland's poetry derive from the importance of the eighteenth century in the conflicts between England and Ireland, though little of this art reflected the ongoing social problems between the English and Irish. That irony is also developed in the poem 'In Which Hester Bateman, Eighteenth-Century English Silversmith, Takes an Irish Commission'.[34] The major image in the poem, a silver spoon, was commissioned from Bateman for a marriage in Ireland. Boland pictures the silversmith, as she has the portrait sitter in 'The Death of Reason', as distant from the battles in the country to which she is sending her work: 'Far away from grapeshot and tar caps/And the hedge schools and the music of sedition/She is oblivious to she pours out/And lets cool the sweet colonial metal.' Images of eighteenth-century Irish life, from hedge schools to artillery, contrast with the 'colonial' art of Bateman.

In spotlighting the work of the silversmith, who subjected the silver to violence as she 'Chased, beat it. Scarred it and marked it', Boland creates a symbol for the oppression of the Irish, the violence necessary to create the spoon compared to the treatment of people and land. The spoon symbolises 'an age-old tension' between England and Ireland, of 'Past and future and the space between/The semblance of empire, the promise of nation', both of which created problems. When this poem was published, in the 1990s, that age-old tension was still in evidence. The wedding spoon, an artistic celebration of union, paradoxically represents the 'mediation/Between oppression and love's remembrance.'

These poems on the visual arts are not isolated from the prevailing themes in Boland's work, in this case her early and continuing distinction between representations of history and the actual past. Histories, whether of time and place, of literature, of art, can give us one view of life and culture, but the past also is full of ghosts that are outside history. This is what we do not always see in the chronicles, in the canons of literary and art history, where a point of view is often determined by an individual who has selected image and narrative, or by a cultural and artistic mindset whose values embody a particular aesthetic. We have to be careful to see that these poems are not so much a condemnation of any artist as much as they are a reflection of a culture's inherent aesthetic values (neoclassical portrait painting being a good example), ultimately one potential disadvantage of even great art.

The poem, 'The Art of Grief',[35] brings together many of the subjects and themes in Boland's ekphrastic poems as she describes a speaker's reaction to a statue of a woman with 'A veil of grief covering her whole face.' Relating the woman to herself, the speaker says that both were of middle age but the statue's image is 'fixed, set and finished in/a mutton-fat creaminess, a seamless flutter in/marble', while her own life is neither set nor finished. Boland stresses the silence of the statue – the face 'had been chiselled out with the veil in/the same, indivisible act of definition/which had silenced her.' The poem connects the statue to a narrative where the speaker has once seen her own mother weep, though the mother never revealed nor did the speaker understand the source of that grief – a silence akin to that of the statue. The final lines highlight the value of the visual arts to Boland. Referring to the three women subjects in the poem, speaker/poet, mother and statue, the speaker describes her response to the woman represented in the statue: 'What she knew was gone and what I/wanted to know she had never known:/the moment her sorrow entered marble –'. As Richard York argues, the poem shows that the speaker's momentary knowledge comes from a visual art, 'but it questions that visual art, too. It conceives it as a violent hypostatization of life which is also process, change in time, memory'.[36]

Blending autobiographical, gender and aesthetic issues, 'The Art of Grief' suggests that weeping has no cadence itself. The poet, however, remedies this in the poem's structure and sound patterns: seven stanzas of eleven lines each, carefully blending end-stopped and run-on lines punctuated with caesuras and emphatic short sentences opening or ending a stanza. Weaving together narrative and lyric, the poem relates the silent statue to both the silent mother and the poet/daughter who says she could not weave into her cadences the grief that made her mother and the woman imagined in the statue weep. The poem, however, ironically undercuts this judgment in some of its most rhythmical and musical lines:

> I could see that weeping itself has no cadence.
> It is unrhythmical, unpredictable and
> the intake of breath, one sob needs to
> become another sob, so one tear can succeed
> another, is unmusical; whoever the muse is
> or was of weeping, she has put the sound of it
> beyond the reach of metric-makers, music-makers.

'The Art of Grief' demonstrates that, on one level, grief is not beyond the reach of art as both the statue and Boland's poem illustrate. In each case, as the final line states, art finds the region where 'grief and its emblems are inseparable'. And a poet, observing a work of art, can, despite what the poem says, create the cadences and enhance that emblem with her metrics and her music.

NOTES

1   *New Collected Poems*, pp 227–8; *NCP*, p. 165. The following abbreviations are used for quotations from Boland's work: NCP – *New Collected Poems*; DV – *Domestic Violence*; WWC – *Woman Without a Country*; OL – *Object Lessons*; JTM – *A Journey with Two Maps*.

2   Bethany J. Smith, 'Ekphrasis and the Ethics of Exchange in Eavan Boland's *Domestic Violence*', *Word and Image: A Journal of Verbal and Visual Enquiry*, 29:2, 2013, pp 212–32.

3   Kelly's portraits of Eavan Boland holding a doll are reproduced in *A Poet's Dublin*, an anthology of Boland's poems edited by Paula Meehan and Jody Allen Randolph (Carcanet, Manchester, 2014).

4   Eavan Boland, 'A Journey with Two Maps', *A Journey with Two Maps* (New York, 2013), pp 3–26. Boland likens this to Manet's reworking of a Berthe Morisot painting, one of her mother's favourite painters, submitted to the 1870 Paris Salon. The poem 'On this Earth' (DV, 38), describes a speaker taking her own daughter to see Morisot's painting of her daughter, Julie Manet, who was, according to the poem, 'wearing her mother's brush strokes.'

5   *OL*, p. 38.

6   *NCP*, p. 127.

7   Alfred Corn, 'Notes on Ekphrasis', www.poet.org/poetsorg/text /ekphrasis-poetry-confronting-art, accessed 10 September 2014.

8   Eavan Boland, 'A Journey with Two Maps', pp 3–26.

9   *Ibid.*, pp xiv–xv.

10 *NCP*, pp 108–109.

11 In a later poem, 'Studio Portrait 1897' (WWC), Boland describes a photograph of her grandmother, imagining her being told by the photographer: *'Keep still quite still not move stir not once'*.

12 Pilar Villar, '"The Text of It": A Conversation with Eavan Boland', *New Hibernia Review*, 10:2 (2006), pp 52–67.

13 Corn, 'Notes on Ekphrasis', p. 4.

14 NCP, p. 114.

15 NCP, p. 110.

16   NCP, p. 17.

17   Villar, 'The Text of It', p. 64.

18   Medbh McGuckian, 'Birds and their Masters' in Anthony Roche
      and Jody Allen Randolph (eds), 'Special Issue – Eavan Boland',
      Irish University Review, 23:1 (1993), pp 29–33. On the other hand,
      McGuckian sees 'Self-Portrait on a Summer Evening' as more
      subversive in that Boland presents herself as both artist and
      subject.

19   OL, p. 253.

20   NCP, pp 129–30.

21   Jody Allen Randolph, 'What Great Art Removes', *Women's
      Review of Books,* 26:2 (2009), pp 21–22. Allen-Randolph's book,
      Eavan Boland (Bucknell University Press, 2013) is a very good
      general introduction to Boland's work.

22   NCP, p. 92–8; WWC, p. 63.

23   NCP, pp 91–2.

24   WWC, p. 57.

25   Memories and mirrors are recurring images in *A Woman
      Without a Country,* emphasising the significance of changing
      views and time passing.

26   NCP, pp 97–8.

27   Andrew J. Auge, 'Fracture and Wound: Eavan Boland's Poetry
      of Nationality', *New Hibernia Review,* 8:2 (2004), pp 121–41.

28   NCP, pp 93–4.

29   DV, pp 19–20.

30   Margaret Crawford, 'The Famine and the *Illustrated London
      News,* 1845–9: Image Versus Reality' in Raymond Gillespie and
      Brian Kennedy (eds), *Ireland, Art into History* (Dublin, 1994), pp
      75–88.

31   NCP, pp 207–8.

32   Catriona Clutterbuck, 'Eavan Boland and the Politics of
      Authority', *Yearbook of English Studies,* 35 (2005), pp 72–90.

33   NCP, pp 205–6.

34   NCP, pp 279–80.

35   NCP, pp 239–41.

36   Richard York, 'Voice and Vision in the Poetry of Eavan Boland',
      Estudios Irlandeses, 2 (2007), pp 205–13.

Sinead Morrissey

THE MAYFLY
i.m. Lilian Bland, 1878–1971

Conspicuously mis-christened—what chink
        in the general atmosphere, what sudden
                lift of bones and breath

allowed you to stand up straight in mechanic's overalls
        (*skirts are out of the question*) and plot
                your escape route into the sky?

Like the right foot of Louis Blériot,
        trapped beside one of his overheating
                engines, like the umpteen previous

biplane extravaganzas that had left the ground
        —gadzooks!—for a couple of minutes
                only to wobble uncontrollably

in recalcitrant space and then nosedive,
        everything flared white hot
                for you until it abruptly ended:

ju-jitsu, shooting, horseracing,
        spending days on remote Scottish
                islands photographing seabirds.

You donned your Donegal cap
        (*the natives, I hear, thought one of the mills*
                had blown up but put it down

to a thunderstorm) and tapped your cigarette ash
        all over Edwardian decorum;
                if Blériot wouldn't let you near

his Channel-hopping aeroplane—
      you'd begged him in a letter
            to crown you as his passenger—

you'd build and fly your own.
      The unflexed, held-aloft wingspan
            of gulls in flight was where you started,

in the Tobercorran workshop,
      your gardener's-son assistant
            holding your tools and worshipping

you from a distance. *I enclose*
      two photos of my biplane,
            the "Mayfly"; she is the first

biplane to be made in Ireland:
      skids of ash, ribs and stanchions
            of spruce, bamboo outriggers

taut beneath unbleached calico,
      more grasshopper than aircraft.
            You ran the finished may-fly,

may-not fly still missing its engine
      and airy as a climbing frame off the top
            of Carnmoney Hill,

Belfast smouldering under its furnaces,
      the Lough a phlegmatic eye,
            casually watching, and hung

as a counterweight four six-foot
      volunteers from the Irish Constabulary
            who saw the ground ripped clear

of their feet in an upward gust
        and were trailed alarmingly over
                heads of astonished livestock

before dropping off.
        In the movie of your life
                they haven't scripted yet

all bets are on from this moment
        (it is quite a new sensation being charged
                by an aeroplane) –

a horizontally opposed two-cylinder
        engine with the help of a whiskey
                bottle and an ear trumpet

gets fitted next and Lord O'Neill
        of Randalstown Park, so struck
                by your exploits, offers up

his level acreage as a refuge
        and launching point.
                (The engine is beautifully balanced

but all the same the vibration
        is enormous ... the nuts
                dance themselves loose.)

Hooked all your life on barter –
        a glider for an aeroplane, an aeroplane
                for a motorcar, England

for Ireland, Ireland
        for Canada—you knew this was
                the single most inflammable

exchange you'd ever risk, the lone bull
standing slack under hawthorn
at the edge of the field,

quick chatter-and-flash
from the hedgerow,
enough of a canopy of willowy light

to finally allow admittance,
and saw, as you climbed up
to your tilted seat and got

those improbable Victorian pram wheels
started, a straggle of farmhands
and scullery maids,

politely assembled, all wishing you
skywards. Once it was finished,
you ran back, over and over,

to the proof it had happened: the tracks
of her passage in the spangled grass,
and then their absence –

your footprint missing on earth for the span
of a furlong, as if a giant had lifted its boot
and then set it down.

THE ANTIPASTORAL IN EAVAN BOLAND'S POETRY

Péter Dolmányos

Eavan Boland's contribution to modern Irish poetry and poetics needs no lengthy introduction. Her reputation is safely established as one of the definitive voices of the contemporary scene. Her position is likewise stable and unchallenged as she boldly lives up to the scope of Dillon Johnston's phrase of 'Irish poets who are also women'.[1] The phrase itself is emblematic of the situation: Boland herself is a living testimony to the Eliotian idea of the tradition that is modified to include new work and which as a result becomes its integral part. This is achieved by a constant dialogue with the tradition of modern Irish poetry, which is in turn also constantly engaged in a dialogue, occasionally in debate with the founding ideologies of the modern Irish state. These ideologies are rooted in what can be identified as a pastoral vision; thus Boland's poetry involves the examination and the refutation of this vision in favour of a more realistic approach to what constitutes everyday experience.

Boland's poems insist on the importance of the temporal constituent of human experience. The events she deals with have a temporal dimension and the locations of the poems are often places in an explicitly stated time. This insistence on time is also present in the pervasive dichotomy of myth and history in her poetry that has a direct relationship with her treatment of the pastoral. Though myth is a story and thus it is a temporal construct, its inclusion of the divine and the supernatural associates it with the impression of timelessness, which prompts Boland to regard history as the proper frame for the expression of human experience. As a result the idealising tendency of the pastoral tradition is passed over in favour of an approach that is concerned with the revision of that tradition and which can be best termed antipastoral.

VARIETIES OF PASTORAL

Terry Gifford distinguishes three main uses of the term pastoral to describe the possible scope of the concept. The original scope of the term is a formal convention that involves the world of country life and within that the figure and experience of the shepherd.[2] The broader understanding of the pastoral is related to content rather than form as it denotes a work that deals with the country in contrast with the urban world. Similarly to the first use of the term, this one retains an idealising tendency in relation to the world it describes. The third and most recent understanding of the pastoral dismisses this feature and relegates the term to pejorative use by suggesting the falsity of the idealised representation of the rural world.[3] The third meaning already indicates the possibility of revision and correction and as long as it explicitly happens the work is regarded as antipastoral.

Jonathan Allison claims that pastoral and antipastoral are intimately related to each other, even to the point of inseparability according to some readers.[4] In his brief account pastoral is described as originally seeing the country and rural life as offering a possibility of renewal for people corrupted by life in the court and the city, involving a tangible tendency to idealise its subject. This concept is broadened to cover a 'poetry of the countryside (however defined)' with or without explicit idealisation, whereas anti-pastoral subverts the idealising drive of the pastoral and suggests the limitations of the tradition.[5] Allison refers to Heaney's distinction as well to support his position: in Heaney's understanding 'pastoral is a matter of "idealised landscape with contented figures," but with antipastoral, "sweat and pain and deprivation are acknowledged"'.[6]

Donna L. Potts mentions that the origin of pastoral is connected with the epic tradition in an indirect way since what is overlooked by the epic can constitute the subject for the pastoral as it is a discourse of 'the unheroic and the everyday'.[7] Among the implications of the pastoral the harmonious relationship between man and nature is a cardinal one. During the development of pastoral classical imagery is replaced by a predominantly Christian one. The new element of the tradition as a result of this change is the garden, which increasingly takes over as the setting of pastoral poems, and the antithesis of garden and city becomes the new central opposition. Later shifts in the approach to the garden as a concept, however, will resituate this image: the neo-classicist tendency of seeing the garden as 'nature methodised' adds human ingenuity to the concept, whereas with the appearance of the suburb as part of the process of urbanisation the garden can even become a type of urban space. This is what is present in Boland's suburbia as well – the earlier antithesis gives way to an in-between category, a type of frontier perhaps where pastoral and antipastoral meet and clash with each other.

The location of Ireland at the westernmost periphery of Europe with its particular landscape and social composition singled it out to become a potential modern western 'equivalent of the ancient world's rural Arcadia'.[8] This was particularly true in the period after the industrial revolution, when the colonised Ireland offered a potential other to an increasingly industrialised and urbanised England. Yet the colonial status of Ireland also means a different situation in the local context since the development of pastoral in colonised areas follows a nostalgic pattern as current power relations necessarily prompt a nostalgic longing for previous states.

The basis of the Irish literary revival is also a pastoral one with its idealising drive of rural life and the figure of the peasant. This, however, is rooted in the paradox of the limited experience of rural life on part of the leading figures of the revival (Yeats, Lady Gregory and Synge): though they were representatives of the Anglo-Irish tradition, they had no real knowledge of the physical world of the peasant. This lack of direct experience brought fairly harsh criticism from writers critical of the revivalist agenda (principally Joyce and Beckett) but there is an intriguing presence of the antipastoral already in the work of Synge. The close entanglement of pastoral and antipastoral is perhaps most salient in the work of Patrick Kavanagh: he offers the most critical revision of the image of the Irish peasant in *The Great Hunger* but his early poetry is firmly rooted and strongly immersed in the pastoral tradition.

Contemporary Irish poetry is still characterised by a tendency for idealising the landscape yet the fact of partition has led to somewhat different paths of development for the pastoral. Despite the differences there is a growing concern with ecological and environmental matters in contemporary pastoral since its fundamental element of retreat is endangered by recent trends of modernisation. This increasing presence of environmental concerns links the pastoral with ecocritical approaches[9] and it points towards what Gifford terms the post-pastoral.[10] These relations represent a certain degree of terminological ambiguity which is also exemplified by Bernard O'Donoghue's assessment of Heaney's work: O'Donoghue uses the term anti-pastoral interchangeably with pastoral or bucolic to refer to the same field.[11]

BOLAND'S PASTORAL REVISIONS

What begins as an account of the promise of the discovery of a new world, or at least of a new beginning, in the early poem 'New Territory' eventually turns into a balanced picture of human life in a broader context which has been carefully relieved of illusions. The act of venturing into a new world is not idealised or romanticised as experience overwrites the possibility of any claims for innocence. Though the dense imagery of the opening of the poem builds up the expectation of something new, the speaker carefully brings this under control by observing that:

Water and air
And fire and earth and therefore life are here,
And therefore death.[12]

The hint at the possibility of pastoral is quickly intertwined with its opposite, recalling the 'Et in Arcadia Ego' motif of the paintings of Guercino and Poussin from the seventeenth century. This act of balancing is characteristic of Boland's poetry as a whole as her carefully constructed stance never allows idealisation to achieve its full potential as it is always countered by tangible reminders of the real.

The natural world is addressed in a similar manner in the poem 'Migration', emblematically dedicated to Michael Longley, a poet frequently engaged in writing about the natural world. On this occasion the migratory birds frequently associated with the romantic tradition are introduced both in their preparations for leaving and in their return. While their outbound preparations are seen as ceremonial, their return is markedly less glorious: they are 'single and ruffled',[13] and many birds are lost along the way, having fallen into the sea. These observations represent the clearly defined sceptical stance of the speaker in relation to the idealising tendency of the tradition of nature poetry.

The proper pastoral setting in Ireland would be the west with its association of unspoilt natural scenery. Yet this very primeval state of nature is what stands in the way of idealisation: in the poem 'On Holiday' the west is a world of 'Peat and salt' with a bawling wind that 'scalds the orchids/of the Burren' and with 'child-stealing spirits'[14] demanding constant sacrificial offerings of milk left on the windowsills. The interior is likewise unfriendly as 'The sheets are damp./We sleep between the blankets.'[15] On another instance, in 'White Hawthorn in the West of Ireland' the speaker sets out to the West with a definite aim:

> All I wanted then was to fill my arms with
> sharp flowers,
> to seem, from a distance, to be part of
> that ivory, downhill rush.[16]

This wish, however, is frustrated by superstition as the touching of hawthorn is thought to bring bad luck. The speaker is caught between the temptation offered by the artistic tradition of the pastoral and the anxiety of popular belief, with the latter eventually overcoming the former.

The frequent location of Boland's poems is the suburb. Though geographically it forms a part of the urban world, it can be considered more of an in-between space that is located at the meeting zone of country and city. The comforts of urban life are available yet the spatial dimension is opened up to include not only the strictly considered living space of a flat or a house, but a garden is present as well. The garden is a patch of nature transformed by enclosure and cultivation: it is a piece of nature domesticated in proportions adequate to human control. A proper image of this is present in 'Nocturne', with the kitchen light overflowing a part of the garden, turning it into 'an electric room – a domestication/of closed daisies',[17] yet the line break implies what becomes immediately explicit in terming the sight 'an architecture/ instant and improbable'.[18] The garden is a humanised space but laws of nature cannot be dispensed with even in this location. The suburban garden thus can become a proper setting for an exploration of the pastoral or the antipastoral as the close perspective can bring the idealising tendency of the pastoral under the control of reflection.

The first of the explicitly suburban-related poems is 'Suburban Woman'. The observation of the speaker of 'Town and country at each other's throat'[19] quickly locates the place in a context of war rather than in the usual association of peace, and this subversive approach remains characteristic of the whole poem: the world of domesticity is entangled in various forms of virulent conflict. Though the place is initially 'a space of truce',[20] the vocabulary of conflict and violence suggests that this is only temporary, and the first section of the poem closes with the image of defeat. The imagery then shifts from the military to the sexual but the implication of violence and violation remains as 'courtesan' and 'brothel' suggest.[21] With time moving on from the early morning moments domestic life takes over but it is understood as sacrifice when the perspective is opened on daily routine and on the broader context of individual life. Household activities require the 'pawning'[22] of her day and even childbirth is seen in business terms:

> [...] she, crying, stilled,
> bargained out of nothingness her child,
>
> bartered from the dark her only daughter.[23]

Though the image of the child implies promise and potential, the cost is made clear too as the new life is 'a seed' but it is simultaneously 'a life ransoming her death'[24] and the motif of April is capable of evoking Eliot as well as Chaucer.

The retreating and fading light of section IV offers a different perspective as the captured moment approximates the ideal concept of suburbia. The impression of time suspended endows the moment with the potential of vision by virtue of its peaceful nature, yet this is also one of 'thieving perspectives' and of 'the last light'.[25] The vocabulary of war returns in the last section but the end of the day is also the end of the conflict. This, however, is only a temporary state as the next day reopens the conflict and:

> […] all her victims then –
>
> hopes unreprieved, hours taken hostage –
> will newly wake[26]

This last section of the poem introduces the figure of a writing woman as well, the identifiable double and other of the woman observed in her daily routine. This conscious distancing of the observing intelligence suggests an emphasis on the act of critical assessment and it marks the sceptical approach to the possibility of a pastoral interpretation of modern suburban life – at least for a woman.

The antipastoral association of the suburb is even more explicitly stated in 'Ode to Suburbia'. In spite of the title neither the tone nor the subject of the poem gives the impression of anything elevated, which is blatantly made clear by the phrase 'ugly sister'[27] in reference to the suburb itself. The vision is claustrophobic: the domestic interior is a prison as the windows turn into mirrors that lock the inhabitant mercilessly inside. The antipastoral is perfectly illustrated by the deficient grammar of the 'sentence' 'No magic here'[28] but this is not the final stance as the spread of the suburb on the expense of the natural world proper is seen as encroachment and is attributed to the seductive powers of the suburban world originating in its 'plainness'.[29] The imagery of love and seduction hints at the essentially human nature of this particular environment, which subverts the possibility of reading this world as the example of human ingenuity complementing natural beauty. This is further illustrated by the final image of the cat that can claim its ancestry from the majestic lion, with the former's occasional ability of causing surprise by revealing something of its majestic ancestry. The irony involved in this parallel is an ample illustration of the relation between the suburb and nature.

The suburban setting is only implied in some poems but their references to the outside world are frequent reminders of the antipastoral. In the poem 'Before Spring' the precarious nature of the outside world is evoked through the image of the wind:

> That hard-blowing
> wind outside
> has a sound
> of spring.[30]

Spring is not automatically benevolent nor is the wind a pleasant harbinger of change. Similarly in 'Hymn' the winter night before dawn offers nothing consoling: 'A lamb/would perish out there'[31] and:

> The cutlery glitter
> of that sky
> has nothing in it
> I want to follow.[32]

In both poems the domestic interior represents the context of home whereas the natural world outside is too hostile for habitation, tilting the balance observably in favour of the former.

On other occasions, however, the garden can stand for the soothing and the miraculous which offer special moments of insight and which can thus be associated with the pastoral rather than with its revision. This happens in the poem 'In the Garden' as the speaker and her daughter explore the world of the garden. The delicate ambiguity of 'I want to show you/what/I don't exactly know'[33] illustrates the speaker's acknowledgement of the lack of perfect human control even in this enclosed piece of nature. The main observation, however, is that of innocence in a kind of prelapsarian world of instinct: the unconcerned happiness of the child finds an analogue in the snail as its wet marks precede the dew, and this in turn is read back on the child:

> [...] this is truth,
> this is brute grace
> as only instinct knows
> how to live it
>
> turn to me
> your little face.
> It shows a trace still,
> an inkling of it.[34]

Such revelatory moments, however, will meet their reconsideration in Boland's poetic world. 'The New Pastoral' is built on the experience of a suburban woman who is fully aware of her position: the opening contrast between a man's world and her own indicates the lack of a proper place for her in the tradition and she considers herself a 'displaced person/in a pastoral chaos'.[35] The 'comely maiden' of de Valera's vision would probably be an adequate person for the pastoral context but the stereotypical confinement of the woman in the world of domesticity as the foundation and guarantee of peace does not fit the modern experience of the speaker: her assertion 'But I'm no shepherdess'[36] and her questions about the supposed powers of idealised pastoral characters make it clear that the tradition is not applicable to her situation and thus it needs a reconsideration and a rewriting. The reality of modern suburban life excludes the possibility of idealisation but once this is accepted there is a chance for a happy life, perhaps not unlike that of the earlier tradition as the speaker's awakening sense of doubt indicates:

I could be happy here,
I could be something more than a refugee

were it not for this lamb unsuckled, for the nonstop
switch and tick
telling me

there was a past,
there was a pastoral,
and these chance sights

what are they all
but amnesias of a rite

I danced once on a frieze?[37]

The highly self-reflexive reconsideration of the pastoral tradition concludes with an intriguing case of doubt. The image of the mythic rite captured on the frieze suggests the suspension of time through its association of art and also through the possible pun on 'freeze', yet this simultaneously implies the severing of ties with reality by eliminating the temporal dimension. The word 'amnesia', however, is a function of time thus the doubt expressed at the end indeed means an act of redefining the pastoral for the modern world, which in turn will perhaps retrospectively lead to a reconsideration of the original tradition itself. The principal direction of the poem points towards the calling into question of the tradition itself, suggesting a false premise at its basis by the oxymoron of the 'pastoral chaos'. The pastoral is only successful if its nature as discourse is acknowledged, yet this also means the acceptance of the fact that idealisation is necessarily falsification at the same time. If continuity is accepted between the pastoral tradition and contemporary suburban life then the tradition needs a thorough revision especially in the light of Boland's accounts of suburban experience.

Reconsideration takes an even broader sweep in 'A Ballad of Beauty and Time' as it focuses on art itself. The context is that of an ageing woman setting out 'to buy some time',[38] visiting a plastic surgeon first and a sculptor after that in the hope of countering the physical effects of passing time yet both encounters yield sobering revelations about the power, or rather, the powerlessness of the chosen agents. While the modern art of the plastic surgeon is carried out on living material and thus it is predictably ephemeral compared to that of the sculptor, the latter's confession about his skill subverts the generally acclaimed notion of the artist's power of immortalising the subject: the sculptor's knowledge consists solely of recognising when to finish the work. The contrast of the two makers eventually serves the purpose of the reconsideration of idealisation and its relation to the real and it boldly deconstructs the Keatsian notion of beauty equalling truth: the captured moment is frozen, deliberately devoid of movement, and consequently of life, the 'immortality' or 'eternity' of art is idealisation which loses its connection with reality in the very moment when it is made. Demythologisation becomes complete in the assertion of the speaker 'I am the brute proof./Beauty is not truth'[39] with its deliberate choice of only approximant rhymes.

The echo of Keats's urn returns in 'Object Lessons' in the rather profane form of a coffee mug with a hunting scene on the side. The details of the scene culminate in the kiss of a lady and the huntsman, offering a modern fulfilment for the yearning pair of Keats's pastoral. The contrast is further elaborated as the sacrificial march of the urn is evoked through the rather commonplace scene of hunting – though both imply violence, the respective contexts are markedly different. With the breaking of the coffee mug the difference becomes even more tangible: the hunting scene, by virtue of the destruction of the object that carried it, becomes the representation of time abruptly stopped rather than time suspended – the twentieth-century antipastoral implies an unfulfilled potential rather than the consciously preferred aestheticised improbable eternity of Keats.

In 'Suburban Woman: A Detail' the autumn scene facilitates a metamorphosis of the location into something that contrasts with the earlier representations of the suburb as a purely functional living space with no mystery involved. The first part of the poem follows the usual demystifying path:

> This is not the season
> when the goddess rose
> out of seed, out of wheat,
> out of thawed water
> and went, distracted and astray,
> to find her daughter.[40]

The speaker sets out to visit a neighbour yet the fading light destabilises her usual perception of the familiar space of the garden and the result is a vision of a tree revealing its human origin, evoking the frequently used Daphne myth. The effect of this on the speaker is similar to the doubt at the end of 'The New Pastoral' as she loses her sense of origin and destination.

In 'The Women' a more controlled process of metamorphosis is outlined with a great deal of self-reflection involved. The facilitator of the change is temporal rather than spatial this time: it is 'the in-between, /neither here-nor-there hour of evening',[41] which results in a similar state of being 'in two minds'[42] for the speaker, yet this is the state of creative work for her too. The emerging vision is grounded in the pastoral and in myth, and the continuity between the ancient and the contemporary is asserted, yet there is a sense of disruption present, paradoxically through the act of reflection and recording: 'the physical force of a dissonance –/the fission of music into syllabic heat'[43] indicates some form of discontinuity. Though the muses may be sisters, the supplanting of music by poetry, or pastoral myth by contemporary suburban life, will involve unavoidable shifts in perspective requiring the conscious participation of the reflective intelligence.

This reflective intelligence becomes the focus of the poem with the rather explicit title 'We Are Human History. We Are Not Natural History'. The setting is the usual garden and the chosen summer evening is special because of the children's discovery of wild bees and the show of light that unfolds as a result of their reaction to the scene. The distinctiveness of this particular evening, however, is only interpretable from the point of view of the human mind as it is the contemplating imagination that finds an elegiac element in what would be an absolutely common summer evening for the bees of the same scene. The elegiac motif reinforces the presence and importance of the temporal constituent of the experience and implies the notion of history – on a small and personal scale but inevitably linking it with particularly human experience and making it a definitive part of that given experience.

The inescapable temporal dimension of life prompts a necessary choice for Boland's speaker in 'Outside History'. The historically unmeasurable timespan suggested by the stars of the January skies renders them 'outsiders'[44] whose function is to facilitate the recognition of temporality and its implications:

> They keep their distance. Under them remains
> a place where you found
> you were human, and
>
> a landscape in which you know you are mortal.
> And a time to choose between them.[45]

The choice that can be made is even more intriguing:

I have chosen:

out of myth into history I move to be
part of that ordeal
whose darkness is

only now reaching me from those fields,
those rivers, those roads clotted as
firmaments with the dead.[46]

Though myth, just as history, is a human construct yet it is
distinguished from history by its incorporation of the
divine and the consequent illusion of the suspension of
time both of which act as redemptive measures as opposed
to the purely human dimension of history. The choice of
history with its conceivable temporal frame is the necessary
response for the sake of artistic honesty and truthfulness.
This is the choice that informs Boland's approach to the
pastoral on the whole: pastoral is associated with myth and
with timeless, yet this is a falsification of human experience
as life is a function of time; the temporal is an inescapable
and essential element of the human world thus the proper
response to it is the antipastoral.

In 'Time and Violence' two regular characters of the
pastoral tradition are finally given an opportunity to
express their own experience of what is regarded as
timeless and idealised existence. The poem employs the
usual suburban setting with the woman contemplating the
scene in the evening on the step. The time is different
though as it is early spring and the natural association of
rebirth witnessed in the garden contrasts with the
speaker's melancholic recognition of ageing. The tension
between the individual human experience of life as a linear
process and the perception of life in the natural world as a
cycle nearly causes the speaker to miss what turns out to
be a vision: a shepherdess appears in the doorway and a
mermaid is spotted by the road. Neither of these two
figures concord with the usual associations of such

pastoral figures as the shepherdess has a cracked smile and some physical injuries and the mermaid displays 'all/ the desolation of the North Sea in her face'.[47] On the speaker's closer scrutiny they are both disappearing but a voice is heard addressing her:

> This is what language did to us. Here
> is the wound, the silence, the wretchedness
> of tides and hillsides and stars where
>
> we languish in a grammar of sighs,
> in the high-minded search for euphony,
> in the midnight rhetoric of poesie.
>
> We cannot sweat here. Our skin is icy.
> We cannot breed here. Our wombs are empty.
> Help us to escape youth and beauty.
>
> Write us out of the poem. Make us human
> in cadences of change and mortal pain
> and words we can grow old and die in.[48]

As earlier, the Keatsian cold pastoral is rejected in favour of the temporal though this time the attribution of this idea to genuine representatives of the tradition lends more authenticity to the act of refusal. The situation is still somewhat paradoxical: the human construct of the pastoral locks these figures in a timeless world which lacks those very elements that constitute fundamental human experience – the heat of passion, childbirth, ageing, pain and death are all missing as lived experience. Aestheticisation is understood as confinement rather than liberation, and these characters experience language as a prison – the discourse of the pastoral turns into its antithesis, in the suburban nightfall the assumed pastoral becomes antipastoral.

CONCLUSION

In Eavan Boland's poetry experience is always carefully framed: it is a function of time and it is linked to a well-defined place. The frequent use of a suburban setting offers a limited space which contrasts with nature proper and this comes with the choice of special times such as the evening, the twilight or the morning, suggesting process and the temporal unfolding of experience. There is often the image of a woman standing in the doorway or a woman writing: both give the impression of the in-between position of contemplation and the latter explicitly implies the transforming of experience into discourse in parallel with the temporal dimension of experience. The contemplation of natural scenery in the human frame of the garden involves the pastoral and that in turn evokes myth yet there is a clear-cut insistence on the presence of a dichotomy as the pastoral is balanced by the antipastoral and myth is challenged by history in the claim for the representation of human experience.

The revision of the pastoral involves both its spatial and temporal dimensions. The spatial constituent of the pastoral has its modern incarnation in the garden in the suburb and the location already suggests ambiguities by its very nature as an in-between category incorporating the human space of town and the natural world of the country. In spite of all the human efforts of domestication, the garden retains much of its relation with nature and as a result it never fully becomes the possible modern equivalent of the scene of the retreat of the pastoral tradition. The temporal constituent is addressed by the repeatedly stated conviction that time is a part of human experience thus its inclusion is an inescapable necessity in the representation of experience. This conviction informs Boland's conscious choice of history over myth in spite of all the artistic temptations of the comforts of an aesthetic tradition.

The preference of history over myth and the mundane experience of suburban life offer the frame for the reconsideration of the pastoral. The pastoral tradition is deconstructed along a dialogue with the tradition itself:

through the examination of events, characters and locations the idealised world of the pastoral is rejected in favour of an antipastoral revision of critical observation. The allusions to myths and the occasional revelatory moments unfolding in that suburban garden indicate that the break is not complete and unredeemable with the pastoral: the implications of Boland's pastoral revisions point toward Gifford's notion of the post-pastoral, the acknowledgement and incorporation of both pastoral and antipastoral elements in the contemporary notion of the tradition itself.

NOTES

1   Dillon Johnston, *Irish Poetry after Joyce* (2nd edition) (Syracuse, Syracuse University Press, 1997), p. 273.
2   Terry Gifford, *Pastoral: New Critical Idiom* (London, Routledge 1999), p. 1.
3   Gifford, p. 2.
4   Jonathan Allison, 'Patrick Kavanagh and the Antipastoral' in Matthew Campbell (ed.), *The Cambridge Companion to Contemporary Irish Poetry* (Cambridge, Cambridge University Press, 2003) p. 42.
5   Allison, p. 42.
6   Allison, p. 42.
7   Donna L. Potts, *Contemporary Irish Poetry and the Pastoral Tradition* (Columbia, University of Missouri Press, 2011) p. 1.
8   Potts, p. 3.
9   Potts, p. 13.
10   Gifford, pp 146–50.
11   Bernard O'Donoghue, 'Heaney's Classics and the Bucolic', in Bernard O'Donoghue (ed.), *The Cambridge Companion to Seamus Heaney* (Cambridge, Cambridge University Press, 2009), p. 106.
12   Eavan Boland, *New Collected Poems* (Manchester, Carcanet, 2005), p. 9.
13   Boland, p. 11.
14   Boland, p. 143.
15   Boland, p. 144.
16   Boland, p. 180.
17   Boland, p. 142.

18 Boland, p. 142.
19 Boland, p. 63.
20 Boland, p. 63.
21 Boland, p. 64.
22 Boland, p. 64.
23 Boland, p. 64.
24 Boland, p. 64.
25 Boland, p. 65.
26 Boland, p. 65.
27 Boland, p. 66.
28 Boland, p. 66.
29 Boland, p. 66.
30 Boland, p. 93.
31 Boland, p. 95.
32 Boland, p. 95.
33 Boland, p. 106.
34 Boland, p. 107.
35 Boland, p. 113.
36 Boland, p. 113.
37 Boland, pp 113–4.
38 Boland, p. 122.
39 Boland, p. 124.
40 Boland, p. 138.
41 Boland, p. 141.
42 Boland, p. 141.
43 Boland, p. 141.
44 Boland, p. 188.
45 Boland, p. 188.
46 Boland, p. 188.
47 Boland, p. 238.
48 Boland, pp 238–9.

REFERENCES

Jonathan Allison, 'Patrick Kavanagh and the Antipastoral' in Matthew Campbell (ed.), *The Cambridge Companion to Contemporary Irish Poetry* (Cambridge, Cambridge University Press, 2003), pp 42–58.

Eavan Boland, *New Collected Poems* (Manchester, Carcanet, 2005).

Terry Gifford, *Pastoral: New Critical Idiom* (London, Routledge, 1999).

Dillon Johnston, *Irish Poetry After Joyce*, 2nd edition (Syracuse, Syracuse University Press, 1997).

Bernard O'Donoghue, 'Heaney's Classics and the Bucolic' in Bernard
O'Donoghue (ed.), *The Cambridge Companion to Seamus Heaney*
(Cambridge, Cambridge University Press, 2009), pp 106–121.
Donna L. Potts, *Contemporary Irish Poetry and the Pastoral Tradition*
(Columbia, University of Missouri Press, 2011).

Paula Meehan

IT IS ALL I EVER WANTED
for Eavan Boland

to sit by this window
the long stretched light of April falling
on my desk, to allow

the peace of this empty page
and nearing
forty years of age

to hold in these hands
that have learnt to be soothing
my native city, its hinterland

and backstreets and river scored
memory of spring
blossom and birds –

my girl-poems
fountaining
over grief and the want of someplace to call home.

Last week I took as metaphor, or at least as sign,
a strange meeting:
a young fox walking the centre line

down the south side of the Square
at three in the morning.
She looked me clear

in the eyes, both of us curious
and unafraid. She was saying –
or I needed her to say – *out of the spurious*

the real, be sure
to know the value of the song
as well as the song's true nature.

Be sure, my granny used say,
of what you're wanting,
for fear you'd get it entirely.

Be sure, I tell myself,
you are suffering
animal like the fox, not nymph

nor sylph, nor figment,
but human heart breaking
in the silence of the street.

Familiar who grants me the freedom of the city,
my own hands spanning
the limits of pity.

from *Dharmakaya* (Carcanet Press, 2000)

A Modern Encounter with 'Foebus Abierat': On Eavan Boland's 'Phoebus Was Gone, all Gone, His Journey Over'

Christine Murray

A poem known as 'Foebus abierat' or 'Phoebus had gone' ascribed to anon and likely written by a woman in northern Italy toward the end of the tenth century, was discovered in 1960 by Peter Dronke, editor of *Medieval Latin and the Rise of the European Love-Lyric*. The original poem is brief and its structure is simple with, as Dronke says, 'rhythmic five line strophes with monorhyme'.[1] 'Foebus abierat' is a song and as such may have been written to be performed. The poem is a dream-vision lyric which, despite its sensuality and apparent secularism, I will argue has an implied homiletic theme.

Eavan Boland's translation of 'Foebus abierat' titled 'Phoebus was gone, all gone, his journey over' was published in *Poetry* (2008).[2] The translation is accompanied by a brief note by Boland which describes her interest in bringing this almost lost poem to a modern audience. The theme and thrust of Boland's 'Phoebus was gone, all gone, his journey over' is one of tension between female transgression and the divine order. As Boland says, in this dream-vision lyric, 'from the first stanza, with its moonlight and wild beasts, it's obvious that the agenda of this poem is magic rather than measure'.[3] In this essay, I will argue that while this opinion has veracity in the poem's translation and mystic overlay, the poem remains tenaciously adherent to the church doctrine of its time, giving this reading a heightened tension.

In a rough prose approximation the poem reads: Phoebus had gone away, his voyage past. His sister was riding high, unbridled, directing her beams into forest springs, and wild beasts at the chase, their jaws agape. Mortals had surrendered their limbs to slumber. At a time in April just passed, a faithful likeness stood before me; calling me softly, he touched me little by little. His voice, overwhelmed by tears, failed him. Sighing, he was not strong enough to speak. At his touch, I trembled fearfully. As if in terror I startled, leapt to rise. With outstretched arms I pressed my body to his. Then froze utterly, drained of blood for he had vanished. I was holding nothing. Freed from slumber, I boldly cried out: 'What escape do you seek? I beg of you, why so quickly? Only wait if you will – I too shall enter for I want to live with you eternally!' Soon I regretted having spoken so. The terrace windows had been opened, Diana's beams poured in with beautiful light while I in my wretchedness grieved so long. Streams of tears flowed down my cheeks. Until the next day, my weeping never ceased.

Eavan Boland's translation of the poem follows on from her earlier translations of Irish and classical lyric poetry centering strong women characters at the heart of these poems. There is a sense that Boland is bringing the reader into a created space where legendary women, like her

Gráinne in 'Song',[4] can have an independent existence and where their perceived transgressions are actually a warrior cry for individuality and growth beyond the societal bounds that oppress them. In the same way, Boland's translation of 'Foebus abierat' brings this work directly into the realm of our contemporary understanding.

Eavan Boland's speech to the Poetry Book Society, 'Gods Make Their Own Importance: The Authority of the Poet in Our Time'[5] delineated the difficulties of being a woman poet in the post-independence period when Ireland's intellectual and creative development was effectively stymied by the Catholic constitution. The imaginative creation of the State was primarily seen as an occupation for the male poet, and traditional poetry forms were the norm in published work. This control over the imaginative creation of the State as well as the expected engagement of the poet with conservative religiosity and the narrow understanding of the role of women led to the radical impotence of the female poet's voice on issues of creative authority, as well as a telling lack of modernist expression and experimentalism in Irish canon.

That poetry is a marginalised artform is a given. That Irish women's poetry has been treated as lacking in authority can seem a national tragedy for which no-one seems able to account. What we, as readers, look for in poetry and in translated work is the expressive authority of the poet. An imaginative Ireland that has a lack of strong public women is an intolerable Ireland. The most important revelation in Eavan Boland's poetry and in her works of translation is that of showing up this tension and, in some cases, of allowing for the possibility of an anarchic transgression.[6] 'Phoebus was gone, all gone, his journey over' demonstrates both.

Myth and legend were important in the creation of Ireland's cultural identity from the very outset of the post-independence period. The intellectual and cultural development of Irish women writers and artists was certainly affected by de Valera's Catholic constitution.[7] While Ireland's historical mythologies are populated with female warriors and powerful queens, they were as good as written from history in the early years of the new State. Literary mothers and grandmothers were virtually inaccessible to the serious poetry reader. Eavan Boland's work in translation has a reinvigorating aspect in this respect. While 'Foebus abierat' was probably written by a woman, it does present us with some difficulty as the speaker-protagonist ultimately submits to what I see as the perception of a dogmatic created order. She recognises her transgressive death wish is opposed to the divine order, which – in the end – she does not wish to transcend.

'Foebus abierat' contains both the sacred and the profane balanced finely within it. The contemporary reader can choose to navigate an early poem like this through historical understanding, or to find her way to the original poem's sense, movement, and symbol cluster without the common knowledge that was available to its listeners when it was first composed. In this translation, Boland decides to bring us fully into world of the poem, but in ways which make its emotional import feel thoroughly contemporary.

'Foebus abierat' draws from the vernacular ballad tradition in its monorhyme and strophic structure. Eavan Boland extends the original poem, making it five full stanzas, while retaining the original intent and thematic drive:

PHOEBUS WAS GONE, ALL GONE, HIS JOURNEY OVER

Phoebus was gone, all gone, his journey over.
His sister was riding high: nothing bridled her.
Her light was falling, shining into woods and rivers.
Wild animals opened their jaws wide, stirred to prey.
But in the human world all was sleep, pause, relaxation, torpor.

One night, in an April which had just gone by,
The likeness of my love stood beside me suddenly.
He called my name so quietly. He touched me gently.
His voice was drowning in tears. It failed completely.
His sighs overwhelmed him. Finally, he could not speak clearly.

I shuddered at his touch. I felt the fear of it.
I trembled as if I knew the true terror of it.
I opened my arms wide and pressed him against my body.
Then I froze: I was ice, all ice. My blood drained into it.
He had fled. Here was my embrace – and there was nothing in it.

Fully awake now, I cried out loudly:
'Where are you fleeing to? Why are you rushing away?
Wait, wait for me. If you want, I can enter there.
Because the truth is, I want to live with you forever'.
But soon I regretted it – that I had spoken out this way.

And all the time, the windows of the terrace had been wide open.
The light of the moon poured down; its beauty, its radiance.
And I grieved and grieved. I grieved for so long.
The tears flowed down my cheeks: tributaries of tears.
It was a whole day before I could stop weeping.[8]

As is immediately clear, 'Foebus abierat' contains worlds –
the spirit world is visiting the fleshly world and the
context also includes the world of religious piety by
implication, as I will argue below. Boland leaves the
material core of the poem unchanged, but she adds a
contemporary perspective, achieved through her use of
language and her manipulation of image.

My own perspective is that our post-modern
relationship to poetry is nullified by our understanding of
what the poem has become; an externalised self-dialogue
foisted upon an unforgiving and uninterested public.
Magazines shoot out neat and tidy forty line poems as a
hen produces her eggs. Ideas and themes contained in the
poetic form are limited by our contemporary approach to
poetry to such an extent that the modern poem can be
merely a shard of narrated experience with little of value

or with little or no recognition of the possibility of universal themes. It could be said that we are alienated from understanding the thrall of once universally held ideas, whether they were informed in poems by either shared religions or via communal moral-philosophical systems.

The triumph of individualism has allowed us create multiple responses to the poetry of the past, often leading to skewed interpretations of the original work. This can sometimes be a good thing however, if it freshens dialogue or widens contemporary perspectives on the poem. The job of the poet-translator though, is to retain as much of the original intent and movement of the poem as possible while contemporising it for a modern audience. Poetry translation can be confrontational, dynamic and ekphrastic. That we have diluted the meaning of poetic ekphrasis, limiting it to a type of poetic collaboration in the visual art and musical fields, does not necessitate that the poet translator should follow suit:

> Ekphrastic poems are now understood to focus only on works of art – usually paintings, photographs, or statues. And modern ekphrastic poems have generally shrugged off antiquity's obsession with elaborate description, and instead have tried to interpret, inhabit, confront, and speak to their subjects.[9]

A contemporary reading of Boland's translation 'Phoebus was gone, long gone, his journey over' is of course wildly different to how the original audience of 'Foebus abierat' would have heard and experienced the work. Boland's engagement with the poem as an art object becomes part of her translation process. The moral and philosophical worldview inherent in the original both contains and forgives the unidentified protagonist's stated transgression against the divine order manifest in the physical hierarchy of the observed world. This suggests to me that the original poem is placed firmly in the religionist and homiletic genre. That the intent of the original poet is supremely retained and understood centuries later is a testament to Boland's skill as a collaborative translator. 'Phoebus was gone, all gone, his journey over' moves swiftly from its mystical opening lines, through the speaker's expression of grief and eventually toward recognition of her earthly exile from the beloved. Exile is of course a common theme in homiletic works, readily observable in the Anglo-Saxon worldview of say, works like *The Seafarer* and *The Wanderer* but here that exile is inscribed differently.

The major themes of 'Foebus abierat' are: transgression against the divine order, the grief of an exile on earth and the loss of love. That the loss of the lover is subsumed beneath the protagonist's ultimate acceptance of her earthly exile points to the poem having moral intent. There are many examples of medieval mystic literature with similar themes but 'Foebus abierat' is different, as the speaker is likely a woman and we are aware that she comes alarmingly close to personal transgression:

> Wait, wait for me. If you want, I can enter there.
> Because the truth is, I want to live with you forever.
> But soon I regretted it – that I had spoken out this way.

The Wanderer, for instance, describes a recognition of personal exile and a yearning for reunion with one's fellows. It paints a crisis of exile and loss. It does not show the main protagonist as personally transgressive, and consequently it could provide comfort to a listening audience. In contrast, the protagonist in 'Foebus abierat' is in danger of losing her immortal soul for love. That she barely survives this almost cataclysmic loss gives the work its inherent tension.

In 'Foebus abierat' we have a grief poem, a lament in which human desire almost rejects the divine will and the hierarchical order from which it stems. 'Foebus abierat' is inherently a moral poem despite the overtones of sorcery or magic in the opening lines. While church doctrine is not overtly mentioned, the core theme of self-rescue from transgression against the understood order of things is clear.

The map of the globe and our understanding of our place in the world has radically altered since this anonymous poem was composed. That we are in another place, that our understanding of the world has expanded way beyond what tenth or eleventh century readers would recognize makes it all the more exciting that we can connect with the spirit of the work. Our previous reliance on the great oral traditions of sung poetry has shifted to the experience of poetry being largely now a private interaction between reader and text. We may have lost our ability to hear poetry at a shared communal level due to the post-enlightenment shift towards individualism in all things.

Contemporising a work such as 'Foebus abierat' allows the reader to connect with a work of the imagination at our own experiential level of understanding. The reader begins to look at the translated work both as a dialogue between original poet and the poet translator as well as being a personal poetic encounter. In effect, readers participate in the translation by contributing our own set of understandings. With the contemporary poet-translator acting as a bridge, a chain of understanding is created that connects us to a visceral sense of literature written centuries ago. As Boland describes in her translator's note:

> I have tried for a plainspoken note so as to make more contemporary this wonderful long-ago cry of a woman, finding and losing a body and soul.[10]

Eavan Boland is part of the tradition of women translators who work with an interest in how texts survive. She has also worked with the marginalia of 'Pangur Bán' (which will be discussed below) and while Dorothy L. Sayers' great translation of Dante's *The Commedia* was left unfinished and was only latterly completed by Barbara Reynolds from Sayers' extensive translator's notes, we could also mention Marion Glasscoe's work on Julian of Norwich in the same context.[11] Contemporary women editors, poets and translators are performing great acts of retrieval and engagement for contemporary audiences.

From the outset of 'Phoebus was gone, long gone, his journey over' we are confronted with Boland's energetic approach to her translation:

> Phoebus was gone, all gone, his journey over.
> His sister was riding high: nothing bridled her.

Boland then sets up a tension between the sleeping world and the light of radical vision enacted through Phoebus' sister, the moon:

> Her light was falling, shining into woods and rivers.
> Wild animals opened their jaws wide, stirred to prey.

The moon, or Diana, functions in the poem both as a symbol and an actor. She is one of the major dramatis personae catalysing the homiletic theme at the core of the poem and in its contemporary translation. The moon is a mystical being, who, by the generosity of her illuminatory gift, allows the meeting between the living woman and her dead lover. The moon is the originator of mythos and an ally to the grieving woman. That the unidentified woman speaker ultimately rejects the moon's gift as transgressive and against the divine order does not lessen the moon's presence in the development of the poem's theme.

It is worth noting however that there is no sense of the moon having to mourn the loss of her brother: instead she continues in her necessary operation: 'nothing bridled her'. Moon appears to open the portal into which the dead

Phoebus can re-enter, be it purely as a vision or in some non-physical actuality. The brief and unaccountable return of Phoebus can be interpreted as a gift from the moon to the lover. That the speaker-protagonist cannot enter into the gift brings her in turn an awareness of her grief and then, of her humanity. A double-edged gift if there ever was one.

Boland returns to the moon image in stanza 5 picking up on the tension initialised in her introductory stanza. The instance of reunion, or allowed moment, closes. The entire action of the lovers reunion appears to occur within seconds. Boland uses the stanzaic form to create and sustain the movement from recognition to loss. That movement gives the illusion of time passing within the poem but this is experienced by the reader rather as an energetic movement, one encapsulating a nanosecond of retrieval:

> And all the time, the windows of the terrace had been wide open.
> The light of the moon poured down; its beauty, its radiance.

The moon's mystical status and divine persona is always other to the speaker here. Boland chooses not to fully personify the moon in stanza 5; she has become 'it', perhaps denoting the difference between the mortal and the divine heroines, or between the speaker and Diana. The moon, as catalyst for the action of the poem, enables the drama to occur. The mystical, or peculiar between-place opened at the beginning allows the reader to adjust their thinking to the possibility of mythos and to side-step concepts like chronological time.

We are invited through 'Foebus abierat' to enter into realms that are other to the human, 'But in the human world all was sleep, pause, relaxation, torpor' (l.5). We recognise that grief is a dominating factor in the poem. We are also aware that the protagonist realises her transgression against nature in her vocalised death wish. As a result of her catalysing meeting with the imagined Phoebus, the speaker-protagonist allows herself to grieve, ultimately recognising and accepting her humanity. While 'Phoebus was gone, all gone, his journey over' is secular-mystical in its overt language and symbolic overtones, it contains within it an affirmation of perceived order and of the medieval worldview.

In this reading, the newly-dead Phoebus has become 'other'. His sister, the moon, endows a moment of grace or momentary reunion to his human lover. She can accept the gift or not. The poem's protagonist avers her living condition:

> I opened my arms wide and pressed him against my body.
> Then I froze: I was ice, all ice. My blood drained into it.
> He had fled. Here was my embrace – and there was nothing in it.

The lover's death-wish is transgressive according to a worldview where sin includes suicide or harm to the created self. The beauty of the world is poignantly illustrated by the rift created between the feeling creaturely world and the momentary visitation of the newly dead. We would have a whole other poem if the speaker protagonist were to go with Phoebus. But the poem that we do have and Boland's translation of it both manage to imply this possibility as subtly enticing.

'But soon I regretted it – that I had spoken out this way' (l.20) represents the protagonist's awareness of her mooted transgression. That recognition abruptly closes the moon-created portal which allowed Phoebus entry. It allows her to grieve, a purely human and creaturely rejection of fantasy. There is no overt religiosity in the poem, but we know that the experience of grief separates us from both the animal and the godly realm. Grief brings us back to earth and we are faced with our own mortality.

The poem is left open-ended. The speaker appears to be alone in the world, neither invited into the mystical, the fantastical nor the religious. The reader keenly feels the sting of self-recognition experienced by the speaker. But we leave the poet in her grief, what else can we do? The world, radiantly lit by Phoebus' sister is a backdrop to her loss and grief. Our hope is that the speaker will find her place in this world. While the action occurs against a moonlit backdrop, and momentary relief is experienced, the speaker's personal transgression is finally cast in a moralistic light and clearly carries a universal lesson.

Boland's 'Phoebus was gone, all gone, his journey over' creates a tableau vivant in its spare visuals; her choice of language creates the energy of the poem's translation. To further explore her methods, we can look briefly at her pacy, almost tenacious translation of 'Pangur Bán', an 11th-century note written into the margins of a manuscript in the Monastery of St Paul, Carinthia, Austria.

'Pangur Bán' has been translated by Robin Flower, Seamus Heaney, Frank O'Connor and others. Boland's translation is energetic and catlike. She cuts away any descriptive superfluity and historical reference. Her rolling words mimic the action of the cat:

> And his delight when his claws
> Close on his prey
> Equals mine when sudden clues
> Light my way.[12]

Action and light are important elements in Eavan Boland's poetic work. Both 'Phoebus was gone, all gone, his journey over' and 'Pangur Bán' evince Boland's relation to revealing the passing of time alongside memorable instants. 'Pangur Bán' can be read as an exposition of the artistic process; we can trace the process through the words of the long dead scribe, who hunts each riddle from dark to light. It speaks directly to us as we know the creative process is a toil. It is isolating, yet the rewards of inspiration far outweigh sedentary isolation. The unidentified author of 'Pangur Bán' transcends his solitude by speaking directly through poetic form to us, his readers. Can poetry can truly capture the sense of a moment, more than any other art? The act of translation certainly appears to re-energise poetry. In 'Pangur Bán', we have a wry introduction to the creative process, its pressures and its challenges:

Neither bored, both hone
At home a separate skill
Moving after hours alone
To the kill

When at last his net wraps
After a sly fight
Around a mouse; mine traps
Sudden insight.

On my cell wall here,
His sight fixes, burning,
Searching; my old eyes peer
At new learning,

And his delight when his claws
Close on his prey
Equals mine when sudden clues
Light my way.

The same immediacy of language in word choice and in rapid movement is evident in stanza 3 of 'Phoebus was gone, all gone, his journey over'; it feels as if there's almost no room for breath in the above. In an instant, a lifetime of desire is shown to the reader. This instant occurs in a dream space that wraps up time and rolls it out again, as we would furl and unfurl a flag. Likewise, in 'Phoebus', reality is bendable:

I shuddered at his touch. I felt the fear of it.
I trembled as if I knew the true terror of it.

I opened my arms wide and pressed him against my body.
Then I froze: I was ice, all ice. My blood drained into it.

The physical setting of 'Pangur Bán' is in direct contrast to'Phoebus' as here the setting is the physical actuality of the monastic cell. The art of the monk creator is exposed with a tenacity likened to the cat's stalking and kill:

When at last his net wraps
After a sly fight
Around a mouse; mine traps
Sudden insight.

The monk's flash of insight elicited by the activity of the hunter cat allows him to enter into another level of creative understanding. Our grasp of the poem's theme is a magnesium flash which illuminates the poetic creative process. That heat is also generated by the collaborative translation process of engagement. The poet translator reaches through time to the poet originator, taking the present reader along for the ride. We are privileged to enter new worlds:

On my cell wall here,
His sight fixes, burning,
Searching; my old eyes peer
At new learning

We noted animal imagery in the text of 'Foebus abierat'. There is a rift between the animal and human realm which creates the fantastic portal for Phoebus to return. The protagonist-speaker's desire for reunion is so strong that her will and the will of the dead have created or allowed a last image of the beloved to appear. In 'Pangur Bán' the setting may be different but the idea of 'sudden clues' captures the moment of transformation in both poems.

'Phoebus was gone, all gone, his journey over' succeeds in translation, as it retains the poem's original tension between the sacred and the profane in a delicate balance.

The contemporary reader is made aware of the tension inherent in the poem from the very outset of Boland's delivery, where a hierarchy is exposed which includes the created world, the human world and the world of beasts. We are made aware that the action of the poem occurs in a no-place where the accepted physical and godly hierarchies can have no impact on human desires. That there is danger in even a momentary abandonment of the medieval worldview is made abundantly clear. While we are at a remove from the homiletic intent of the poem, we can appreciate its inherent tension and theme: transgression against the divine order is subtle and requires moral strength and self-recognition to oppose.

At the outset of this essay I remarked on a narrowing of the possible remits of poetic endeavor, especially in relation to how we view ekphrastic and collaborative approaches to translation. A close encounter with translations of 'Foebus abierat' confirms instead the power of translation as a form of engagement with text which can reanimate and amplify.

Dorothy L. Sayers, Marion Glasscoe, Barbara Reynolds and Eavan Boland have succeeded in bringing many works of art to contemporary audiences, and while the form of the work and our level of expectation is vastly different from how an original audience experienced and understood it, we are privileged to receive some understanding of that quickening of human emotion that links us through the centuries. This can only be achieved through an intelligent and sensitive approach to the art of poetry translation.

The most important revelation in Eavan Boland's translation of 'Phoebus was gone, all gone, his journey over' is that raising the (even momentary) possibility of anarchic transgression against the perception of the ordained order. In many ways this subtle little poem translation exposes the tension at the heart of Boland's overall work. Unlike the speaker protagonist of 'Phoebus was gone, all gone, his journey over' who ultimately capitulates to the divine order because she is weighted against a mindset which she will never quite transcend, Boland consistently challenges the status quo and questions the Irish cultural narrative on issues of authority and of absence. It is hugely important for the poet who is a woman to bring her perspective to the national narrative and to become visible in our culture. Eavan Boland has achieved increased visibility for Irish women poets through her work in poetry, in editing and in translation.

NOTES

1   Peter Dronke (ed.), *Medieval Latin and the Rise of the European Love-Lyric*, (Oxford, Clendon, 1968), 2nd edition, p. 169.

2   *Poetry* (Chicago) available at www.poetryfoundation.org/poetrymagazine/poem/181312, accessed 24 November 2015.

3   Boland, 'Translator's Note', at www.poetryfoundation.org/poemcomment/181312 accessed 24 November 2015.

4   'Song' by Eavan Boland from *The War Horse* (1975).

5   The Ronald Duncan Lecture for the Poetry Society, Poetry Library, South Bank, October 1994 subsequently published by Poetry Book Society Productions as *Gods Make Their Own Importance: The Authority of the Poet in Our Time* (1994).

6   Article 41.2 of Ireland's Constitution states that 'in particular, the State recognizes that by her life within the home, woman gives to the State a support without which the common good cannot be achieved' and that 'The State shall ... endeavour to ensure that mothers shall not be obliged by economic necessity to engage in labour to the neglect of their duties in the home.'

7   In *Poetry* (April 2008), Eavan Boland 'Phoebus was gone, all gone, his journey over', Poetry Foundation, http://www.poetryfoundation.org/poetrymagazine/poem/181312, accessed 24 November 2015.

8   From *Ekphrasis: Poetry Confronting Art*, Academy of American Poets at https://www.poets.or/poetsorg/text/ekphrasis-poetry-confronting-art accessed 24 November 2015.

9   Eavan Boland: translator's note. Accessed at Poetry Foundation https://www.poetryfoundation.org/poems-and-poets/poems/translator-notes/detail/50915.

10   *Ibid.*

11   *Julian of Norwich:* A *Revelation of Divine Love*, edited by Marion Glasscoe (Exeter, 1976, revised 1993).

12   'Two translations of a poem from Old Irish' 'Pangur Ban' http://homepages.wmich.edu/~cooneys/poems/pangur.ban.html which gives Frank O'Connor's translation and Eavan Boland's translation.

Michael Longley

THE HEBRIDES
for Eavan Boland

I

I shall have left these rocks within the week –
Itinerant,
large awhile, I came on spec
And shiver on the quays,
Taking in how summer on the island
Is ill at ease.

The winds' enclosure, Atlantic's premises,
Last balconies
Above the waves, The Hebrides –
Too long did I postpone
Presbyterian granite and the lack of trees,
This orphaned stone,

Day in, day out colliding with the sea.
Weather forecast,
Compass nor ordinance survey
Arranges my welcome
For, on my own, I have lost my way at last,
So far from home.

In whom the city is continuing,
I stop to look,
To find my feet among the ling
And bracken – over me
The bright continuum of gulls, a rook
Occasionally.

II

My eyes, slowly accepting panorama,
            Try to include
        In my original idea
            The total effect
Of air and ocean – waterlogged all wood –
            All harbours wrecked –

My dead-lights latched by whelk and barnacle
            Till I abide
        By the sea wall of the time I kill –
            My each nostalgic scheme
Jettisoned, as crises are, the further side
            Of sleep and dream.

Between wind and wave this holiday
            The cormorant,
        The oyster-catcher and osprey
            Proceed and keep in line,
While I, hands in my pockets, hesitant,
            Am in two minds.

III

Old neighbours, though shipwreck's my decision,
    People my brain –
  Like breakwaters against the sun,
    Command in silhouette
My island circumstance – my cells retain,
    Perpetuate

Their crumpled deportment through bad weather,
    And I feel them
  Put on their raincoats for ever
    And walk out in the sea.
I am, though each one waves a phantom limb,
    The amputee,

For these are my sailors, these my drowned –
    In their heart of hearts,
  In their city, I ran aground.
    Along my arteries
Sluice those homewaters petroleum hurts.
    Dry dock, gantries,

Dykes of apparatus, educate my bones
    To track the buoys
  Up sea lanes love emblazons
    To streets where shall conclude
My journey back from flux to poise, from poise
    To attitude.

Here, at the edge of my experience,
    Another tide
  Along the broken shore extends
    A lifetime's wrack and ruin –
No flotsam I may beachcomb now can hide
    That water-line.

IV

Beyond the lobster pots, where plankton spreads,
Porpoises turn.
Seals slip over the cockle beds.
Undertow dishevels
Seaweed in the shallows – and I discern
My sea levels.

To right and left of me there intervene
The tumbled burns –
And these, on turf and boulder weaned,
Confuse my calendar –
Their tilt is suicidal, their great return
Curricular.

No matter what repose holds shore and sky
In harmony,
From this place in the long run I,
Though here I might have been
Content with rivers where they meet the sea,
Remove upstream,

Where the salmon, risking fastest waters –
Waterfall and rock
And the effervescent otters –
On bridal pools insist
As with fin and generation they unlock
The mountain's fist.

V

Now, buttoned up, with water in my shoes,
    Clouds around me,
  I can, through mist that misconstrues,
    Read like a palimpsest
My past – those landmarks and that scenery
    I dare resist.

Into my mind's unsympathetic trough
    They fade away –
  And, to alter my perspective,
    I feel in the sharp cold
Of my vantage point too high above the bay,
    The sea grow old.

Granting the trawlers far below their stance,
    Their anchorage,
  I fight all the way for balance –
    In the mountain's shadow
Losing foothold, covet the privilege
    Of vertigo.

1964

'THE ONLY LEGEND I HAVE EVER LOVED':
CLASSICAL MYTHOLOGY AND THE CERES MYTH
IN THE POETRY OF EAVAN BOLAND

Nessa O'Mahony

On 3 September 1994, on the eve of the declaration by the
IRA of their historic ceasefire, the Saturday edition of *The
Irish Times* published Michael Longley's poem 'Ceasefire',
which gives an account of the painful process of peace-
building that immediately follows the end of the Trojan
War, according to the various narratives that followed it.
The poem appeared in a larger font than the surrounding
reviews, encased by a text box to make it stand out. It
wasn't the first time, nor would it be the last in the history
of the Northern Ireland conflict, that poetry was used as a
means of commenting on contemporary events, or where
classical mythology was mined for contemporary
resonances.

Longley's adaptation of classical mythology to offer a
parallel with the contemporary might be seen as an
example of what Deborah Sarbin has described as the use

by male poets of myth and legend to create a 'usable past'. She continues: 'This emphasis on legendary figures has created distance, a tendency to remove history from the realm of the every day'.[1] She goes on to argue that female poets such as Eavan Boland have moved in an opposite direction, seeking to move away from a 'distant idealized object to the real'[2] and to make use of the mythic to focus on 'intimate moments and/or empowerment of women'.[3] In this essay I shall explore the treatment of classical mythology in the work of Eavan Boland, specifically the treatment of the myth of Ceres, to assess the extent to which her classical references are intended to bring history back into the realm of the every day in general, and the quotidian life of the woman in particular.

As a precursor, I want to mention a fascinating conversation (republished here) that took place between Eavan Boland and Paula Meehan on the Peacock Theatre stage in Dublin in June 2014 to mark the publication of Boland's new volume of poems and photographs, *A Poet's Dublin*. During that event, Meehan asked Boland about her life-long preoccupation with re-discovering a place for woman's experience in a poetry dominated by male subjectivity. Boland immediately referenced Adrienne Rich's poem 'Diving into the Wreck':

> We are, I am, you are
> by cowardice or courage
> the one who find our way
> back to this scene
> carrying a knife, a camera
> a book of myths
> in which
> our names do not appear.[4]

Rich was voicing the dilemma of many women writers who had failed to find themselves, or their own stories, in mythology. The gap forced them to explore alternatives, or, as Rich puts it in her poem 'The Stranger', to find 'the living mind you fail to describe/in your dead language'.[5] So this essay also seeks to explore the extent to which Boland, in her own work, explores that 'book of myths' to find a living language there and I will use Adrienne Rich's essay, 'When We Dead Awaken: Writing as Re-vision' as the starting point for discussing how Boland offers an alternative mythology to describe the 'living mind' of women's experience.

Rich published this influential essay in *College English* in 1972. It was readily adopted as an important contribution to the evolution of feminist literary theory. Rich used a critique of Ibsen's play *When We Dead Awake* to focus on a wider exploration of the 'awakening consciousness' of women in the second half of the twentieth century and issued a clarion call to all feminist critics:

> A radical critique of literature, feminist in its impulse, would take the work first of all as a clue to how we live, how we have been living, how we have been led to imagine ourselves, how our language has trapped as well as liberated us; and how we can begin to see – and therefore live – afresh … We need to know the writing of the past, and know it differently than we have known it; not to pass on a tradition but to break its hold over us.
>
> For writers, and at this moment for woman writers in particular, there is the challenge and promise of a whole new psychic geography to be explored. But there is a difficult and dangerous walking on the ice …[6]

For Boland, a writer whose evolution was strongly influenced by a sense of geographic displacement due to her peripatetic upbringing as a diplomat's daughter, the lure of a new psychic geography was very strong. She had already sensed the barriers that tradition placed on her self-realisation, as she explains in the introduction to her 1995 memoir, *Object Lessons*: 'I know now that I began writing in a country where the word *woman* and the word *poet* were almost magnetically opposed'.[7] Thus she saw the exciting potential of Rich's critique to carve out a new language that might end that binary opposition, as she suggested in that Abbey Theatre discussion with Paula Meehan.

Many critics have discussed Boland's indebtedness to Rich. As Albert Gelpi says, Boland has 'singled Rich out for special notice as an empowering forebear', although Gelpi points out that Boland 'committed as she also was to comprehending the intersections of personal and national identity, forged a different poetry and a different image of the poet'.[8] Part of that difference may lie in the two women's different focus on the past, and the literary traditions of that past, as Gelpi goes on to argue:

> Her purpose became ... to write of 'the life of a woman in a Dublin suburb with small children' and to make 'a visionary claim ... for that life' (Allen Randolph, *Interview*, 119). The move was at once literary and political: to enter 'the tradition at an oblique angle' (Lannan Literary Videos, #42: Eavan Boland), and thereby alter the tradition henceforth.[9]

In Boland's case, tradition focussed on Irish history and literature, but also on the classical mythology so beloved of her childhood. In *Object Lessons*, she describes how learning Latin as a teenager honed her awareness of the power of the written word, how words were 'a sinuous path to clarity and safety'.[10] It is not therefore surprising that Latin literature would exert such a powerful influence, providing a lifelong source of imagery and narrative. Of reading *The Aeneid* for the first time, she writes: 'It was a slow magic, an incantation of images and structures, a pounding syntax'.[11] How, then, did the narratives found in classical literature offer a vein of archetype for a writer seeking to find analogues for her own experience as a woman?

Boland references classical mythology in her poetry from the very beginning. *New Territory*, her first collection published in 1967, includes the poem 'The Gryphons', in which she is already interrogating the received versions of classical narratives. 'The story goes' she begins, before asking 'how do these perennial stones/Endure the prospect of a living feast?'[12] Another poem from that first collection, 'Athene's Song', sees Boland already presenting what would become a recurring theme: the removal of the woman's voice from the story being told and, as Stef Craps puts it, the complicity of all artists in that removal:[13]

> Beside the water, lost and mute,
> Lies my pipe and like my mind
> Remains unknown, remains unknown[14]

The 1975 collection *War Horse* features only one explicitly classically-themed poem, 'The Greek Experience', but once again we find the theme of a story-teller silenced by a louder voice: 'My name means nothing here, his, Herodotus/Towers in Babylon, salts the Aegean/Is silted into each Ionic ear'.[15] By the time Boland publishes *Night Feed* in 1982, focussing more of her energy on carving out a specifically feminine poetic, her classical frame of reference has shifted to a more domestic setting and she is actively asserting a new ownership of old archetypes. Thus the Muse Mother of the poem of the same title is seen 'hunkering –/her busy hand worrying a child's face,/ working a nappy liner'[16] while the speaker in 'The New Pastoral' can no longer tolerate the subjectification of tradition. Having asserted that 'I'm no shepherdess',[17] the poem's speaker continues:

> I could be happy here,
> I could be something more than a refugee
> were it not for this lamb unsuckled, for the nonstop
> switch and tick
> telling me
>
> there was a past,
> there was a pastoral,[18]

She is suggesting that for every human experience, there has been an observer seeking to turn that into art and she cannot exempt herself from that charge.

Boland's 1986 collection *The Journey and Other Poems* sees her once again evoking that earliest classical influence in the classroom. Sheila Conboy describes how in the title poem, taking Virgil's *The Aeneid* as the model:

> Boland exploits the form of Virgil's journey for a two-fold purpose: first, to recover and express the miseries of real women of the past – women who have suffered through children's illnesses just as the speaker suffers while her own children lie with fevers – and second, to celebrate the poetic bond she shares with Sappho, her guide to the underworld.[19]

As the poet undergoes her own descent to hell, in the company of Sappho, she there encounters women who are not the idealised objects of old, but rather living, breathing women for whom she is warned not to 'define these women by their work' but rather to remember that 'these are women who went out like you'[20] and for whom a new poetic utterance is required:

> I have brought you here so you will know forever
> the silences in which are our beginnings,
> in which we have an origin like water,[21]

According to Deborah Sarbin, it is in poems such as 'The Journey' that Boland, in common with Eileán Ní Chuilleanáin:

> focuses on intimate moments and/or empowerment of women. It is not a flight from history to myth, but a reclamation of the same sense that they seek to reclaim history as well.[22]

Gerardine Meaney, discussing the same poem, adds that Sappho's answer here reinforces the idea that:

> the role of public voice of the mute past is not available to the woman poet and, on another, that it is only available to the woman poet. An antithesis between speech and love is

established and it is her access to the latter which apparently distinguishes the woman poet.[23]

For Meaney, Boland's writing here can be seen as 'an act of loving remembrance and a search for "an origin"'.[24]

The poet's sense of wordlessness in the face of this imperative to find a new subject matter and a new language finds echo in the next collection, *Outside History* (1990), where in 'The Latin Lesson' the poet once again revisits Virgil's epic poem and leaves with a question of how she will 'keep a civil tongue/in my head'.[25] It is significant that this poem acts as a prologue for the long titular sequence of poems in which the fates are explored of various mythic and historical women who have been silenced or written out of history altogether. It is in this sequence that we get the first close focus on Ceres, the figure who features prominently in the poem that is the subject of this chapter and whose story may offer 'an origin' of a sort. In the poem 'The Making of an Irish Goddess', Boland explicitly links her own sense of motherhood with that of the Goddess, who 'went to hell/with no sense of time'.[26] For Boland, whose body is now 'neither young now nor fertile,/and with the marks of childbirth/still on it',[27] the mythological narrative is the link to the everyday present:

> myth is the wound we leave
> in the time we have
>
> which in my case is this
> March evening
> at the foothills of the Dublin mountains,[28]

In her persona of Goddess turned Dublin housewife, Boland closes the poem with an explicit reference to the mother-daughter myth of Ceres and Persephone as she espies her own daughter in the distance, 'her back turned to me'. She will return to that central trope once again in the poem, 'The Pomegranate'.

Before taking a closer look at that poem, I wish to pause to explore the mythological figure of Demeter in order to discover what her myth tells us about ancient and contemporary attitudes to death and loss and how this fits into Boland's developing personal poetic. Demeter (called Ceres by the Romans), daughter of Cronus and Rhea, was the Goddess of corn and 'thus the great sustainer of life for men and beasts alike'.[29] Demeter was usually associated with her daughter, Persephone (Proserpina); they were often called the 'Two Goddesses' or even 'the Demeters' and were depicted together 'holding torches and wearing crowns, sometimes holding sceptres and stalks of grain'.[30] The cult of Demeter and Persephone was celebrated at Eleusis, on the outskirts of Athens, for over a two thousand year period.[31]

One of the principal elements of the Demeter myth concerns her daughter's abduction by the god of the Underworld, Hades, and Demeter's grief at her loss. The earliest reference to the myth is in Hesiod's *Theogony* (c. 700 BC) but the story is best known from the seventh century BC poem, the *Homeric Hymn To Demeter*.[32] It tells of Hades' abduction of Persephone and Demeter's frantic search for her; she spends nine days and nights wandering the earth, carrying 'flaming torches' (line 47 in the edition being cited) before deserting Olympus to live among the mortals.

The *Hymn* links Demeter's role as Goddess of Corn and her responsibility for cultivation; having left Olympus for Eleusis in Attica, Demeter nurses Triptolemos, son of King Celeus, to whom she promises one day to give the secret to cultivation of grain. But because of her grief for her daughter, the earth has become barren and no corn will grow: 'The earth would not send up a single sprout, for Demeter of the lovely crown kept the seed covered' (lines 304–5). It is this sterility that forces Zeus to take action;

fearing a famine that would wipe out humankind and thus deprive him of sacrifices, he finally promises to retrieve Persephone from Hades although, because Hades persuaded her to eat some pomegranate seeds, she is obliged to return to the Underworld for four months of each year. The *Hymn* thus gives the aetiology for the passage of the seasons; the joyful reunion between mother and daughter, with growth and fertility returning to the earth, represents spring and summer, with winter represented by the four months Persephone must spend in the Underworld. But the poem places this natural cycle in a framework of life and death; Demeter's emotion foregrounds the human dimension of a mother who has lost her daughter and who grieves for her.

However it is Ovid's version of the story of Ceres and Proserpina that has influenced subsequent renderings of the tale. His account occurs in Book 5 of *Metamorphoses*, and is also treated in Book 4 of his *Fasti*. In *Metamorphoses*, Pluto's abduction of Proserpina is seen as a result of some mischief on the part of Venus who sends her son Cupid to 'extend/the empire of Venus and Cupid' (5.371–2) by shooting the god of the Underworld with one of his arrows, thus ensuring that Proserpina does not follow the example of Minerva and Diana by rejecting Venus. Ovid presents Ceres as the very embodiment of the grief-stricken mother searching tirelessly for her daughter. Once Ceres discovers the true fate of her daughter, when she finds her daughter's girdle in the nymph Cyane's pool, her anguish and fury are clear. Ovid's Ceres is an avenging angel: 'as the first shoots sprang from the earth, they would perish/at once, destroyed by the scorching sunshine or torrents of rain' (5.482–3). There is no reference to Eleusis, no sub-plot involving Celeus or the Eleusinian Rites; Ovid focuses on the domestic squabble between the gods and goddesses – 'A bandit husband is hardly a match /for a daughter of yours, if she is no longer a daughter of mine' Ceres tells

Jupiter (5.521–22). As with the *Hymn to Demeter*, the daughter is prevented from being wholly restored to her mother because she has eaten some pomegranate seeds – but Jupiter solves the problem by deciding to split 'the rolling year into equal parts' (5.565), with Proserpina spending six months with her mother and six with her husband. The agricultural theme is no longer the centre of this myth in Ovid's telling of it; there is no reference to the Eleusinian Mysteries, nor the integral link between the seasons and the cycles of birth and death. By the time of Ovid's writing, agriculture had been established as a way of living for centuries; the Demeter/Ceres myth no longer needed to play the aetiological role. So Ovid focuses on the human dimension, the grief of a mother's loss and the joy at her daughter's recovery.

This has been the focus of most subsequent narrators. Karen Bennett's discussion of more recent reception of the myth may help to clarify why it appears to remain so resonant with contemporary women writers, in particular:

> To my mind, the most fruitful approach to the Demeter/Persephone myth has been the psychological perspective assumed by Jung, Kerényi and Neumann, according to which mythological figures are reflections of archetypes existing deep within the collective unconscious. Proof of the resonance of this theory is the prolific stream of feminist psychoanalytical literature produced in recent decades which give a central place to the motif of Demeter's quest for her lost child, usually interpreted as the female quest for psychic wholeness. In many cases, Hades is seen as representing patriarchal society which estranges woman from her deeper Self and enslaves her; and wholeness is interpreted as consisting of reunion with the powerful Goddess archetype. Indeed, a whole body of feminist thought is centred on the notion that, before the onset of patriarchy, there existed a universal fertility Goddess figure … that represented the power of the feminine principle in its purest form.[33]

I agree with Bennett's reading that Eavan Boland's version of the myth in 'The Pomegranate' locates 'her focus of interest in the personal relationship between mother and daughter'.[34] For me, the poem personalises the universal, allowing the poet to explore her relationship with her own daughter, now grown to an age where she is ready to make her own way in life and depart the safety and security her parents have provided for her. Given that the poet's previous interrogation of myths and narratives has sought to reverse the expunging of women's role from history, it is significant when, in the opening lines, she announces that the Ceres-Persephone story is the 'only legend I have ever loved'.[35] This statement alone should be enough to make the reader sit up and listen intently; it seems to represent a shift in Boland's treatment of mythological narrative, as if only this story of a mother's search for her daughter resonates most fully with her. Perhaps it is because, for the poet, the Ceres myth is one that can mean something different to a woman at various stages of life: 'I can enter it anywhere. And have./As a child in exile …'[36] As a child, she is herself Persephone, responding to the daughter's experiences of exile; as a mother of her own daughter, she experiences the fearfulness of Ceres realising that her daughter may not come back to her:

> […] at first I was
> an exiled child in the crackling dusk of
> the underworld, the stars blighted. Later
> I walked out in a summer twilight
> searching for my daughter at bed-time.
> When she came running I was ready
> to make any bargain to keep her.[37]

Shara McCallum describes this as an 'interesting departure' from more typical treatments of the myth by poets such as Louise Glück or Rita Dove:

> The poet or narrator of that poem does not speak in the voice of either Persephone or Demeter but rather reflects on her

varying personal encounters with the myth over time. Because she can and does 'enter the story anywhere,' she shows us how the world looks on either side of the river.[38]

Or, as Bennett puts it, the:

duality of the role emphasises the cyclical nature of the legend that has been so stressed by feminist psychoanalysts, and suggests the story may form part of the archetypal female experience.[39]

While Bennett's statement could in truth be applied to most mythology formed as a way of making sense of human experience, I believe that the Ceres myth resonates particularly for mothers and daughters at all stages of their lives. In Boland's rendering, there is no place for a Pluto in this narrative to distract from the intensity of the mother-daughter link. Indeed, rather than being fed the seeds by her husband, Boland's Persephone reaches, Eve-like, for the forbidden fruit herself: 'but she reached/out a hand and plucked a pomegranate' (lines 31–32) and, like Eve, inherits the knowledge of loss known by all mothers and daughters: 'The legend will be hers as well as mine./She will enter it. As I have' (lines 50–51). It is as if the Ceres story offers Boland in this poem a sort of mythological hall of mirrors that provides the poet with a simultaneous glimpse of past, present and future.

Given the emblematic nature of the Ceres myth for Boland and given her description of it as a story that could be entered into at any stage by the writer, it can be no surprise that she was to return to the narrative in later work. She does so in her next collection, *The Lost Land* (1998) in a series of short lyrics such as 'Daughter' and more specifically, 'Ceres Looks at the Morning', where once again we are given the sense of timeless circularity identified by critics such as Bennett:

Beautiful morning
look at me as a daughter would

look: with that love and that curiosity –
as to what she came from.
And what she will become.[40]

These lines support Rosemary Wilkinson's assertion that
Eavan Boland uses classical material to 'critique the
emblematic use of female imagery in national literature or
to readdress the relationship between the reality of
women's experience and its mythologised representation'.[41]
I would argue that, in doing so, Boland offered a useful
model to other contemporaries, such as Eiléan Ni
Chuilleanáin, who in poems such as 'Odysseus Meets the
Ghosts of the Women' and 'The Second Voyage' also
turned to classical mythology to interrogate representations
of women, or Nuala Ní Dhomhnaill, whose alternative Mer
People mythology allowed her to explore both feminist and
linguistic issues.

For younger generations of women poets, mythology
continues to provide a source of inspiration, although it
might be argued that for them it is just one of a range of
narratives that can be mined. For example in Sinead
Morrissey's most recent collection, *Parallax*, her poem
'Daughter' references the Persephone myth alongside
Timothy Leary's psychedelic theories, contemporary
picture books and Japanese pictographs.[42] Perhaps one of
Boland's greatest legacies is that, by showing how she
could use one mythical narrative as a valuable point of
entry and departure in charting her own experience as
daughter and mother, she opened the door on a whole
other range of entry and departure points for her
successors.

NOTES

1   Deborah Sarbin, 'Out of myth into history: The Poetry of Eavan
     Boland and Eileán Ní Chuilleanáin', *Canadian Journal of Irish
     Studies*, Vol 19, No 1 (July 1993), p. 87.
2   Sarbin, p. 88.

3   Sarbin, p. 90.

4   Adrienne Rich, 'Diving into the Wreck' in *Diving into the Wreck: Poems 1971–72* (New York, Norton, 1973), lines 87–94.

5   Adrienne Rich, 'The Stranger', Poetic Orphanage website, accessed 4 August 2015. http://snarkattack-gracenotes.tumblr. com/post/20639211860/the-stranger-by-adrienne-rich.

6   Adrienne Rich, 'When We Dead Awaken: Writing as Re-Vision', *College English*, Vol 34, No 1, *Women, Writing and Teaching* (October 1972), pp 18–19.

7   Eavan Boland, *Object Lessons* (Manchester, Carcanet Press, 1995), p. xi.

8   Albert Gelpi, '"Hazard and Death": The Poetry of Eavan Boland', *Colby Quarterly*, Vol 35, Issue 4 (December 1999), p. 2.

9   Gelpi, p. 4.

10 Eavan Boland, 1995, p. 76.

11 Eavan Boland, 1995, p. 79.

12 Eavan Boland, 'The Gryphons', *New Collected Poems* (Manchester, Carcanet, 2005), p. 8.

13 Stef Craps, '"Only Not beyond Love": Testimony, Subalternity and the Famine in the Poetry of Eavan Boland', *Neophilologus*, 94 (2010), p. 166.

14 Boland, 2005, p. 23.

15 Boland, 2005, pp 61–2.

16 Boland, 2005, pp 102–3.

17 Boland, 2005, p. 113.

18 Boland, 2005, pp 113–4.

19 Sheila C. Conboy, '"What You Have Seen Is Beyond Speech": Female Journeys in the Poetry of Eavan Boland and Eiléan Ní Chuilleanáin', *The Canadian Journal of Irish Studies*, Vol 16, No 1 (July 1990), p. 69.

20 Boland, 2005, p. 149.

21 Boland, 2005, p. 150.

22 Deborah Sarbin, '"Out of Myth into History": The Poetry of Eavan Boland and Eiléan Ní Chuilleanáin', *The Canadian Journal of Irish Studies*, Vol 19, No 1 (July 1993), p. 90.

23 Gerardine Meaney, 'Myth, history and the politics of subjectivity: Eavan Boland and Irish women's writing', *Women: A Cultural Review*, 4, 2 (1993), p. 139.

24 Meaney, p. 139.

25 Boland, 2005, p. 172.

26 Boland, 2005, p. 178.

27   Boland, 2005 p. 179.
28   Boland, 2005, p. 179.
29   J. March, *Cassell Dictionary of Classical Mythology* (London, Cassell, 2000), p. 130.
30   J. March, *Cassell Dictionary of Classical Mythology*, p. 130.
31   Karen Bennett, 'The Recurrent Quest: Demeter and Persephone in Modern-Day Ireland', *Classical and Modern Literature*, 23, 1 (2003), p. 15.
32   Bennett, p. 17.
33   Bennett, p. 18.
34   Bennett, p. 23.
35   Boland, 2005, p. 215.
36   Boland, 2005, p. 215.
37   Boland, 2005, p. 215.
38   Sharea McCallum, 'Eavan Boland's Gift: Sex, History, and Myth', *The Antioch Review*, Vol 62, Issue 1 (Winter 2004), p. 39.
39   Bennett, p. 24.
40   Boland, 2005, p. 265.
41   Rosemary Wilkinson, 'Classical receptions in the work of two late twentieth-century female poets: Eavan Boland and Olga Broumas', *Classical Receptions in Drama and Poetry in England Project Site* (Milton Keynes, Open University, 2008). Accessed 4 August 2015. http://www2.open.ac.uk/ClassicalStudies/Greek Plays/PoetryDB/BolandBroumas/BolandBroumasIintro.htm
42   Sinead Morrissey, 'Daughter' in *Parallax* (Manchester, Carcanet, 2013), pp 33–7.

BIBLIOGRAPHY

The Homeric Hymn to Demeter, translated by M. Morford and R. Lenardon, in Morford, M. and R. Lenardon, *Classical Mythology*, International Eighth Edition (2009), pp 327–338.

The Homeric Hymn to Demeter, translated into English Hexameters by Brian Kemball-Cook (Hitchin, Herts, Calliope Press, 2001).

Bennett, K., 'The Recurrent Quest: Demeter and Persephone in Modern-Day Ireland', *Classical and Modern Literature*, 21, 1 (2003), pp 15–32.

Boland, E., *New Collected Poems* (New York, Norton, 2005).

Boland, E., *Object Lessons: The Life of the Woman and the Poet in Our Time* (Manchester, Carcanet, 1995).

Conboy, S., '"What You Have Seen Is Beyond Speech": Female Journeys in the Poetry of Eavan Boland and Eiléan Ní

Chuilleanáin', *The Canadian Journal of Irish Studies*, Vol 16, No 1 (July 1990), pp 65–72. Stable URL http://www.jstor.org/stable/25512810 accessed 05/02/2015.

Craps, S., '"Only Not beyond Love": Testimony, Subalternity, and the Famine in the Poetry of Eavan Boland', *Neophilologus*, 94 (2010), pp 165–176.

Gelpi, A., '"Hazard and Death": The Poetry of Eavan Boland', *Colby Quarterly*, Volume 35, No 4 (December 1999), pp 210–228.

Grimal, P., *Dictionary of Classical Mythology*, translated by A.R. Maxwell-Hyslop; edited by Stephen Kershaw (London, Penguin Books, 1991).

McCallum, S., 'Eavan Boland's Gift: Sex, History, and Myth', *The Antioch Review*, Vol 62, Issue 1 (Winter 2004), pp 37–43.

March, J., *Cassell Dictionary of Classical Mythology* (London, Cassell, 2000).

Meaney, G., 'Myth, History and the Politics of Subjectivity: Eavan Boland and Irish Women's Writing', *Women: a cultural review*, Vol 4, No 2 (Oxford, Oxford UP, 1993).

Morford, M. and R. Lenardon, *Classical Mythology*, International Eighth Edition (Oxford, Oxford University Press, 2009).

Morrissey, S., *Parallax* (Manchester, Carcanet, 2013).

Rich, A., 'When We Dead Awaken: Writing as Re-Vision', *College English*, Vol 34, No 1, Women, Writing and Teaching (October 1972), pp 18–30. Stable URL: http://www.jstor.org/stable/375215 accessed 4/8/2015

Sarbin, D., '"Out of Myth into History": The Poetry of Eavan Boland and Eiléan Ní Chuilleanáin', *The Canadian Journal of Irish Studies*, Vol 19, No 1 (July 1993), pp 86–96. Stable URL: http://www.jstor.org/stable/25512952 accessed 05/02/2015

Wilkinson, R., 'Case Study Two: Classical receptions in the work of two late-twentieth century female poets; Eavan Boland and Olga Broumas', *Classical Receptions in Drama and Poetry in England Project Site* (Milton Keynes, Open University, 2008). Accessed 4 August 2015. http://www2.open.ac.uk/ClassicalStudies/Greek Plays/PoetryDB/BolandBroumas/BolandBroumasIintro.htm

Dermot Bolger

WEDDED
For Bernie

This is what I am wedded to:
The bus journey in the dusk,
Tailbacks, roadworks, queues.
Tired commuters gazing into space,
Thrown forward in our seats
Every time the driver brakes;
As inane strangers on mobile phones
Make us eavesdrop on their lives.

The name carved on a boulder
At the entrance to our estate,
The sweep of curving rooftops,
The bicycles left on the path,
Hopscotch marked out in chalk.

The light in the kitchen window
When she gets home before me,
The bustle of pots, the radio
Blathering about the outside world;
A scent of spices as she says hello,
Busy stirring some dish at the stove.

The voice of the woman I wed,
Who makes every aspect blessed:
This kitchen, this suburban street,
This bus trip like a pilgrimage
Back to where I may finally lie
With my bride amid shoals of roofs,
Amid the vast galaxies of estates,
Amid the myriad specks of light,

In the place where I am safe,
Where I wake deep in the night
And touch her sleeping face.

EAVAN BOLAND AND THE DEVELOPMENT OF A POETICS: 'IT MAY BE BEAUTY/BUT IT ISN'T TRUTH'[1]

Siobhan Campbell

The poems in Eavan Boland's first volume *New Territory* (1967) have antecedents among the Metaphysical poets as well as the Romantics, and W.B. Yeats is a presiding spirit. Themes are adumbrated here which arise in the later work. Critics have cited 'Athene's song' as a poem which marks Boland's territory of concern with becoming a poet as a woman and the difficulties therein.[2] 'From my father's head I sprung/Goddess of the war,' acknowledges the heroic tradition in poetry and foreshadows the subject of the difficulty for women in entering that sanctum, something she will return to in both poetry and prose. In the line 'Peace became the toy of power', she foregrounds an understanding of how rhetoric and its associated rhythms can be misused, knowing that there are – as she will say much later in 'Violence Against Women',

> arranged relations,
> so often covert, between power and cadence[3]

Boland thus introduces early the question of how best to write a socially-engaged poem within the lyric imperative. Addressing the ideals of violence in the service of a cause and of sacrifice for aspirational liberation, a poem like 'A Cynic at Kilmainham Gaol' captures her developing poetics. Initially the atmosphere of the poem, referring to the leaders of the 1916 rebellion (fourteen of the sixteen were shot at Kilmainham Gaol where they had been imprisoned), seems reverend and sombre:

> Autumn dark, no worship, mine or yours
> Can resurrect the sixteen minds,[4]

But soon a dichotomy is explored which undermines that initial feeling. The 'dual sight' of the rebels is noted, with 'one eye' on the guns and the other on the 'magic, tragic town, the broken/Countryside, the huge ungenerous tribe/Of cowards'. Boland seems to imply that the rebels knew how the majority of the Irish people were not supportive of the rebellion and that moreover they 'chose' the 'magic' anyway, and even, as the syntax used allows this interpretation, that they are operating with a certain self-consciousness 'with the tears they chose/Themselves'. The title gives a hint at corroborating this interpretation of the poem and in this reading it becomes clear that Boland's freighting of possible meanings is often carried by her sly use of syntax for effect.

With *The War Horse* (1975), Boland's themes of interest to this study begin to more fully emerge. The title poem places the speaker as 'safe' within a suburban house as something wild and inexplicable, the 'war horse' invades that peace, bringing with it an intimation that neither the safety nor the peace are solidly based:

> Only a leaf on our laurel hedge is torn –
>
> Of distant interest like a maimed limb,[5]

This, along with 'why should we care' acts to make an almost unbridgeable chasm between those who watch, apparently unmoved, from relative safety, and those who partake of this danger.

The half lines 'a volunteer//You might say,' uses the word that the IRA used for those who signed up to its cause and it is likely to also be referring to the Irish Volunteers before then. The speaker maintains that 'no great harm is done' and yet the 'maimed limb' and the 'screamless dead' belie that. There's an interesting line where the 'unformed fear of fierce commitment' is characterised as 'gone', seeming to imply a move towards what the horse may represent. And this is borne out as the actual physicality of the horse is conveyed well in the first two thirds of the piece but once he passes ('He stumbles on like a rumour of war, huge,/Threatening;'), the speaker leans on the sill in 'relief' and describes her blood as still with 'atavism'. If the latter is taken as the recurrence of a feature of a distinct culture or tribe though it has been genetically absent for generations, it leads to the final lines requiring to be taken as knowingly ironic – 'recalling days//Of burned countryside, illicit braid:/A cause ruined before a world betrayed'.

'Child of Our Time' a poem dated the day of the Dublin-Monaghan bombings, 17 May 1974, in which three infants died, shows Boland dealing with actual contemporary violence. Here she writes an elegy but also questions 'idle talk' and its relation to the rhymes, rhythms and legends she mentions. Boland admits that the poem takes 'its tune', 'its rhythm from the discord of your murder,' but hopes in the final lines to find a 'new language' which is able for the task ahead. The poem appeared in *The Irish Times* but within two weeks Boland had written 'The Weasel's Tooth' (a self-consciously Yeatsian title), an essay in *The Irish Times*, where she retracted the poem, appealing 'for writers now in Ireland to liberate themselves from the myths, the hallucinations of cultural unity'.[6] Jody Allen Randolph interprets this 'important turn' as indicative of the poet recognising that 'Yeats's fantasy of cultural coherence' had continued in Ireland and was in compromised relation to the continuing violence; she sees Boland here as 'freeing herself to seek out a new political poem'.[7] This new poem would interrogate such compromise with a distinct wariness of rhetoric and an investigation into the source of authority to do the 'telling'. That investigation animates several poems in the *The Journey and Other Poems* and *Outside History*, published in 1986 and 1990 respectively.

In the title poem, 'The Journey', we see the poet being brought to an underworld by Sappho. The speaker has already been addressing issues of aesthetics and of the 'proper' subject for poetry: '"there has never"/I said "been a poem to an antibiotic:"' and her concern is that there would be a separation between the ability of language and the necessity of the task in hand, 'every day the language gets less//"for the task and we are less with the language"'. The placement of 'language gets less' means it is also read as statement in its own right. This is amplified by the rest of the poem which has Sappho showing the speaker diseased women and children in a nightmare scene of suffering. The speaker asks, 'let me at least be their witness', only to be told that what she has seen is 'beyond speech' and 'beyond song' – surely a problem for a poet. Sappho's reply is that the poet is here precisely to learn the 'silences in which are our beginnings' and that all there is to do is to 'remember it'. This dilemma of the poet committed to a socially-engaged poem is one to which Boland returns continually, answering it with varied poetic strategies. She is determined to craft a lyric that can incorporate images of the abuse of power as well as conveying the dangers of both nostalgia and complacence/ lack of vigilance.

The Journey and Other Poems brings together several poems which continue to explore both the 'consolations of the craft' and the psychic trap within that consolation. In 'Listen. This is the noise of myth', the poet links the lies, the tricks and the legends that a culture may hold dear:

> This sequence of evicted possibilities.
> Displaced facts. Tricks of light. Reflections.
>
> Invention. Legend. Myth. What you will.[8]

And in 'Fond memory', Boland draws attention to the thrall of nationalist sentiment, here exerted in the guise of a Tom Moore song which has an emotional effect. The listener has to fight back tears but comes to a realisation, deciding that such a reaction is 'wrong':

> I thought this is my country, was, will be again,
> this upward-straining song made to be
> our safe inventory of pain. And I was wrong.[9]

Here the word 'safe' takes a reader back to the compromised safety explored in 'The War Horse' and what appeared to be an impulse to question it in that earlier poem has now blossomed into a whole sequence of poems which set out the inherent problem of beautiful rhetoric used to service a cause.

Boland's subject then is partly the problem of presenting a wariness of beautifully-crafted rhetoric within the lyric poem which is often committed to just that. Her ancillary subject of how to establish herself as a poet within the patriarchal tradition is amply discussed by critics such as Allen Randolph, Meaney, Wills *et al* and by Boland herself in her prose essays. What is of interest here is Boland's concern to find an artistically and morally sound set of poetics when writing from a violently-contested island where the very source of art itself may be suspect.

With these elements in mind 'Mise Eire' in *The Journey and Other Poems* warrants re-reading. It appears after the poem 'I Remember' which may itself be a statement of intent for the poet:

I was the interloper who knows both love and fear,
[...]
beyond the need to touch, to handle, to dismantle it,
the mystery;[10]

The 'dismantling' predicated here can be seen to take place in 'Mise Eire'. The title, ostensibly means 'I am Ireland' and has been taken to have this meaning by critics (see Meaney and Goodby).[11] However, in Irish grammar, this phrase could read '*is* mise Éire' which both names, as in 'I name myself Éire', as well as containing an element of 'me=Ireland' as in 'me Tarzan', implying that the *me* and the *Ireland* are one and the same.

Éire as used in the 1937 Constitution named the State of Ireland, even though the State did not include the six counties of Northern Ireland (though Articles Two and Three laid claim to those). The Constitution was taking the historical name for the island of Ireland/Éire and therefore to some, the aspiration of the state including the 'six counties' area is inscribed within this word, perhaps even more so when rendered in Irish. This naming causes commentators (especially from the UK) pause for thought when writing of Ireland as the impulse can be toward disambiguation with some using 'the Republic of Ireland' with others using Éire to specifically denote the 'Irish' area of 'southern Ireland'.

In the very title of this poem, Boland draws our attention to the problem of language construction, thereby implying that nothing that follows afterwards should be taken as literal. As my reading assumes intentionality, I maintain this even while knowing that this title is also that of the 1912 piece by Pádraig Pearse and it simultaneously refers to the 1959 Seán Ó Riada score for the George Morrison movie celebrating revolutionary nationalism. Of many possible title variations available, Boland chose 'Mise Eire' and her intent in doing so becomes clearly interrogatory. The poem opens in the negative:

I won't go back to it –

my nation displaced
into old dactyls,[12]

Dactyls, being the metrical foot of Greek elegiac poetry, have that powerful forward movement via the stressed syllable followed by two unstressed syllables. The word 'poetry' itself is often used as a mnemonic for this. Is Boland implying an older heroic poetry toward which hers will certainly not return?

Having established that the speaker will not go back to 'oaths' made in the past, the second stanza begins with a litany:

land of the Gulf Stream
the small farm,
the scalded memory,

That the Gulf Stream is a constant (though currently weakening) seems to imply that the small farm and the sense of a painful past invoked by 'scalded' are also constants and even that they may be 'natural' to the land in question. The following lines invoke 'songs' and 'words' that seek to re-make, obfuscate or otherwise apply a balm to historical event:

the songs
that bandage up the history,
the words
that make a rhythm of the crime

where time is time past.

These lines might seem to say that time in this 'land' is never experienced in the present but is freighted with the 'crime' of history and that the poets (if we read 'poetry' for 'words') are ill-serving of the real injury, preferring to 'make a rhythm' of it.

Clair Wills posits that Boland suggests a revisionist aim of challenging the orthodox version of the past in that this would be preferable to the 'bandage' of words she mentions.[13] And that does seem possible if we allow that such orthodox accounts may not include characters such as the two females invoked in the next sections, a garrison prostitute and an emigrant mother leaving Ireland with her 'half-dead' baby. But what to make of the twice-negative line 'No. I won't go back.' followed by the line 'My roots are brutal.'? In the former, it could be argued, is a fatalistic sense that no matter how much the 'no' is meant or emphasised, the speaker may well be drawn 'back'. In the latter, the use of 'roots' – knowledge of which is often seen as a positive, strengthening force – followed by 'brutal' could be seen as both a statement of historical fact and as a burden which continues to be carried in the present.

A colon leads into the final pair of sections, implying that these two are the 'roots' of the poem that we read in our own present moment, our 'time' which, as readers, has to be time present. The first 'I am the woman' section equates the speaker with she who 'practises/the quick frictions' – perhaps another form of metaphorical 'bandage' in the peddled falsity of the 'rictus of delight' and one which women find themselves able to perform perennially. Is there anything as humanly constant as transactional sex and faked female pleasure? In the second of these sections, the speaker becomes the emigrant listening to an 'immigrant/guttural', and missing the 'vowels' of home, though neither knowing or caring that any 'new language' is 'a kind of scar' that heals 'into a passable imitation' of what has gone before. The two dactyls of 'immigrant/guttural' could perhaps offer a new form of the old inheritance if they were not seen immediately to be compromised. So an imitation of the previous dispensation is all this emigrant woman has to show for her journey away from the 'land' in question, surely implying that the orthodoxies of the 'songs' and 'words' may go on making a 'rhythm of the crime' as will the rhythms of sex, no better or no worse than before. The reader is left to ask what the difference is between this description and a going 'back to it'?

With this in mind, I am sent back to those 'old dactyls' to hear the possibility of two dactyls in the line, 'I won't go back to it', and then to hear how they are undone in the re-working of that line as 'No. I won't go back'. Boland may be putting down a marker that her poem will deal with the ostensibly unheroic experience of women even as she uses the prostitute and the mother as emblematic and not individualised. But we know from the end of the poem's 'imitation' of 'what went before' that the poet may also be admonishing herself as a writer using the 'words' she initially seems to complicate to subsequently work against the very thing she describes. There's a pessimistic view of the power of poetry in this poem which may indeed be all an 'imitation' of what has gone before despite the effort of the poet to re-work the received heroic poem. And all this is discussed within the kind of poem which might lend itself to being interpreted as a kind of political tract. However, that interpretation may miss the full range of focus while also taking the poem to be linguistically simpler than it is. I am suggesting that there is a double-bluff here as she plays with the shifting locus of authority. Edna Longley may therefore have the emphasis wrong then when she says that the piece destabilizes *Mise* but not *Eire* as here, we see that Éire is standing for any repeated falsity, in itself certainly an unstable name for a contested political State but almost more importantly a name that also doubles for a problematic state of poetic mind or a problematic set of poetics.[14]

Moreover, we understand the *Mise* to be incontrovertibly linked in a me=Jane way to the *Éire*, thereby the problems of one are the problems of the other. When Longley praises Paul Muldoon for distinguishing between 'dead and living tradition, between apparent and real breaks with the past', could it be that she has not allowed that Boland implies there's no way of breaking with a 'past' which has had no substance in the 'words' that should perhaps have inscribed it?[15] Could Boland be suggesting that if such a break was to be in evidence, it might mean that the 'imitation of what went before' would have stopped somehow and for this poet, at least in this poem, that is not the case? Instead, the poet appears doomed to repeat, much like the archetypal characters who peopled the classical poetry she invokes. While the poetic line she uses may be variable and free of fixed metre, and while her archetypes may instead be women who compromise and carry on, the problem of rendering anything in a 'new language' remains intractable. 'My roots are brutal' this poem seems to say, and brutal – it implies – they will remain.

As Boland develops this aesthetic over several books, she explores not only the danger of beautiful rhetoric whether in speech or in 'songs crying out their ironies' ('The Achill Woman') but also the question of whether any so-called 'healing' of these kinds of fractures is possible or even desirable. As she says at the end of 'In Exile' (from the sequence 'Outside History'): 'my speech will not heal. I do not want it to heal'.[16] This is an insight earned by listening to the 'sense of injury' in the speech of two exiled German girls who spoke 'in their own tongue: syllables in which pain was/radical, integral'. Indeed, the repetitions of motif that Boland performs might even become monotonous were it not that they are freighted with the idea of the 'imitation' of what went before. It is as if with re-working her subject matter, Boland gets closer to this notion, mentioned in 'We are Always too Late' as 'the re-enactment. Always that.' In this poem, that idea is qualified by the notion of continuously being too late. The speaker, who is 'always' going towards the character in the poem, tries to demonstrate that the trees stand for the 'beautiful upstagings of/what we suffer by' but the result is a defeated attempt as the piece ends 'she never even sees me.'

The artistic dilemma for Boland is to match an acute sense of how history pervades the present with the need to also address the silenced suffering of the voiceless. These imperatives couple with the knowledge that any attempt to work them into art may be doomed even as she expresses the demand for that attempt to be continued.

The problem is clearly inscribed in the volume, *In a Time of Violence* (1994). 'Inscriptions' for instance, addresses the issue of the dead:

> For years I have known
> how important it is
> not to name
> the coffins, the murdered in them,
> the deaths in alleyways and on doorsteps –
> in case they rise out of their names[17]

The poem is ostensibly talking about one child, 'Peter', who is long gone but whose named cot is among the belongings in a rented holiday cottage but it moves this thought outwards to suggest that there is no comfort in knowing that 'his sign is safe tonight'. The reader has to work hard to find any relation between the deaths in alleyways and the beloved child but the link appears to be in the lines, 'Someone knew/the importance of giving him a name'. Could the poet here be admonishing herself for a lack of attention to the actual victims of violence even though her professed poetic aesthetic is ostensibly developing as quite the opposite? When she professes in the sequence 'Outside History', 'out of myth into history I move to be/part of that ordeal', might a reader not have expected more of the actual murders, real suffering and visceral brutality to have appeared within the work? 'The Dolls Museum in Dublin' which appears beside 'Inscriptions' is also about problematic commemoration and Boland here begins to employ the strangeness of sentence structure which will become characteristic:

> To be the hostages ignorance
> takes from time and ornament from destiny. Both.
> To be the present of the past. To infer the difference
> with a terrible stare. But not feel it. And not know it.[18]

The stanza is a grammatician's nightmare and arguably also fails to engage the reading ear even as it serves to show up the problems of individuality and the illusions around it – both explored in the poem. Here is Boland at her most syntactically torturous when she grapples with the most intractable poetic problems. She finishes this sequence with 'Beautiful Speech', warning the reader that her 'speech' will move away from the 'dear vowels/*Irish Ireland ours*' (which she has unpicked in all their attractive dangers) and that we should come with her on that journey, or, as she will eventually write in 'Instructions' (*Domestic Violence*, 2007): 'Now take syntax. Break that too.' The poems in *In a Time of Violence* are thus a kind of primer for entering the dilemmas that pervade the 2001 volume *Code* (published by Carcanet in the UK as *Code* and by Norton in the USA as *Against Love Poetry*).

The book begins with the poem 'In Which Hester Bateman, 18th Century English Silversmith Takes an Irish Commission'. It is the first in a sequence entitled 'Marriage'. Eleven poems make up this group and their obsessions reflect a poetics dedicated to addressing issues of history, of art, of nation, within a framework which accentuates the individual conscience, the individual life, particularly the female life, as really lived.

In this book, as here in the initial poem, the question of what kind of linguistic structure is fit for the task becomes central to the work itself:

> Hester Bateman made a marriage spoon
> And then subjected it to violence.
> Chased, beat it. Scarred it and marked it.
> All in the spirit of our darkest century:
>
> Far away from the grapeshot and tar caps
> And the hedge schools and the music of sedition
> She is oblivious to she pours out
> And lets cool the sweet colonial metal.[19]

The 't' sounds in the opening force the ear to hear that 'violence' and it's a relief to move to the more assonantal second stanza. But there, the third line refuses to be easily read. 'She is oblivious to she pours out' is given without an internal comma so that 'She' can be both object and subject and the verse can be read both upwards and downwards, something forced by the syntax — asking a reader to look again, to establish what exactly is being poured out and to what 'oblivious to' may apply. The syntactical play of *Code* may imply that there are at least two ways of reading everything, that nothing is given, that the onlooker could end up seeing double, questioning the layering that makes the notion of marriage resonate to include art and intention, empire and nation, 'past and future and the space between'. Here the inner working of language itself is drawn into arguments posited more discursively in Boland's earlier poems.

This first poem, along with the ode that closes the book, brackets a collection that includes some poems explicitly concerned with the parts of language, exploring for instance, how the 'Old Monks' used vowels and consonants and also investigating the stance of Standard English towards Hiberno-English. In this light the final verse of the first poem can be read to be as much about language as about the marriage spoon:

> Until resistance is their only element. It is
> What they embody, bound now and always:
> History frowns on them: yet in its gaze
> They join their injured hands and make their vows.[20]

The capitalisation of the first word in each line draws the eye to the enjambment: 'It is/What they embody'. The poet seems to be asking the reader to look longer, to ensure that linguistic difficulty and the feeling this conveys is noticed. The use of non-sentences like 'Chased, beat it.' is a recognisable trait from earlier collections. In 'Outside History' from the book of that title, 'An old steel engraving' may foreshadow the themes of this Hester Bateman piece, not only in the 'spaces' which it tries to illuminate between the 'unfinished action' captured in the object, and how the onlooker's own moral space is included by the artefact, but also by ending with the stanza:

> Is this river which
> moments ago must have flashed the morse
> of a bayonet thrust. And is moving on.[21]

To find the subject of that first 'Is', a reader must travel back up the poem. And, there's playfulness in the fact that the subject appears movable: ostensibly it continues from, 'this is/what happened and is happening and history', but visually and aurally it connects to 'the word/nothing can stir'. This kind of linguistic 'resistance', partially already formed in previous collections, becomes clearly a parallel project with the publication of *Code*. Boland is interested in exploring the tension within the syntax, within the cadence of Hiberno-English (as opposed to merely the words used), and in employing those conflicts to her own poetic ends.

Where ever-present tensions are at their highest, the poet turns to prose as in the second piece in the 'Marriage' sequence, 'Against Love Poetry'. Written in short sentences, it presents some characteristic Bolandisms: 'Why do I put these words side-by-side? Because I am a woman'.[22] Apart from the mysterious story that this small piece tells, it is certainly a coda for *Code*. 'It is to mark the contradictions of a daily love that I have written this. Against love poetry.' This might be read as the poet working within recognisable 'meaning-laden' language wishing simultaneously to show up the perilous nature of assumptions that she too can make about the efficacy of language in a poem. Yet the resonance of the story in which a condemned man, a great king, breaks down and weeps in front of his victorious enemy only when his old servant is paraded in front of him, seems to hint at the larger theme of the poet as servant only to her own muse.

In a poem like 'Quarantine', Boland's ambition is viscerally felt. She expressly takes on the love poem and yet writes one here. She has said that poetry must take account of the human endeavour to make a good life and yet never avoid the 'accurate inscription/of that agony'. She loads this twenty-line piece with conflict-ridden words and themes: 'north' (twice), 'the toxins of a whole history', two famine deaths in the worst of circumstances and the wish/statement: 'Let no love poem ever come to this threshold.' And she ends with two sentences beginning with the Irish-English use of 'and' acting like *agus* with connotations of *while/although/as* plus an 'and then' quality when used as a sentence starter by traditional story tellers in Irish while also linked to the use of the continuous present tense in Hiberno-English.[23] Used thus, 'And' could seem to refer to a whole linguistic and human history while opening out within the sense to embrace the importance of a relationship of care and the difficulty of expressing that care which may reside in a place language has yet to reach:

> And what there is between a man and a woman.
> And in which darkness it can best be proved.[24]

The titular poem 'Code' is an ode that draws attention to itself as artefact by veering from its iambics, varying line length and stanza shape in alternate stanzas. It takes up the issue of Creation (once with a capital, and once with a lowercase 'c') affirming: 'let there be language/even if we use it differently:' and it appears to give primacy to 'word' over the natural world which, as in many Boland poems, makes its appearance as a perfect metaphor for time. Addressed to Grace Murray Hopper, verifier of COBOL, it concludes with the large statement:

> I am writing at a screen as blue
> as any hill, as any lake, composing this
> to show you how the world begins again:
> One word at a time,
> One woman to another.[25]

And in trying to replicate the placement of one line underneath the other as it appears on the printed page, it's clear the hidden computer code would be useful. And in re-reading, with code-breaking in mind, the lines 'The given world is what you can translate' and 'I never made it numerate as you did./And yet I use it here to imagine' seem important. Implied here is that it may be the power of imagination that informs language, itself a metaphor for our 'code' as individuals, and that this code is transformative, and even capable of creation.

Boland, over a number of collections before *Code*, had addressed the whole question of memory in terms of a real or received history, in terms of truth and imagination, and in relation to the whole issue of time: passing, recalled, stalled and revived within the poem. The moral space, that Boland insists her poems inhabit, exists precisely because she refuses to write the historical moment out of memory or to make the real lived moment solely emblematic. Since rejecting her own poem, 'Child of Our Time' (omitting it from several collected editions), there's been a commitment to exposing the moment where the latter movement might happen, where language 'is perilous'. This shift is also demonstrated by Boland's emphasis on the syntactic slipperiness of language. Twin themes of the unreliability of 'memory' and almost intractable problems of 'making' thereby become explicitly linked. 'Making money' re-imagines the mill workers of Dundrum, a suburb of Dublin:

> if you can keep
> your composure in the face of this final proof that
> the past is not made out of time, out of memory,
> out of irony but is also
> a crime we cannot admit and will not atone
> it will be dawn again the rainy Autumn of the year.[26]

The poem then moves to its final lines where the action of the past is looked forward to in the future tense:

> The air will be a skinful of water –
> the distance between storms –
> again. The wagon of rags will arrive.
> The foreman will buy it. The boxes will be lowered to the path
> the women are walking up.
> as they always did, as they always will now.
> Facing the paradox. Learning to die of it.[27]

Looking at this section, the awkwardness of the enjambment from 'path' to 'the women are walking up' has the effect of jolting the reading mind, momentarily slipping the noose of time. This then may be what is meant by 'paradox' in the final line where the paradox of 'time travel' (undertaken by the poet in the poem) meets a paradox like that of the Ship of Theseus (will this ship be the same object if its wooden parts are replaced over time?). In that moment, forced to contemplate these women in a way managed by the poem, the reading mind becomes conscious of itself, thereby becoming strangely more aware of their presence, now actual women (since there's no difference within the mind between imagined and actual in this moment), walking 'as they always did, as they always will now'. Boland may be playing the kind of poetic mind-game that we associate more with Paul Muldoon. The argument is clear. Boland wants the language she chooses, her placement of it on the page including her use of resonant non-sentences ('Learning to die of it.') to form part of her insistent themes in order to rise poetically to the challenge of the difficulty she describes.

'Irish Poetry', the ode for Michael Hartnett with which *Code* concludes, uses 'it' in the first stanza to be that created, that made 'it' which also appeared in the opening poem of the book:

> We always knew there was no Orpheus in Ireland
> No music stored at the doors of hell.
> No god to make it.
> No wild beasts to weep and lie down to it.[28]

And, within the recollection of, and the image of people talking, this poem moves in short bursts as if it is coming to an understanding of itself as it is being written, to describe what Boland's verse may have done for the reader:

> You made the noise for me.
> Made it again.
> Until I could see the flight of it:

But this is the sound of a 'bird's wing in a lost language'; a curiously anatomical natural image which is difficult to match to intended expression except perhaps as a reference to 'The Black Lace Fan My Mother Gave Me', another poem where wing and/or fan takes on the time-stopping resonance of a moment, of place, of feelings deeply felt between people. On reading the poem aloud however, on making its noise again, it is possible to hear a certain grief within:

> how the sound
> of a bird's wing in a lost language sounded.

Here indeed is a distance. Reader and writer may only have the possibility of hearing an imitative sound of how something sounded (which itself is another form of Hiberno-English hyperbaton). This poem is written to the poet Michael Hartnett, whose own *Farewell to English* (and his subsequent return to writing in that language) may also inform it. Eavan Boland has him make the 'noise' so real that an 'as if' can develop which is the closest, she seems to say, that art can get to where any or all of the conflicts traced in this book, and by extension – in her oeuvre – might be resolved. The revelation, such as it is, applies as easily to what Boland has been doing throughout her poetry. Here, even with an always less-than-perfect language, even with the distances the poet has described, we can, through the fruit of the imaginative mind, become that thing, compromised and problematic, but nonetheless desired as the best poetic that her aesthetic can produce:

> and the savage acres no-one could predict
> were all at ease, soothed and quiet and
>
> listening to you, as I was. As if to music, as if to peace.[29]

Boland brings what has been seen as 'savage' towards an 'as if' that allows for 'peace' even though the problems therein are clearly observed. Here, as is her way, she allows for the poem as an accommodation and not as a solution. She suggests that the poem, standing for art, can hold within it an aesthetic reply to a contested culture and a violent state as well as implying the transcendence of a momentary creation within art, however compromised that might be.

NOTES

1   This quote is from the poem 'Tirade for the Lyric Muse' in Eavan Boland, *Collected Poems* (Manchester, Carcanet, 1995), p. 130.

2   For example, John Goodby in *Irish Poetry Since 1950: From Stillness into History* (Manchester, Manchester University Press, 2000) discusses the fact that Boland's 'apprenticeship was prolonged' citing 'Athene's Song' as a turning point and quoting Derek Mahon on the poem as sounding a 'proleptically "feminist" note' which Goodby opines is returned to in the poem 'The War Horse'. p. 178.

3   Eavan Boland, *New Collected Poems* (Manchester, Carcanet, 2005), p. 24, hereafter *NCP*.

4   *NCP*, p. 16.

5   *NCP*, p. 40.

6   Eavan Boland, 'The Weasel's Tooth', *The Irish Times*, 7 June 1974.

7   Jody Allen Randolph, *Eavan Boland: Contemporary Irish Writers* (London, Rowman and Littlefield, 2013), p. 51.

8   *NCP*, p. 154.

9   *NCP*, p. 156.

10   *NCP*, p. 127.

11   Gerardine Meaney, 'Myth, History and the Politics of Subjectivity: Eavan Boland and Irish Women's Writing', *Women: A Cultural Review*, 4.3 (1993), pp 136–153. John Goodby, *Irish Poetry Since 1950: From Stillness into History* (Manchester, Manchester University Press, 2000), p. 231.

12   *NCP*, p. 128.

13   Clair Wills, *Improprieties: Politics and Sexuality in Northern Irish Poetry* (Oxford, Clarendon Press, 1993), pp 57–58.

14   Edna Longley, *The Living Stream: Literature and Revisionism in Ireland* (Tarset, Bloodaxe, 1994). 'Eavan Boland's feminist poem 'Mise Eire' (I am Ireland) destabilises Mise but not Eire – "my nation displaced/into old dactyls"', p. 173.

15   *Ibid.*, p. 172.

16   *NCP*, p. 185.

17 *NCP*, pp 210–11.
18 *NCP*, p. 209.
19 *NCP*, p. 279.
20 *NCP*, p. 280.
21 *NCP*, p.184.
22 *NCP*, p. 280.
23 For a discussion of the various uses of 'agus', see Patrick S. Dinneen, *Foclóir Gaedhilge agus Béarla: An Irish-English Dictionary* (Dublin, M.H.Gill and Son, 1904) accessible as an e-book at <http://www.ucc.ie/Celt/Dinneen1sted.pdf> [accessed 31 January 2015], p. 14.
24 *NCP*, p. 282.
25 *NCP*, p. 291.
26 *NCP*, p. 293.
27 *NCP*, p. 293.
28 *NCP*, p. 307.
29 *NCP*, p. 307.

REFERENCES

Abrams, M.H. and Stephen Greenblatt, *The Norton Anthology of English Literature* (New York, Norton 1999).

Allen Randolph, Jody, 'Ecriture Feminine and the Authorship of Self in Eavan Boland's *In Her Own Image*', *Colby Quarterly* 27.1 (1991), pp 48–59.
'The New Critics: The Analytical Prose of Adrienne Rich and Eavan Boland', *PN Review*, 22.2 (1995), pp 15–17.

Berg, Stephen, David Bonanno and Arthur Vogelsang, *The Body Electric: America's Best Poetry from the American Poetry Review* (New York, Norton, 2000).

Boland, Eavan, 'The Weasel's Tooth', *The Irish Times*, 7 June 1974.

Clutterbuck, Catriona, 'Irish Critical Responses to Self-Representation in Eavan Boland 1987–1995', *Colby Quarterly* 25.4 (1999), pp 275–287.

Conboy, Sheila C, 'Eavan Boland's Topography of Displacement', *Éire/Ireland: A Journal of Irish Studies*, 29.3 (1994), pp 137–146.

Damrosch, David, Kevin J.H. Dettmar and Jennifer Wicke, *The Longman Anthology of British Literature: The Twentieth Century* V.2C (London, Longman, 2005).

Dietz, Maggie and Robert Pinsky, *Americans' Favorite Poems* (New York, Norton, 1999).

Gelpi, Albert, 'Hazard and Death: The Poetry of Eavan Boland',

Colby Quarterly 35.4 (1999), pp 210–228.

Haberstroh, Patricia Boyle, *Women Creating Women: Contemporary Irish Women Poets* (New York, Syracuse University Press, 1996).

Hagen, Patricia L. And Thomas W. Zelman, '"We were never on the scene of the crime" – Eavan Boland's Repossession of History', *Twentieth Century Literature*, 37.4 (1991).

Longley, Edna, *The Living Stream: Literature and Revisionism in Ireland* (Tarset, Bloodaxe, 1994).

Meaney, Gerardine, 'Myth, History and the Politics of Subjectivity: Eavan Boland and Irish Women's Writing', *Women: A Cultural Review*, 4.3 (1993), pp 136–153.

O'Connor, Mary, 'Chronicles of Impeded Growth: Eavan Boland and the Reconstruction of Identity', *Post Identity*, 2.2 (1999), pp 45–76.

Salter, Mary Jo and Jon Stallworthy (eds), *The Norton Anthology of Poetry* (New York, Norton, 1998).

Somerville-Arjat, Gillean and Rebecca E. Wilson (eds), *Sleeping with Monsters: Conversations with Scottish and Irish Women Poets* (Edinburgh, Polygon 1990).

Villar-Argáiz, Pilar, *The Poetry of Eavan Boland: A Postcolonial Reading* (Palo Alto, California, Academica Press, 2008).

Wills, Clair, *Improprieties: Politics and Sexuality in Northern Irish Poetry* (Oxford, Clarendon Press, 1993), pp 57–58.

Thomas Kinsella

WESTLAND ROW

We came to the outer light down a ramp in the dark
Through eddying cold gusts and grit, our ears
Stopped with noise. The hands of the station clock
Stopped, or another day vanished exactly.
The engine departing hammered slowly overhead.
Dust blowing under the bridge, we stooped slightly
With briefcases and books and entered the wind.

The savour of our days restored, dead
On nostril and tongue. Drowned in air,
We stepped on our own traces, not on stone,
Nodded and smiled distantly and followed
Our scattering paths, not stumbling, not touching.

Until, in a breath of benzene from a garage-mouth,
By the Academy of Music coming against us
She stopped an instant in her wrinkled coat
And ducked her childish cheek in the coat-collar
To light a cigarette: seeing nothing,
Thick-lipped, in her grim composure.

Daughterwife, look upon me.

'DAYS OF BURNED COUNTRYSIDE':
PUBLIC AND PRIVATE WARS, 1975–1985:
A RETROSPECTIVE

Gerald Dawe

In 'A Final Thought',[1] her fond and neatly thought-out epilogue to the 60th anniversary edition of *Icarus*, the well-known student literary magazine from Trinity College Dublin, Eavan Boland cast her mind back to her years as an undergraduate in the early 1960s, publishing her first poems:

> I wasn't active in getting [*Icarus*] out, or distributing it. Other students, some of them friends of mine, did all the heavy-lifting. I was much more a prowler at its margins, eager to see the poems in it, and occasionally pleased to see my own.

Describing the magazine of the time as 'elegant', Boland considers to 'this day, however, nameless or not, I remember how that font set off poems that might have looked ragged and unofficial without it'. The sense of authorisation, of the first telling steps into a public endorsement, something every poet recalls with both excitement and trepidation, is etched in the epilogue's recollection of each physical detail of how the poems *looked* on the page, 'in the graceful slant of those particular block capitals or printed stanzas, every lyric looked as if it had landed safely'.

Following on from the impressions of the appearance of her poems in *Icarus* (in 1964) Boland reflects on her own literary self-consciousness as a young student-poet: 'I don't think I had the slightest idea ... what it means to have a College magazine with its own strong, vivid and established literary tradition'. Nor the 'particular hard-to-define sense of esteem it hands out to fledgling poets and yearning talents. On the contrary, I took it for granted'. It is an important point of realisation for, as the established and much praised senior poet writing in 2010 looks back fifty years, the phrase that resonates here is surely, 'took it for granted'.

If Boland's development as a poet is characterised by anything as directly definitive as a 'theme' it is surely in her *not* taking anything for granted. For Boland as poet and essayist is driven by an over-riding critical desire to challenge, revise, revisit and (eventually) restore much that is or was taken for granted in Irish literary terms and circles of the 1960s and 1970s. Perhaps this is what she means when in summarising 'A Final Thought' Boland admits that:

> Maybe the fact that I am writing this at a distance means that some fraction of the value and privilege did get through to me. I was – in this I might have been in the majority of students – not at all sure what part of me would be confirmed or denied by my education. I was certainly unsure what place my hit-and-miss but nevertheless stubborn determination to be a poet would have once I went through Front Gate. Like other students I looked for signs and guarantees that the world of knowledge would not frown on the world of imagination – however unformed the second might be.

Icarus, the student magazine, provided 'one of those signs, one of those guarantees' and 'even across so many years,

I'm still grateful for that' Boland concludes. Naturally only so much can be read into an epilogue to a commemorative celebratory anthology; nonetheless there are several important underlying 'signs' in Boland's short prose piece that bear thinking about in a retrospective essay such as this.[2] Simply put, the 'prowler at the margins' was much more at the centre of things even while recalling the general vulnerabilities of 'esteem' which were to remain central to Boland's 'stubborn determination to be a poet'. A determination that brought into its ambit Boland's private and public interrogation of the role of womanhood and the suburban places of self-definition in Ireland; as well as the pressures on and of female sexuality in the tragically protracted separation of the morally dominant Catholic Church from the civic and cultural institutions of the Irish Republic. Often overlooked, however, is Boland's initiating engagement with and opening-up to the political and ideological conflict of the northern Troubles, which erupted only a few years after her graduation from Trinity in 1966. Eavan Boland anticipated as much as participated in these difficult and at times painful challenges.

It is beyond the remit of the present essay to do justice to each and every one of these important early influences on Boland's personal and poetic development. I would however like to connect these general introductory remarks to my own understanding of Boland's substantial contribution to what could be called 'the debates' of the 1970s and 1980s as a kind of historical sketch by a younger contemporary who was greatly impressed by the focus and intensity of Eavan Boland's early collections: *The War Horse* (1975), *In Her Own Image* (1980) and *Night Feed* (1982).

Most of the dedicatees of these publications are drawn from Boland's time at Trinity College[3] and the Dublin-based poets she met during the sixties. Eamon Grennan ('The Pilgrim'), Michael Longley ('Migration'), Derek

Mahon ('Belfast vs. Dublin') and Brendan Kennelly ('The Flight of the Earls') feature alongside Philip Edwards[4] and David Norris[5] and her long-time friend, Mary Robinson.[6]

This sense of an identifiable literary college community is nothing new but it is clear from her later reflections published in *Object Lessons*[7] that Boland was very aware of the non-academic literary world and practice taking place in the local pubs and cafes, the 'inner city', which was becoming a home from home within a few paces of Trinity:

> Dublin was a coherent space then, a small circumference in which to be and become a poet. A single bus journey took you into college for the day. Twilights over Stephen's Green were breathable and lilac-coloured. Coffee beans turned and gritted off the blades in the windows of Roberts' and Bewleys. A single cup of it, moreover, cost nine pence in old money and could be spun out for hours of conversation. The last European city. The last literary smallholding. Or maybe not.[8]

After spending much of her girlhood and teenage years in the UK and United States before returning to Dublin as a fourteen year old, Dublin became her home. By the time she was an undergraduate at Trinity she also had to find room for herself in the city's literary culture. Portraits of Patrick Kavanagh[9] and Padraic Colum[10] paint a telling picture of the young poet's difficult attempts to connect with the city. 'On reflection', her contemporary Derek Mahon, remarked in 1993:[11]

> I now realise that she was struggling to assert herself in what she correctly perceived to be a male-dominated literary culture. Was it, for her, a necessary struggle? She had only to look at a door and it flew open.

Boland's first substantial volume, *New Territory* appeared in 1967 when she was 23. In the eight years which led into the publication of *The War Horse* (1975) the Irish poetry scene was increasingly viewed (at least from outside) through the perspective of what would become known as 'Northern Poetry' with the 'Belfast Group' as its incubator.[12]

The second, third and fourth volumes of Longley, Mahon and Heaney were appearing[13] alongside the work of older contemporaries including John Montague, John Hewitt, Roy McFadden, Robert Greacen and Padraic Fiacc, among others. By the time *In Her Own Image* and *Night Feed* appeared in 1980 and 1982, the sense of a literary 'movement' in the north had gathered both critical momentum in the media and cultural definition with the publication of Frank Ormsby's wide-selling and definitive anthology, *Poets from the North of Ireland*, the first edition of which appeared in 1979.

The publication of senior figures in Irish poetry from the south of the country such as Thomas Kinsella and Richard Murphy seemed to be finding their level in terms of how Irish poetry was now being increasingly viewed in the UK and US as 'the North'; an ascription underpinned in the Anglophone literary world by the controversial reception for Seamus Heaney's fourth collection, *North* (1975).[14] Heaney's inclusion and central presence in the talismanic *Penguin Book of Contemporary British Poetry* (1982), along with five[15] fellow northern poets and the well-charted reactions to that, including Heaney's 'An Open Letter', point to heightened 'tensions' of the 1970s and 1980s. The laid-back optimism that people experienced with the late arrival of 'the sixties' in the Irish republic, had to be quickly (and reluctantly) re-adjusted to the starkly local ('northern') crises of the seventies. Its destabilising spill-over into the south, when huge numbers of refugees evacuated from the sectarian mayhem of Belfast and other cities in the north sought emergency housing along the border, was a chastening reminder of what the future might hold.

Eavan Boland was a key artistic presence in urging publicly that certain elements of Irish national public discourse needed to be recalibrated in order to match the radically changing conditions of Irish political reality; a call for revisionism not at all common at the time. With the foundation of Field Day (1980) – a response to these political challenges and the perceived need to engage with them – and the ideological and cultural discussions at play in a journal such as *The Crane Bag* (1977–1985) and the women's platform, Arlen House, reflected an intellectual ferment of revisionism, nationalism and feminism which suggested that the legacy and lifestyle of Patrick Kavanagh's generation, never mind W.B. Yeats and the Literary Revival, was fast breaking up. What was taking its place was the question.

Boland's role in focussing these discussions in the southern state fulfilled the role of what would be called today 'the public intellectual'. This was demonstrated through her literary journalism. Boland wrote trenchant reviews for *The Irish Times*, which, along with her 'Poetry Anthology' and 'Poet's Choice' radio series and various television appearances on the national broadcaster RTÉ as well as her numerous readings and moderating of workshops in the Republic, reveal a range of commitment that by any standard is exceptional for the time.

Her characteristically robust review in *The Irish Times* of the first flush of Field Day pamphlets was deeply questioning for the time and proposed an integrating view of the island of Ireland rather than deferring to the partitioned and divided states it had, in many ways *unwittingly*, become:[16]

> A new Ulster nationalism is not my idea of what Irish poetry needs, but I would be quite willing to lay aside this prejudice if the new nationalism contained all the voices, all the fragments, all the dualities and ambiguities of reference; but it doesn't. Judging by the Field Day pamphlets here in front of me, this is green nationalism and divided culture.

While concluding her review of Seamus Heaney's poem, *An Open Letter*, the second of the three pamphlets, Boland declared:

> Poetry is defined by its energies and its eloquence, not by the passport of the poet or the editor; or the name of the nationality. That way lies all the categories, the separations, the censorships, that poetry exists to dispel.[17]

Six years later, six more years we should recall of The Troubles and the dreadful daily toll of violence visited upon ordinary life in the north, Edna Longley's response to Eavan Boland's 1989 pamphlet, *A Kind of Scar: The Woman Poet in a National Tradition*,[18] chastises her for 'not questioning the nation'[19] and:

> was surprised that *A Kind of Scar* ... ignored the extent to which the North has destabilised the 'nation'. Boland holds to unitary assumptions about 'a society, a nation, a literary heritage'. Troubled about 'the woman poet' she takes the 'national tradition' for granted.

A few years previously in 1982 I had tried to represent the shifting of these poetic grounds in an anthology I edited, *The Younger Irish Poets*.[20] The book opened with three 'southern' poets – Paul Durcan, Eavan Boland and Richard Ryan – in an effort to exhibit what else was going on throughout the country as well as the resurgence of poetry in/from the north. The anthology sold remarkably well and went into three reprints in 1983 and a little later in 1985 before going out of print.[21]

Boland was represented in the anthology by six poems – 'Belfast vs. Dublin', 'The War Horse', 'Child of Our Time', 'Conversation with an Inspector of Taxes', 'Solitary' and 'A Ballad of Beauty and Time'. The poems, drawn from her three books to date, had their own story to tell; at least that was my intention.

I had met Eavan in the late 1970s as a raw graduate poet from Belfast living in Galway, grappling with the fall out of the northern violence and the accompanying political storms. There had been some exchanges of views and I was greatly taken by the tension in her work between the public voiced concerns of *The War Horse* and the demeanour of family life and the contained impressionism composed in the 'suburban' poems of *Night Feed*. I had also made an intermediary connection between the poet and the artist Constance Short for an interim broadsheet publication featuring some of the poems which ultimately became *In Her Own Image*.

Boland's independence and dedication was impressive but there was a kind of fearlessness too which, in those intensely focussed years set her apart from the often sentimentalised responses or bewildered indifference in the Republic to what was going on 'up north'.

Looking back over three decades since that anthology was first published, the selection of Boland's poems seemed to reproduce a distinctive meta-narrative all of its own. From the somewhat stylized opening poem of 'Belfast vs. Dublin' through the poignant and moving poems 'The War Horse' and 'Child of Our Time' to the sophisticated translation from Mayakovsky's 'Conversation' to the much edgier tones of 'Solitary' and the confident dramatization of 'A Ballad', it looked as if this introductory sample of Boland's poetry revealed a fascinating movement; a 'mini' inner history. Between the stereotypically-freighted inherited past of 'Belfast vs. Dublin' to the shocking disclosure of 'Solitary' and its scene of masturbation, within these (unstated) parameters sat centre-stage one of the finest poems of the seventies, 'The War Horse':[22]

> But we, we are safe, our unformed fear
> Of fierce commitment gone; why should we care
>
> If a rose, a hedge, a crocus are uprooted
> Like corpses, remote, crushed, mutilated?

He stumbles on like a rumour of war, huge,
Threatening; neighbours use the subterfuge

Of curtains.

The poem's conclusion bears the rhetorical flourish in mind on this occasion with justice, I think:

/.../That rose he smashed frays
Ribboned across our hedge, recalling days

Of burned countryside, illicit braid:
A cause ruined before, a world betrayed.

In *Object Lessons*, Boland reflects:

I wrote the poem ['The War Horse'] slowly, adding each couplet with care. I was twenty-six years of age. At first, when it was finished, I looked at it with pleasure and wonder. It encompassed a real event.[23]

However, her sense of the poem altered over time as she relates some twenty years later:

In a time of violence it would be all too easy to write another poem, and another. To make a construct where the difficult 'I' of perception became the easier 'we' of a subtle claim. Where an unearned power would be allowed by a public engagement.

But the political poem was not what Boland was after; the gesture was wrong-headed:

I would learn that it was far more difficult to make myself the political subject of my own poems than to see the metaphoric possibilities in front of me in a suburban dusk.

And of course this is precisely what *Night Feed* records in its atmospherics of surprise, at-homeness and an amazed joy while coping with the fissures of a self-divided from these very stabilities which drive the fragmented lyrics of *In Her Own Image* into a form of despair. No-one else writing in Ireland carried these contrary and contradictory pulses in their poems. The scrutiny that

Boland entered into of what constituted(s?) a soulscape of contemporary womanhood was relentless and, one can only assume, costly in its emotional and psychic draw.

But the wonder of these poems has never left them: 'How my flesh summers,/How my mind shadows, /Meshed in this brightness'.[24] Such engagements were bound, eventually, to produce a reaction both within the work itself and in its reception. Risks are run in such self-consciousness too, of tracking the poetic pathways to self-construction, although it could be said that Boland was following a pattern laid down well before her by W.B. Yeats in his *Autobiographies*. But this transparent 'angle of approach' has been questioned by, among others, Caitriona O'Reilly in her review[25] of Boland's follow-up publication to *Object Lessons*, *A Journey with Two Maps: Becoming a Woman Poet*:[26]

> ... given that Boland has declared that her approach is self – rather than fact-based, what critic can feel comfortable about contending directly with Boland's narratives of her own poetic development and the necessarily partial version of literary history propounded through those narratives. The precise validity of this method is open to debate.

Indeed it is; but given O'Reilly's injunction that 'one of the main problems with Boland's approach is its basic ahistoricity', it might be all the more necessary a requirement to see Boland in the contexts of *her* own time; in other words the historicity of Boland's early achievement.

It may also be the case, as Caitriona O'Reilly justly remarks, that Boland's 'habit of continually checking her pulse by submitting all threads into her narrative of personal witness becomes, by its very insistence, a distraction'.[27] In contrast, Boland's 'compelling' account of translating the German poet Elisabeth Langgässer and her 'empathetic and illuminating' reading of the German-

Jewish writer Else Lasker-Schüler show Boland at her less 'self'-centred best.

However, there are systemic risks of what O'Reilly sees as 'false witness and intellectual fuzziness'. This is often the fate of post war recollections it has to be said. Indeed Boland notes as much in the 'Introduction' to *After Every War*,[28] the anthology of her translations from nine German poets:

> During the Troubles in Ireland the political life of the island was endlessly on view – violent, oppressive, and often cruel. Gradually, act by murderous act, a country I had once known, once understood to have existed, disappeared. With that disappearance, a world of familiar signs – of memories and explanations – was displaced. What's more, as that land disappeared there was little enough to register its previous existence. The delicacy and actuality of a place in its time can quickly be overwritten.

She continues with a poignant and moving resolution that, while not intending to 'compare what happened on one island to the mid-century cataclysm', Boland states:

> ... the violation of our island went so deep, was so toxic, that the private could no longer find shelter from the public. Everything was touched. Nothing was spared. A buckled shoe in a market street after a bombing. A woman looking out of window at an altered street – they were all emblems, images, perhaps even graffiti of the new reality. Overnight, so it seemed, the division between the public and private imagination ceased to be meaningful. Both were interchangeable ways of grasping and rendering a new reality. The political poem became a map of dissolving boundaries.

The achievement of Eavan Boland resides in the courage and willingness she demonstrated to say the things she said as poet and critic in a much less liberal and liberated Irish society than the one we currently live in; an advance and advantage that she and other women of her generation in large part made possible.

NOTES

1   Eavan Boland, 'A Final Thought' in *Icarus: 60 Years of Creative Writing from Trinity College* edited by Dan Sheehan, Joanne O'Leary, Eoin Nolan, Anna Kinsella (Dublin, DU Publications, 2010), p. 241.

2   Jody Allen Randolph (ed.), *Eavan Boland: A Sourcebook* (Manchester, Carcanet Press, 2007) contains a useful bibliography of 'Selected Articles by Eavan Boland', particularly relevant here, pp 192–207.

3   Boland attended Trinity College 1962–1966 and was appointed junior lecturer in English, a post from which she resigned in 1968.

4   Philip Edwards was Edward Dowden Professor of English Literature (1867) in the Department of English, Trinity College Dublin (1960–1966).

5   David Norris was a Lecturer in English at TCD (1968–1996) and is a member of Seanad Éireann (1987– present).

6   Mary Robinson was Reid Professor of Law, TCD and subsequently, President of Ireland (1990–1997).

7   Eavan Boland, *Object Lessons: The Life of the Woman and the Poet in Our Time* (Manchester, Carcanet Press, 1995).

8   *Object Lessons*, p. 249.

9   *Object Lessons*, pp 98–100.

10 *Object Lessons*, pp 138–140.

11 Derek Mahon, 'Young Eavan and Early Boland', *Irish University Review: Special Issue – Eavan Boland* (Spring/Summer 1993), p. 24. Mahon would recall these days in prose reminiscences including 'Yeats and the Lights of Dublin' and 'Icarus in the Ignorance Age' in *Selected Prose* (Oldcastle, Gallery Press, 2012), pp 64–75, 241–243 and, on a slightly earlier frame of reference, in the sequence 'Decadence 4: "shiver in your tenement"', *New Collected Poems* (Oldcastle, Gallery Press, 2011), pp 201–2.

12 See Edna Longley's rebuttal of 'the origin-myth' in 'Encryptions: Stephen Enniss, *After the Titanic: A Life of Derek Mahon*', *The Yellow Nib* (No 10, Spring 2015), p. 55.

13 From her Trinity College contemporaries – *Night-Crossing* (1968), *Lives* (1972), *The Snow Party* (1975) by Derek Mahon; *No Continuing City* (1969), *An Exploded View* (1973), *Man Lying on a Wall* (1976) by Michael Longley; *Acts and Monuments* (1972), *Site of Ambush* (1975) *The Second Voyage* (1977) by Eiléan Ní Chuileanáin; and *My Dark Fathers* (1964), *Getting up Early* (1966),

Selected Poems (1969), *Shelley in Dublin* (1974), *A Kind of Trust* (1975) by Brendan Kennelly who had also edited *The Penguin Book of Irish Verse* in 1970 and which included Boland as the penultimate poet: 'Her book *New Territory* put her with the leading younger poets of Ireland' ran the editorial note (p. 27).

14 A year prior to *North* appearing Boland moderated and published in *The Irish Times* (5 July 1974) 'The Clash of Identities', an important round table of discussions with poets, politicians and paramilitaries which forty years later, deserves republication.

15 Andrew Motion and Blake Morrison (eds), *The Penguin Book of Contemporary British Poetry* (Harmondsworth, Penguin, 1982). The other poets from Northern Ireland were Michael Longley, Medbh McGuckian, Derek Mahon, Paul Muldoon and Tom Paulin.

16 The first series appeared in 1983: Tom Paulin, 'A New Look at the Language Question'; Seamus Heaney, 'An Open Letter' and Seamus Deane, 'Civilians and Barbarians'. Boland's review 'Poets and Pamphlets' was published in *The Irish Times,* 1 October 1983.

17 *The Irish Times*, 1 October 1983.

18 Eavan Boland, *A Kind of Scar: The Woman Poet in a National Tradition* (Dublin, Attic Press, 1989, LIP pamphlet).

19 Edna Longley, *From Cathleen to Anorexia: The Breakdowns of Irelands* (Dublin, Attic Press, 1990, LIP pamphlet).

20 Gerald Dawe (ed.), *The Younger Irish Poets* (Belfast, Blackstaff Press, 1982).

21 A second edition, *The New Younger Irish Poets* edited by the present writer was published by Blackstaff Press in 1991.

22 'The War Horse', *New Collected Poems* (Manchester, Carcanet Press, 2005), p. 39.

23 Eavan Boland, *Object Lessons: The Life of the Woman and the Poet in Our Time,* pp 176–179.

24 'Solitary', *New Collected Poems*, p. 79.

25 Caitriona O'Reilly, 'Notes to Self', *The Irish Times*, 4 June 2011.

26 Eavan Boland, *A Journey with Two Maps: Becoming a Woman Poet* (Manchester, Carcanet Press, 2007).

27 See the present writer's 'The Suburban Night: On Eavan Boland, Paul Durcan and Thomas McCarthy', *Contemporary Irish Poetry: A Collection of Critical Essays* edited by Elmer Andrews (London, Macmillan, 1992), pp 168–193 and republished in *The Proper*

Word: Collected Criticism (New York, Fordham University Press, 2007), pp 276–297.

28 Eavan Boland, *After Every War: Twentieth Century Women Poets* translations from the German (New Jersey, Princeton University Press, 2004), pp 5–6.

John Montague

Sibyl's Morning

1

She wakes in a hand-painted cot,
chats and chortles to herself,
a healthy small being, a happy elf,
sister to the early train whistle,
the bubbling dawn chorus along
the wisteria of Grattan Hill.

No complaints as yet, enjoying
through curtains the warm sunlight,
until she manages to upend herself.
Then the whine starts. Is it anger
or lust for the bottle?

Lift her up, warm and close
or held at arm's length —
that smell, like a sheep pen,
a country hedge steaming after rain.
As the bottle warms the decibels increase,
the scaldie's mouth gapes open;
head numb, coated tongue,
cortex ends squealing, no
thirsty drunk at a bar, nursing
a hangover, manages such concentration.

Daughter, dig in, with fists like ferns
unfurling, to basic happiness!
Little one, you are now
nothing but the long music of the gut,
a tug of life, with halts
for breathing, stomach swelling.

2

On your throne afterwards
bang your heels, examine your new
and truly wonderful hands,
try out, warm up, your
little runs of satisfaction.

Day by day they also grow,
sound experiments in the laboratory
of the self, animal happiness,
the tonal colour of rage, cartoon
attempts to communicate, eyes beaming,
burbles rising. Best of all when

like any bird or beast waking,
you wail to yourself, with whoops,
finger stuffed gurgles, and my reward
for the morning, your speciality
(after the peristaltic hiccup)
when you smile and squeal with
sudden, sharp whistles —
O my human kettle!

SHAPE-SHIFTING INSTABILITIES:
USING BLENDING THEORY TO
UNDERSTAND METAMORPHOSIS AS METAPHOR
IN EAVAN BOLAND'S POETRY

Nigel McLoughlin

This essay explores Eavan Boland's use of metaphor in a
number of poems drawn from various points across her
work. The essay will analyse the means by which she
develops different manifestations of metaphors related to
metamorphosis and how her use of these metaphors has
changed over the course of her career. Much critical work
on Eavan Boland relates to the post-colonial, historical and
cultural themes that are developed in her work.[1] In
connection with these, Andrew Auge has responded to
various manifestations of 'fracture and wound' in her
poems.[2] Critics have also analysed her exploration of the
gender politics involved in representing Irish women's
cultural roles and the personal in relationship to feminist
discourse.[3] Still others have examined the use of voice and
vision to reconcile the political and personal and self-

knowledge through self-exteriorisation and narration[4] or analysed Boland's use of embodiment in particular relation to historical and contemporary depictions of trauma and pain.[5] This touches on metaphor theory through the fact that conceptual metaphors are thought to develop from embodied processes grounded in *being in the world*.[6]

Marta Miquel-Baldellou studied images of transition, some of which can be related to metamorphosis, through focusing on three poems titled 'Suburban Woman', 'Suburban Woman: A Detail', and 'Suburban Woman: Another Detail', to depict transitions embodied by the same woman at three different points in her life.[7] While I have previously made use of Text World Theory as a cognitive poetic approach to Eavan Boland's work,[8] there has been no study to date that has deployed theories of conceptual blending (usually shortened to blending theory) in a cognitive poetic study of her poems. In the essay that follows I will make use of blending theory as described by Fauconnier and Turner, and further developed by Brandt and Brandt,[9] in order to analyse the cognitive operations involved and how they produce metaphoric interpretations of the poems in which they are found.

CONCEPTUAL BLENDING

Fauconnier and Turner's blending theory offers a way to understand conceptual phenomena in terms of the conceptual mappings between mental spaces that are created by counterfactual ideas, jokes and metaphors. Such blending of different mental spaces allows novel connections to emerge and form coherent new mental structures. From these, we can hold in mind similarities between disparate items, differences between expected and actual conditions and the insights that often emerge from these. Mental spaces are often described as temporary representational structures which are constructed in the minds of those who participate in language exchanges, in order to represent perceived, remembered or imagined situations which may occur in the present or be marked as occurring at some other time.[10]

In their model, Fauconnier and Turner, assert that metaphors may be represented by four interconnected spaces: the two input spaces of the model represent the two basic parts of the metaphor and contain the specific features which describe the two separate images or ideas contained in the tenor and vehicle of the metaphor. A third generic space is formed from the abstract representation of common structure, represented through the common generic features of the two input spaces; and a fourth blend space represents a compression of common features and also any emergent details which arise from the combination of specific features from the two input spaces.

In their 2005 paper, 'Making Sense of a Blend', Line and Per Aage Brandt investigated mental spaces, with particular regard to metaphor, by combining conceptual metaphor theory and blending theory with cognitive semiotics. They see this as a necessary development since metaphor and the expressive blends that they necessitate are essentially signs. In Brandt and Brandt's version, the two input spaces are referred to as presentation (which contain the metaphoric vehicle) and reference spaces (which contain the entity being described). This preserves the directional qualities of 'tenor' and 'vehicle' in the metaphor. The blend/emergence space of Fauconnier and Turner is separated by Brandt and Brandt into a virtual space (where one thing is imagined acting as another) and a meaning space (where qualities may be abstracted or emerge from the compression or blend in the virtual space). These emergences and abstractions can be mapped back to a semiotic space containing situational and contextual knowledge and accrue resonance as a sign. Brandt and

Brandt advocate the omission of the generic space of Fauconnier and Turner's model, but their model accounts for the shared structure contained in the generic space through the interaction between the virtual space and a relevance space, which holds context dependent information and where schema can be abstracted from the virtual space and used to inform the emergent meaning.[11] The examples analysed below will demonstrate more meaningfully how this operates.

Blending theory has previously been used to examine the mapping of complex metaphors in poetry, for example Margaret Freeman applied it to Sylvia Plath's 'The Applicant'. Freeman asserts that 'blending theory makes explicit the conceptual tools we use in creating and interpreting texts'.[12] In the section that follows, I present an analysis, using Brandt and Brandt's model, of a selection of Boland's metaphors related to metamorphosis. The metaphors in Boland's work provide a good test as to how well the framework can be applied to poetic metaphors and the framework offers a structurally principled way of analysing the metaphors in terms of their cognitive structure, meaning and contextual relevance and provides further understanding of how readers may go about making meaning from them. I have generally omitted the situation from the analysis since, in all cases, the situation is circumscribed by the reader's engagement with a poem, however, consideration of the reader's contextual knowledge is included in the analysis.

Poems have been selected for analysis from an initial reading of Boland's *Collected Poems* (1995) and the next three single volume collections which followed that publication: *The Lost Land* (1998), *Code* (2001) and *Domestic Violence* (2007). In selecting the metaphors to review in detail, I have chosen from across the poet's chronological output and examined examples of the use of metamorphosis as metaphor in order to best demonstrate the breadth and complexity with which poetic metaphor is used. Given the aims of this essay, this strategy is preferable as a means of illustrating the breadth and distribution of the use of metamorphosis as metaphor throughout the work, rather than focusing exhaustively on one or two examples that may not be representative of the poet's work as a whole. Many of the metaphors I analyse can be understood as being constructed from text-worlds in metaphoric relation. Text worlds are mental structures whereby 'worlds' are imagined consisting of enactors, actions, intentions, spaces and times, that can be mentally integrated and understood as coherent wholes or worlds. Blending theory can be used to track the metaphoric connections and mappings between these worlds and the meanings that emerge from those mappings.

METAMORPHOSIS AS METAPHOR IN EAVAN BOLAND'S POETRY
Boland uses metamorphosis as metaphor in several ways. The first of these may be grouped broadly as 'metamorphosis is diminution, decay, reversal or loss of power'; the second may be grouped broadly under 'metamorphosis is usurpation, empowerment, or move towards the place of power' and the third may be classified as 'metamorphosis is renewal or repetition'. Several of the metaphors are complex and may include features of more than one of the basic types.

Metamorphosis is diminution, decay, reversal or loss of power
An early example of the first of these types of metaphor, 'metamorphosis is diminution or loss of power', occurs in 'Ode to Suburbia'[13] originally published in *The War Horse* (1975), where Boland asserts that suburbia's power is 'defined/By this detail':

By this creature drowsing now in every house –
The same lion who tore stripes
Once off zebras. Who now sleeps,
Small beside the coals. And may,
On a red letter day,
Catch a mouse.[14]

The excerpt begins by constructing a reference space consisting of a sketched text-word where an, as yet, unidentified creature drowses 'in every house'. The time is taken to be present, due to the deictic marker 'now'. The presentation space is drawn into analogous relation through the assertion that this is 'the same lion' but the deictic marker 'once' signifies that the text-world of the presentation space is not the same text-world of the reference space and is in fact a past world. In this past text-world a predator-prey relationship is formed between lions, which we contextually recognise as 'big cats' and zebras. The setting for the implied hunt is an implied 'wild space', which the reader supplies through their contextual knowledge of lions hunting zebras. The reference space is then further developed. The reader's attention is switched back to the present text-world of the drowsing creature by the deictic marker 'now', which marks it as the same text-world as the original reference space. This can be envisaged to contain a present text-world where the enactors of cat and mouse form a similar relation of predator and prey, but where the cat only periodically catches the mouse, otherwise it spends its time dozing in domestic comfort. Two mental spaces are being evoked here, the reference space of 'suburban comfort' and the presentation space of the 'savanna'. These and the other spaces analysed may be represented diagrammatically in Figure 1:

Figure 1: Ode to Suburbia

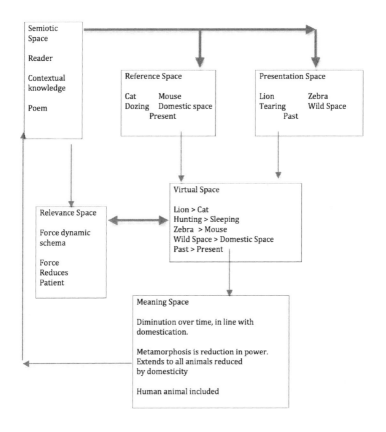

The resolution of the metaphor depends on the reader blending the presentation and reference spaces and making the direct comparison between the 'animal' in both situations. The virtual space maps each of the enactors or conditions represented in the presentation space onto its corresponding enactor or condition in the reference space. The relevance space adds to this the abstract structure of both worlds, with regard to the points at which they mirror each other in structural relation. This may be represented by a force-dynamic schema in which 'agent hunts patient'.

So our points of comparison from the virtual space: predator, prey, action and arena, form the ground for the metaphor and as they are mapped against each other, there is in each case a reduction in stature of the animal, which now hunts smaller prey much less successfully and dozes lazily in a small space of 'man-made' comfort, rather than in the wild. So even the sense of physical space has been shrunken. This in turn influences what will emerge in the meaning space, because we understand this diminution as a loss, because the powerful lion, master of her domain is reduced to a family pet. The thrill of the chase and the necessity of hunting zebra in a daily struggle for survival is reduced to the killing of the occasional mouse as an act unnecessary to actual survival, because what we know about pet cats tells us that food is provided on a daily basis. In the semiotic space it is illocutionally relevant for this utterance in a poem to be construed as signifying something more universal. So when the meaning space maps back to the semiotic space, it offers a frame whereby meaning can be extended from animal to human, acting as a sign that the human inhabitants of this suburban world are similarly diminished 'creatures'.

In a poem from much later in her career, Boland reverses the classical metamorphosis of women to constellation in the poem 'How the Earth and all the Planets were Created' from *Code*:[15]

> as the constellations rose overhead,
> some of them twisted into women:
>
> pinioned and winged
> and single-handedly holding high the dome
> and curve and horizon of today and tomorrow.

The image evokes several legendary figures who, according to mythology, were placed among the stars. The line 'pinioned and winged' is ambiguous, because the word 'pinion' can mean to have the wing clipped to prevent flight, or also to have one's arms held in order to restrict movement or restrain someone. Similarly, 'winged' can mean 'wounded' as well as 'possessing wings'. This ambiguity may on its own be enough to suggest the legend of Andromeda, who was restrained by the arms to prevent 'flight' from the monster Cetus and was rescued by means of a winged horse. In relation to the neural theory of metaphor, if the concepts of 'pinioned', 'winged' and 'constellation' are activated in the context of 'women' and 'legends' and if the reader is aware of Greek mythology and basic astronomy, then the chances are that this is enough to activate the whole legend by spreading activation.

The reference space can be seen as consisting of a text-world in which female constellations are 'twisted' into women. This act of embodiment is a reversal of the mythological 'setting among the stars' of the heroines of Greek mythology, such as Andromeda. It constitutes a movement from sky to earth, from celestial to terrestrial being. In this text-world the woman, made mortal, is burdened with holding the present and future in place. The presentation space here is alluded to, rather than explicitly stated, but the mythological reference frame and actions described evoke the story of Atlas, who held the sky upon his shoulders in Greek mythology. The commonality between these two myths is represented in the relevance space, where a person of a certain gender must bear a burden for a certain length of time. This can be represented either as a force-dynamic schema 'force burdens patient', or as a source-path-goal schema where a burden is transferred from source to goal.

In the virtual space the entities are mapped against each other and what happens when these worlds are blended is the change from the increase of Atlas' power, where a terrestrial being is magnified through his burden into a mountain, to the female, who is diminished from a celestial being to a terrestrial one. While Atlas once held aloft the sky, including, one supposes, the firmament within which the mythological women were set, the women bear the weight of present and future time. What emerges into the meaning space is the reduction of the woman, the entrapment of the female that releases the male and we understand this as a disempowerment of the female. The metaphor, 'metamorphosis is reduction in power', here feeds back to the semiotic space, informed by our contextual knowledge of the poet's politics and the purpose of poetry, to suggest that Boland is using the metaphor to exemplify the fact that women have historically borne and continue to bear the greater burden in society through their entrapment and through their unrecognised labour of maintenance and nurturing (present and future). The unrecognised nature of female labour is suggested because the present and future are invisible burdens. Male burdens by contrast, are like the sky; they are highly visible and easily recognised.

Metamorphosis is usurpation, empowerment or movement towards the place of power
Boland also uses metamorphosis as reversal to signify an empowerment, for example, in the poem 'The Art of Grief',[16] originally published in the collection *In a Time of Violence* (1994). In addition, the poem deals with the transformative power of art and of the artist:

> the moment her sorrow entered marble –
> the exact angle of the cut at which
> the sculptor made the medium remember
> its own ordeal in the earth, the aeons
> crushing and instructing it until it wept itself
> into inches, atoms of change.[17]

Here, Boland uses an underlying metaphor of 'metamorphosis is taking on power', through the marble taking on the human emotion of sorrow and embodying it, and seeming to understand it through the power of the sculptor to make the medium remember its own metamorphosis. Boland is also playing on the fact that marble is a metamorphic rock.

The excerpt begins by constructing a reference space that contains a text-word in which the sculptor allows the emotional state of the subject to be represented in the marble, through the ordeal of cutting. The presentation space alludes to a past text-world in which marble was formed through the compression of limestone. This ordeal of formation not only changes the nature of the stone itself, but also adds value to the stone, since marble is more valuable than limestone. These two worlds share a basic structure, represented in the relevance space, in which force and action change a base material to a more valuable one through their application or agency. In the process, the material acted upon can be said to undergo some ordeal through a violent procedure; this can be represented by another force-dynamic schema: force/agent transforms patient.

The virtual space allows these parallels to be drawn into direct relation so the natural force becomes a sculptor (and the sculptor a force). Compression can be seen as sculpting and the process of making marble from limestone directly analogous to the process of making art out of marble, with the concomitant increase in value.

The ordeal of metamorphosis in rock is metaphorically equated to the ordeal of artistic metamorphosis. The ideas that emerge from this blend in the meaning space are: force causes change; change is painful, but that art can capture that pain and transform it. This means that artistic metamorphosis is ultimately empowering. When mapped back onto the semiotic space, again given our contextual knowledge as readers of Boland's work, this offers the reading that the ability of the artist to capture pain and render it visible in the artefact, in effect transforming pain into beauty, is an act of great power. The poet is similarly an artist, who seeks to empower herself and other women, to claim the title of artist and transform their own griefs into art. While the poem also speaks to what Coffey identifies as 'how the female body has been disempowered through reification',[18] it offers an empowering vision through the poetic voice's determination 'to know what [the reified female] had never known',[19] how to become the agent of their own representation rather than merely a subject to be represented, while for Richard York this image acts as a metaphor for 'the pain that comes into new life and becomes a reflection of the poet's own sensibility'.[20]

This metaphor may be directly compared with a very similar metaphor from earlier in the poet's work which is initially much more negative in its application and connotation. In the poem 'In His Own Image'[21] which originally appeared in the collection *In Her Own Image* (1980), the sculptor and work of art motif also appears:

> He splits my lip with his fist,
> shadows my eye with a blow,
> knuckles my neck to its proper angle.
> What a perfectionist!
> His are a sculptor's hands:
> they summon
> form from the void,
> they bring
> me to myself again.
> I am a new woman.[22]

The poem uses a subversion of the Pygmalion myth in which the sculptor falls in love with the statue he carves. The underlying metaphor in one reading of this poem is 'metamorphosis is loss of power'. The 'sculptor' in this work uses violence to make a 'new woman'; the tone of the poem suggests an ironic admiration for the 'skill' with which she is 'moulded'. In terms of blending theory, and taking into account our earlier discussion, the metaphor may be analysed as shown in Figure 2:

Figure 2: How the Earth and all the Planets were created

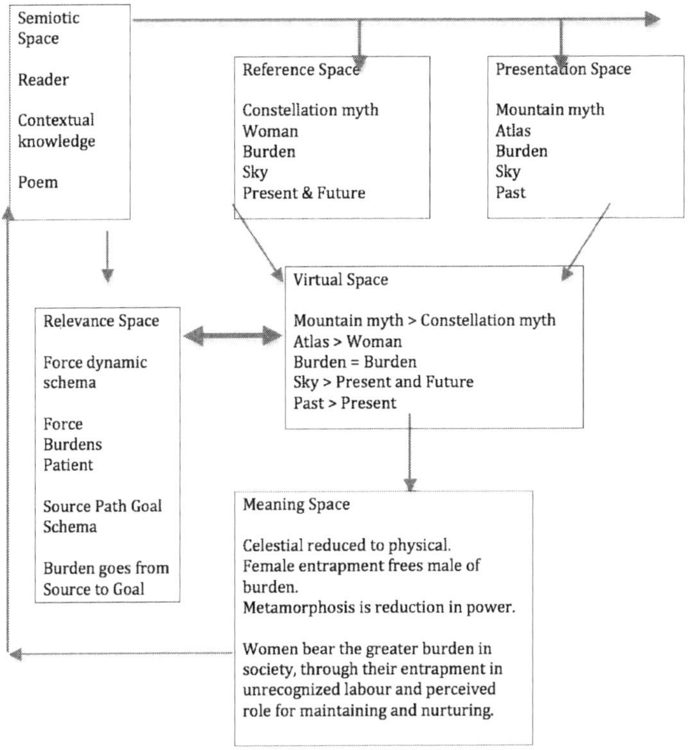

Semiotic Space

Reader

Contextual knowledge

Poem

Reference Space

Constellation myth
Woman
Burden
Sky
Present & Future

Presentation Space

Mountain myth
Atlas
Burden
Sky
Past

Virtual Space

Mountain myth > Constellation myth
Atlas > Woman
Burden = Burden
Sky > Present and Future
Past > Present

Relevance Space

Force dynamic schema

Force
Burdens
Patient

Source Path Goal Schema

Burden goes from Source to Goal

Meaning Space

Celestial reduced to physical.
Female entrapment frees male of burden.
Metamorphosis is reduction in power.

Women bear the greater burden in society, through their entrapment in unrecognized labour and perceived role for maintaining and nurturing.

In the text-world represented in the reference space an abusive man carries out a violent attack against a woman, this is described in terms which evoke a separate text-world of a sculptor working on marble to create a work of art in the presentation space. Again there is a common structure to both of these acts, in that a force acts upon a 'source' material in order to change it into something which is 'valued' through an 'ordeal', so again the relevance space may be said to contain a force-dynamic schema (agent transforms patient). But the mappings between these two worlds in the virtual space are very different. This time the abuser maps to the sculptor, the woman to the block of marble, the act of beating maps to the act of sculpting.

This creates an analogy that the act of abuse which changes the woman is paralleled with the process of sculpting art. One inference that emerges from the blend in the meaning space is that the change wrought by the intentional act of abuse will be as pleasing to the abuser as the artwork is to the sculptor and that the abuse is intended to create a new woman in line with the abuser's view of what she should be (her 'proper' state) rather than her natural state. This act of metamorphosis is disempowering. Again when this is mapped back onto a semiotic space, it becomes a wider sign for the violence wrought on women by the paternalistic culture which shapes them. This reading is in line with critical insights such as Coffey's assertion that the female body is 'contextualised as an artefact constructed through a process of disassembly and reassembly [...] in acts of social and rhetorical violence'.[23] This violence is also rhetorically emphasised in the poem 'How the Earth and all the Planets were Created', analysed earlier, through the use of language such as 'pinioned' and 'winged' and the description of constellations being 'twisted into women'.[24]

However, the last two lines afford an ambiguity which offers the potential to understand this metaphor more positively. Another possible emergence from blend and the resulting mapping back to the semiotic space in that this 'new woman' can also be read as a woman, who having survived the abuse, has found the strength to speak out against it. Her ordeal has not silenced her, but strengthened her. Metaphorically speaking, she has been sculpted into something stronger through her ordeal. Earlier in the poem, the female speaker intimates that she 'needed' 'a hand to mould' her mouth. The ordeal has indeed 'moulded her mouth' but not as the abuser intended. The ordeal has brought her from the void and made a new woman capable of bringing the disempowering abusive acts into the open. In that sense, the speaker of the poem acknowledges that the ordeal has made her what she is now: a stronger and empowered voice, reversing the metaphor's polarity. Coffey remarks that Boland's self-sculpture poems 'replicate the violence' of masculine processes, but also evoke the attempt 'to establish their own agency' by the poems' speakers.[25] The binary Coffey notes, between being the object of violence and taking on agency, also emerges rather strikingly from the analysis in the poem above.

One of Boland's most complex metaphors of 'metamorphosis as taking of power' is found in the poem 'Imago'[26] from the collection *The Lost Land*. Auge reads the title 'Imago' as referring to the idealised image of Ireland,[27] but because 'imago' also refers in a biological sense to the adult stage, indicating full maturity, Boland can play these meanings off against each other. In the poem, Boland lists the various symbols of 'Ireland' that are culturally associated with the country. Of them she says:

All my childhood
I took you for the truth.

I see you now for what you are.

My ruthless images. My simulacra.[28]

I read 'you' here similarly to Auge, as referring to a vision of Ireland, which is constructed by the list of items which precede it. It could be collectively addressed to the plural 'you' comprising all the cultural symbols, but the line 'I took you for the truth' would indicate that the 'you' is something that can be taken for a singular truth and is therefore more likely to be the 'idea' or 'vision' of Ireland represented by those collection of symbols. Boland then asserts that she sees that 'idea' of Ireland for what it is. The final line identifies this as 'the way to make pain a souvenir'. Yet she claims these images and simulacra as hers, perhaps as acknowledgement of her own cultural inheritance.

But with such recognition comes also the potential for growth and change. The poem may be interpreted as an attempt to make explicit the purpose of these distortions, so that the 'reader' may see the truth. Through this process they can be recognised as a 'substitution of signs of the real for the real itself'.[29] A more Deleuzean interpretation of simulacra here suggests that Boland has become aware that a ruthless examination of the symbols has the potential to challenge the cultural representations of Ireland that they symbolise and expose the 'foul skill'[30] they represent. This in turn may result in a metamorphosis of what others see as Ireland.

The reference space creates a world where a child comes to reappraise her view of Ireland as she reaches maturity. This is analogous to the contextually active text-world of the imago emerging from the cocoon into the adult insect implied as the presentation space by the title of the poem. The virtual space maps these correspondences, so the child is analogous to the insect, the cocoon maps to the cultural surroundings, the act of realisation is analogous to the act of emergence and the changed adult form maps to the changed adult view. The relevance space abstracts the mapping in the virtual space and represents the common structure: in both source worlds an entity emerges from a 'cocooned' state to maturity (a source-path-goal schema), or is altered by the force of growth (a force-dynamic schema). What emerges from such mappings in the meaning space is that the act of metamorphosis is empowering; new knowledge is attained through it. This is realised in mapping back to the semiotic space, through the reader's contextual knowledge, as an assertion that power accrues when one realises that one's own representation of truth is just as important and valuable as the prevailing representations which one has culturally received. The metaphoric metamorphosis then is two-fold, it is the metamorphosis of the writer as they mature into the titular 'Imago' stage where they now understand the idea of Ireland as it is represented for tourism and commerce and its relation to her own view of those representations as an artist and as a woman. This process also implies realisation of her own power as both creative artist and as a woman to generate her own representation of 'truth' in relation to what her vision or idea of Ireland actually is and this begins with the realisation that 'the fault of representation lies in not going beyond the form of identity, in relation to both the object seen, and the seeing subject'.[31] Given the arena in which this statement is made, this can be taken to act as a sign that the female representation of what is culturally important in Irish society (and the canon of Irish poetry) can be empowered and given voice, as women (and female poets) realise that they do not have to accept the versions of either handed down to them by the prevailing and predominantly male viewpoint. This analysis resonates with McMullen's observation that Boland challenges the prevailing symbology and 'constructs an Irish past that is not definitive, a national identity that is multiply inflected'.[32]

Metamorphosis is renewal or repetition

In one of the examples previously analysed, Boland hints that metamorphosis is a repetitive process: where constellations (which were mythologically metamorphoses) twist themselves back into women, therefore completing a kind of cycle. As well as this example, there are more overt examples of metamorphosis as a repetitive and as a renewing force. In the poem 'The Woman Changes Her Skin'[33] from *Night Feed* (1982) we have the lines:

> How often
> ...
> have I done this.
> Again and again this.[34]

As the rest of the poem makes clear, the metaphor is one of sloughing off skin as a snake does during the process of growth. This image is reinforced by the final lines:

> Look at the hood
> ...
> And how, quickly
> over my lips
> slicked and cold
> my tongue flickers.[35]

The poem likens the process of removing make-up to that of shedding skin. In so doing it sets up an emergent blended space, where the metaphor is given a sense of renewal and growth.

The reference space of the poem creates a text-world in which a woman removes make-up. However the lexical set implies a world in the presentation space where a snake is sloughing off its skin. The common structure of these worlds is represented in the relevance space where an entity undergoes some repetitive renewing action through a force-dynamic schema (agent sheds patient). The virtual space evoked maps the woman onto a snake, the make-up onto a skin and the removal onto shedding and renewal. In the meaning space, what emerges from this mapping is the fact that the woman is refreshed and renewed, perhaps even rejuvenated, by the act of sloughing off her make-up, which might be envisaged as a mask, hiding the real woman or a cultural imposition that is seen as necessary for fulfilment of her culturally assigned role. The act of removal frees her from this and becomes an act of metamorphosis as regeneration and renewal. In the relevance space, because the speaker of the poem is the agent of her own renewal, the reading emerges that women can be agents of their own metamorphosis. This is made clear through the first person narration and the active verbs.

However in the same collection, we find that 'The Woman Turns Herself Into A Fish'[36] uses the imperative form of the verb in the first half of the poem, so the agent of the transformation is less clear, only the title suggests that she is the agent. Even the conclusion of the process is expressed in the passive voice. Only from that point on, after the process is completed, does the speaker employ the first person:

Slap
the flanks back.
Flatten

paps.
Make finny
...
Pout
the mouth,

brow the eyes
...
It's done.
I turn
I flab upward[37]

The metamorphosis, once achieved, is also less positive and suggests yearning to undo the metamorphosis 'still/I feel//a chill pull' even though this change was something that she 'set [her] heart on'.[38]

CONCLUSION

Metamorphosis as metaphor is a powerful and pervasive trope in Boland's work. She deploys it in a variety of ways, some of which are contradictory and designed to problematise the themes she explores as a poet. Blending theory can be used to analyse the metaphors and to offer an understanding of the mechanisms by which they achieve their effects, to expose the ambiguities that may be found in their construction and explain how those ambiguities may be resolved. Another noticeable feature, which is traceable in the examples above, is the shift in complexity of her metaphors as Boland's work matured. Many of the early metaphors first published in collections up to *In Her Own Image* (1980) used metamorphosis to deal with disempowerment and tended to have external agents of change, which acted either on the narrating persona of the poem or one of the characters in the poem. This trope was present even in very early work, in such poems as 'The Winning of Etain' (1967). In the middle phase, in *Night Feed* (1982), *The Journey and Other Poems* (1986) and *Outside History* (1990), her metaphors became more complex, the tropes of empowerment and renewal became more prevalent and the locus of the agent of change became much more ambiguous or internal. In Boland's more recent work including and after *In a Time of Violence* (1994), this theme of empowerment becomes stronger and the metaphors become more complex and less easily classified. The locus of the agent of metamorphosis is often the persona of the poem or the metamorphosis arises through an act initiated by the persona in the poem. This trajectory is in line with Boland's political development from a young poet realising the disempowered position of women in Irish letters and society, through her determination to represent and change the role of women both in the canon and in our culture, to her position as one of the senior figures of Irish poetry, who has become an empowered role model for poets in Ireland and beyond.

NOTES
1 Pilar Villar-Argaiz, *The Poetry of Eavan Boland: A Postcolonial Reading* (Waltham, MA, Academica Press, 2008); Kim McMullen, '"That the science of cartography is limited": Historiography, gender, and nationality in Eavan Boland's "Writing in a Time of Violence"', *Women's Studies: An Inter-Disciplinary Journal*, 29:4 (2000), pp 495–517; Deborah Sarbin, 'Out of myth into history: The poetry of Eavan Boland and Eiléan Ní Chuilleanáin', *The Canadian Journal of Irish Studies*, 19:1 (1993), pp 86–96.

2 Andrew J. Auge, 'Fracture and wound: Eavan Boland's poetry of nationality', *New Hibernia Review*, 8:2 (2004), pp 121–141.

3 Sheila C. Conboy, 'What you have seen is beyond speech: Female journeys in the poetry of Eavan Boland and Eiléan Ní Chuilleanáin', *The Canadian Journal of Irish Studies*, 16:1 (1990), pp 65–72; Catriona Clutterbuck, 'Irish critical responses to self-representation in Eavan Boland, 1987–1995', *Colby Quarterly*, 35:4 (1999), pp 275–291; M. Louise Cannon, 'The Extraordinary within the ordinary: The Poetry of Eavan Boland and Nuala Ní Dhomhnaill', *South Atlantic Review*, 60:2 (1995), pp 31–46.

4 Richard York, 'Voice and vision in the poetry of Eavan Boland', *Estudios Irlandeses*, 2 (2007), pp 205–213.

5 Donna Coffey, '"Crewel needle": Eavan Boland and bodies in pain', *Contemporary Women's Writing*, 6:2 (2012), pp 102–121.

6 Gilles Fauconnier and M. Turner, *The Way We Think: Conceptual Blending and the Mind's Hidden Complexities* (New York, Basic Books, 2002).

7 Marta Miquel-Baldellou, 'Women in the twilight and identity in the making: The concept of transition in Eavan Boland's poetry', *Estudios Irlandeses*, 2 (2007), pp 128–134.

8 Nigel McLoughlin, 'Negative Polarity in Eavan Boland's 'The Famine Road', in *New Writing: The International Journal for the Practice and Theory of Creative Writing*, 10:2 (2013), pp 219–227.

9   Line Brandt and Per Aage Brandt, 'Making sense of a blend: A cognitive-semiotic approach to metaphor', *Annual Review of Cognitive Linguistics*, 3 (2005), pp 216–249.

10 Grady *et al* quoted in Brandt and Brandt, 'Making sense of a blend', p. 216.

11 *Ibid*, pp 234–237.

12 Margaret H. Freeman, 'The poem as complex blend: conceptual mappings of metaphor in Sylvia Plath's "'The Applicant'"', *Language and Literature*, 14:1 (2005), p. 21.

13 Eavan Boland, *Collected Poems* (Manchester, Carcanet, 1995), pp 44–45.

14 Boland, *Collected Poems*, p. 45.

15 Eavan Boland, *Code* (Manchester, Carcanet, 2001), p. 44.

16 Boland, *Collected Poems*, pp 208–210.

17 *Ibid*, p. 210.

18 Coffey, '"Crewel Needle"', p. 108.

19 Boland, *Collected Poems*, p. 210.

20 York, 'Voice and vision in the poetry of Eavan Boland', p. 206.

21 *Ibid*, pp 57–58.

22 *Ibid*, p. 58.

23 Coffey, '"Crewel Needle"', p. 104.

24 Boland, *Code*, p. 44.

25 Coffey, '"Crewel Needle"', p. 113.

26 Eavan Boland, *The Lost Land* (Manchester, Carcanet, 1998), p. 18.

27 Auge, 'Fracture and wound: Eavan Boland's poetry of nationality', p. 134.

28 Boland, *The Lost Land*, p. 18.

29 Jean Baudrillard, *Simulations,* trans. P. Foss, P. Patton, and P. Beitchman (New York, Semiotext(e) Inc., 1983), p. 4.

30 Boland, *The Lost Land*, p. 18.

31 Gilles Deleuze, *Difference and Repetition*, trans. by Paul Patton (Columbia, Columbia University Press, 1968), p. 68.

32 McMullen, '"That the science of cartography is limited"', p. 515.

33 Boland, *Collected Poems*, pp 85–86.

34 Boland, *Collected Poems*, p. 85.

35 *Ibid*, p. 86.

36 Boland, *Collected Poems*, pp 83–84.

37 *Ibid*, p. 83.

38 *Ibid*, p. 84.

BIBLIOGRAPHY

Auge, Andrew J., 'Fracture and wound: Eavan Boland's poetry of nationality', *New Hibernia Review,* 8:2 (2004), pp 121–141.

Baudrillard, Jean, *Simulations* trans. P. Foss, P. Patton and P. Beitchman (New York, Semiotext(e) Inc., 1983).

Boland, E., *New Territory* (Dublin, Alan Figgis, 1967).

The War Horse (London, Victor Gollancz, 1975).

In Her Own Image (Dublin, Arlen House, 1980).

Night Feed (Dublin, Arlen House, 1982).

The Journey and Other Poems (Dublin, Arlen House, 1986).

Outside History (Manchester, Carcanet, 1990).

In a Time of Violence (Manchester, Carcanet, 1994).

Collected Poems (Manchester, Carcanet, 1995).

The Lost Land (Manchester, Carcanet, 1998).

Code (Manchester, Carcanet, 2001).

Domestic Violence (Manchester, Carcanet, 2007).

Brandt, Line, and Brandt, Per Aage, 'Making sense of a blend: A cognitive-semiotic approach to metaphor', *Annual Review of Cognitive Linguistics,* 3 (2005), pp 216–249.

Cannon, M. Louise, 'The extraordinary within the ordinary: The poetry of Eavan Boland and Nuala Ní Dhomhnaill', *South Atlantic Review,* 60:2 (1995), pp 31–46.

Clutterbuck, Catriona, 'Irish critical responses to self-representation in Eavan Boland, 1987–1995', *Colby Quarterly,* 35:4 (1999), pp 275–291.

Coffey, Donna, '"Crewel needle": Eavan Boland and bodies in pain', *Contemporary Women's Writing,* 6:2 (2012), pp 102–121.

Conboy, Sheila C., 'What you have seen is beyond speech: Female Journeys in the Poetry of Eavan Boland and Eiléan Ní Chuilleanáin', *The Canadian Journal of Irish Studies,* 16:1 (1990), pp 65–72.

Deleuze, Gilles, *Difference and Repetition,* translated by Paul Patton (Columbia, Columbia University Press, 1968).

Fauconnier, Gilles and Mark Turner, *The Way We Think: Conceptual Blending and the Mind's Hidden Complexities* (New York, Basic Books, 2002).

Freeman, Margaret H., 'The poem as complex blend: conceptual mappings of metaphor in Sylvia Plath's "The Applicant"', *Language and Literature,* 14:1 (2005), pp 25–44.

McLoughlin, Nigel, 'Negative Polarity in Eavan Boland's "The Famine Road"', in *New Writing: The International Journal for the Practice and Theory of Creative Writing*, 10:2 (2013), pp 219–227.

McMullen, Kim, 'That the science of cartography is limited: Historiography, gender, and nationality in Eavan Boland's "writing in a time of violence"', *Women's Studies: An Inter-Disciplinary Journal*, 29:4 (2000), pp 495–517.

Miquel-Baldellou, Marta, 'Women in the twilight and identity in the making: The concept of transition in Eavan Boland's poetry', *Estudios Irlandeses*, 2 (2007), pp 128–134.

Sarbin, Deborah, 'Out of myth into history: The poetry of Eavan Boland and Eiléan Ní Chuilleanáin', *The Canadian Journal of Irish Studies*, 19:1 (1993), pp 86–96.

Villar-Argaiz, Pilar, *The Poetry of Eavan Boland: A Postcolonial Reading* (Waltham, MA, Academica Press, 2008).

York, Richard, 'Voice and vision in the poetry of Eavan Boland', *Estudios Irlandeses*, 2 (2007), pp 205–213.

Katie Donovan

DOORS

('Our children are our legends'
– Eavan Boland, from 'Legends')

The room of salt claims her
in crusted white
and subterranean blue:
my tender-cheeked girl
frosted into effigy.
Shuffling in ice dust,
I crunch through
to pull her free.
Lips puckered in salt,
we move like blind yetis
towards a Spring sky, a red car,
the calling of passersby,
the opening of doors
with their come-hither songs.

THE HABIT OF LAND:
EAVAN BOLAND'S IRISH AMERICAN VOICE

Eamonn Wall

One of the most heart-wrenching moments in Eavan Boland's work is located in the 'A Fragment of Exile' chapter in *Object Lessons: The Life of a Woman and the Poet in Our Time*, her 1995 volume of memoir, family history and a recounting of life in the poetry business and among poets. At the outset, in a voice that reaches from the present back into childhood, Boland describes, in the plain, understated speech of the obituary, her moment of separation from Ireland and, perhaps, from childhood:

> I had no choice. That may well be the first, the most enduring characteristic of influence. What's more, I knew nothing. One morning I was woken before dawn, dressed in a pink cardigan and skirt, put in a car, taken to an airport. I was five. My mother was with me. The light of the control tower at Collinstown Airport – it would become Dublin Airport – came through the autumn darkness. I was sick on the plane, suddenly and neatly, into the paper bag provided for the purpose.[1]

Though fortunate to have enjoyed a privileged upbringing – as her biography makes clear – as the daughter of a diplomat and an artist raised in a secure, loving and well-connected family, Boland, like all children, was not the director of her own life; instead, entrusted into her parents' care, she was brought to London and then New York, the family group following the father's overseas postings.[2] For many migrants, shunted from one location to another, the new country will often offer little improvement on the place that had been left behind; Boland, however, was transported from one safe environment to another. Nevertheless, as she has documented in her poetry and prose, her removal from Ireland was traumatic and has had a profound effect on how she understands the world. 'Exile', she points out, 'is not simple', and can be felt equally, though nuanced differently, across race, gender, nationality and social class.[3] In addition, one would suppose, there will always be something impermanent for the child about the ambassador's residence, the sense that, for all of its seeming luxury and prestige, it is a temporary dwelling rather than a home; that its rooms, just when they become familiar, will be handed over to others. Post-war London, a city of derelict buildings where wartime food rationing continued until 1954, was hardly glamorous. British children of this period, as Dominic Sandbrook reminds us:

> still wondered what their parents meant when they reminisced about eating oranges, pineapples and chocolate; they bathed in a few inches of water, and wore cheap, threadbare clothes with 'Utility' labels.[4]

The Boland family's living conditions and arrangements were rather cold, particularly when contrasted with the warm atmosphere of the Dublin home they had left behind:

> After the domestic warmth of the family home in Lesson Park, the embassy seemed austere by comparison, a

'compartmentalized' state reception building as opposed to a home ... Upstairs, one side of the building looked out over the grounds of Buckingham Palace, where the young Irish girl, who sometimes watched Prince Charles play with his nanny, turned an armchair over on its side and rode it 'away from this strange house' with its 'fiction of home in the carpets on the floor'. At home, the upstairs rooms where the family lived seemed cold after the intimacy of the children's lives in the family home in Dublin.[5]

The flight from Ireland, therefore, is an exit from the security of childhood, as well as a breaking of the connection with place. Though young, Boland must begin to find her way in the world as an adult might, and seek to deflect, as has often been the experience of the Irish overseas, points of view voiced to make her feel, simultaneously, inferior and Irish:

[...] becoming the language of the country that
I came to in nineteen-fifty-one:
barely-gelled, a freckled six-year-old,
overdressed and sick on the plane
when all of England to an Irish child

was nothing more than what you'd lost and how:
was the teacher in the London convent who
when I produced 'I amn't' in the classroom
turned and said – 'you're not in Ireland now'.[6]

The Irish voice is borne by distinct accents and it is telling that Boland, who as an adult would become a poet of resistance and empowerment, recalls an insult that goes to the heart of language, nationality and identity. For Boland, as a writer, exile will be a significant influence on her life and work. Irish people inherit 'emigrant songs which make it [exile] sound so simple; they speak of green shores and farewells' though what is handed down does not quite fit the nuances and cadences brought on by separation.[7] A priority in Boland's work is to provide an account of exile that is realistic, personal and rooted in contemporary times.

The trauma revealed in Boland's account of her involuntary departure from Ireland can be gauged by how deeply ingrained its details have been soldered into her poetry and prose. The vomiting on the airplane is a reminder that exile is equally physical and psychic, with the body responding in its own manner to being removed from its native and natural place. In Boland's poetry, particularly in such extended meditations as 'Anna Liffey', we are always aware of the passion and power that is invested in Dublin as the city being recovered as we – poet and readers – search for the markers of lost time:

> I came here in a cold winter.
>
> I had no children. No country.
> I did not know the name for my own life.
>
> My country took hold of me.
> My children were born.
>
> I walked out in a summer dusk
> To call them in.
>
> One name. Then the other one.
> The beautiful vowels sounding out home.[8]

Boland, living in Dublin as a grown woman, writes with the passionate commitment of a returned exile though she does so without unwarranted sentiment. Her fierce embrace of suburbia, for example, marks one of her original contributions to Irish writing. In *Brooklyn*, Colm Tóibín, through his protagonist Eilis Lacey, explores a similar sense of the physical revulsion brought on by the rawness of displacement:

> … she had no idea how far under the sea she was except that her cabin was deep in the belly of the ship. As her stomach began dry heaves, she realized that she would never be able to tell anyone how sick she felt. She pictured her mother

standing at the door as the car took her and Rose to the railway station ...[9]

Though Tóibín's portrait is more visceral than Boland's, this is the result of Eilis's journey to America being undertaken by boat on a rough sea in contrast to the brief plane ride that Boland describes. In *Brooklyn*, as in many representations of exile in Irish and Irish American writing, *choice* is complex. Boland had no choice but to travel with her family to London; in her journey we can observe both the luxury of being drawn away from a narrow parochial world into a wider cosmopolitan one as well as the pain that Boland recounts in *Object Lessons* and in her poetry. Eilis Lacey's situation is equally complex. Although she does choose to leave County Wexford for New York, she is quite a passive young woman with the result that her emigration is engineered by Fr Flood rather than pressed by her own desires. Fr Flood is an energetic Irish priest who oversees a parish in New York and is a mover and shaker who has established many connections throughout his parish's hinterland – his power is difficult to resist. Eilis understands that she is not likely to enjoy good job opportunities at home and she is also the second and least-favoured sister, both sharing a house with their widowed mother. Eilis, like many American immigrants, would probably have preferred to remain at home, though she makes the decision to leave in the face of economic necessity – among other reasons. In the period before her departure, Eilis resolves to pretend:

> ... at all times that she was filled with excitement at the great adventure on which she was ready to embark. She would make them believe, if she could, that she was looking forward to America and leaving home for the first time. She promised herself that not for one moment would she give them the smallest hint of how she felt, and she would keep it from herself if she had to until she was away from home.[10]

Whether such life-altering decisions are being made on one's own behalf or on behalf of a child, necessity and choice can never be made congruent. Though *Object Lessons* and *Brooklyn* are explorations of the lives of quite different women composed in distinct literary genres, they both hinge on defining moments of separation from Ireland, moments that linger long into the future. How such events manifest themselves as lifelong gyres is defined clearly by Alistair MacLeod in one of his short stories:

> Something like when you cut your hand with a knife by accident, and even as you're trying to staunch the blood flowing out of the wound, you know the wound will never really heal totally and your hand will never look quite the same again. You can imagine the scar tissue that will form and be a different color and texture from the rest of your skin.[11]

In Boland's poetry and prose and in Tóibín's and MacLeod's fiction, great interest is expressed in the theme of exile from islands and areas close to the sea – Ireland and Nova Scotia – though there is equal importance given to the complex issue of return. Perhaps the exile has had no choice but to leave, but the manner of departure does not preclude the positive influence that life in the new place will have on the formation of the exiled woman or man. The exile/emigrant/immigrant scar is complex; on the one hand, it can be a marker of enduring pain while on the other it can equally signify independence, growth and liberation. It is often the case that an individual will experience both in oscillating waves.

Jody Allen Randolph has provided a chronology of Boland's childhood spent overseas (though she and Boland differ on the age of Eavan upon leaving Dublin for London):

> Boland, who was born in 1944 in Dublin, lived in London from the ages of five or six to eleven; she then lived in New York City from ages eleven to fourteen when she returned to

Dublin to attend school, 'her mother enrolled her in the Holy Child Convent in Killiney … in order to pass the GCSE'.[12]

The tone Boland uses to describe this return to Dublin, compared to that utilized in the narrative of her departure nearly a decade before, is open and expansive and a narrative of deliverance:

> I came back to Ireland when I was fourteen. I saw unfamiliar sights: horses and lamplight and the muddy curve of the Liffey. I grew to know street names and bus timetables. I went to live with my sisters in a flat outside the city. I went to boarding school. I studied for exams. I started to explore the word Irish, not this time as a distant fact but as a close-up reality of my surroundings. As a word which painted letter boxes and colored trains. Which framed laws and structured language.[13]

Later, in 'A Habitable Grief', a poem from *The Lost Land* (1998), she casts light on what she has brought back with her from exile:

> Long ago
> I was child in a strange country:
>
> I was Irish in England.
>
> I learned
> a second language there
> which has stood me in good stead –
>
> the lingua franca of a lost land.[14]

Two of the impulses that drive Boland's artistic enterprise are the desire to recreate what has been lost, personally and nationally, by exclusion and exile, and the need to communicate what she has absorbed from displacement for the benefit of others. In *Brooklyn* Tóibín represents this same process though in another way: what Eilis has absorbed from New York is identified by others in her hometown when she returns there upon her sister's death.

It is arguable that Eilis's transformation is more superficial than the one that Boland describes in *A Lost Land* and elsewhere; hers is an influence communicated by look and gesture rather than through language, the given medium of the writer.

Writing in his introduction to *Ireland in Exile: Irish Writers Abroad*, his 1993 anthology of Irish writers living overseas, Dermot Bolger noted that nowadays 'Irish writers no longer go into exile, they simply commute' and that 'while editing this anthology my major problem was remembering who was now back and who was away'.[15]

On one level, Bolger's hypothesis makes sense because it is certainly a fact that Irish writers, like many Irish living overseas who follow a variety of professions, wander back-and-forth between Ireland and sundry international destinations. From construction workers to diplomats to writers, we can trace patterns of years or decades spent in the US or elsewhere that are broken up, or linked, by years spent in Ireland. Many Irish writers have either emigrated to America, or have spent considerable periods of time there. These writers can be divided into two main groupings: established writers who have come to the US to take up top-tier university appointments such as Seamus Heaney, Paul Muldoon, Thomas Kinsella and Colm Tóibín, to name a few, and writers who have come to America as more fledgling artists: Colum McCann, Greg Delanty, Mary O'Donoghue, Belinda McKeon and others. In this regard, Boland is more difficult to place. Her appointment at Stanford University, where she serves as Bella Mabury and Eloise Mabury Knapp, Professor in Humanities and Director of Creative Writing, is a prestigious one; however, she is also a writer who, because she spent such important formative years in New York, has been shaped as a child by immersion in American place.

At fourteen, Boland moved with her family again, this time to Manhattan. In *Object Lessons* she describes looking out the window from her new home:

> sixteen stories down, the East River flows towards the city. The freighters and barges make their way across a surface where light is broken up into patches and squares of dazzle.

Unlike the London of her childhood, New York was a place Boland grew to appreciate, 'with its finned cars and theatrical weather. The carousel in Central Park. The metal-colored freeze-up of the lake. The bricks too hot to walk on in summer'. Picking up the habits of American teenagers, Boland describes eating hot dogs and listening to Buddy Holly songs and, in a poem by the same title, 'watching old movies when they were new'. Her poems 'Lights', 'The Carousel in the Park' and 'Traveler' all relate to events from this period of her life.[16]

It is unlikely that any Irish writer, no matter if she/he is raised in Ireland or elsewhere, will remain untouched by American cultural and literary influence – the American reach is so pervasive. In Boland's case, to have spent part of her adolescence in New York was to have had a privileged opportunity to absorb and to understand America first-hand. In this respect, Boland's experience is more akin to that of John Montague's and Padraic Fiacc's than to such writers as Muldoon and McKeon given the importance of childhood and adolescence in the individual's formation. Montague was born in Brooklyn in 1929 and returned to Ireland to be raised by relatives in 1933 while Fiacc was born in Belfast in 1924 and raised in Hell's Kitchen in New York from 1929 until 1946 when he returned to Belfast. For all three poets, an American childhood was a part of their upbringing and independence a feature of their work as is clear from Montague's *The Rough Field* (1972),[17] Fiacc's *The Wearing of the Black* (1974),[18] and Boland's poetry and prose. Guinn Batten has written of *The Rough Field* that it:

> is an exile's, and an orphan's, elegiac farewell, a passage from private attachment to the public performance that may at last seal the tomb of the dead and the past. Such a working through of attachment, as Freud has observed, is necessary if the melancholic son – or, one might argue, nation – is to work through the inevitable traumas that characterize the childhood of the orphan as they do the infancy of so many modern states.[19]

Gerald Dawe has written of Fiacc's 'troubled and broken course' as an important governing factor in his work and psychology and these are also aspects of his back-and-forth early life between Ireland and America that stand as foundation stones of his aesthetic and moral viewpoints.[20] In his poems of The Troubles Fiacc's gaze shakes like a lantern in the breeze from Belfast to New York and back again, particularly when his own family's experiences are captured in poems:

> Our father who art a Belfast night
> -pub bouncer had to have
> A bodyguard, drilled recruits for
> The IRA behind the scullery door in
> The black back yard,
> > died
> In your sleep, in silence like
> The peasant you stayed
> Never belonging on Wall Street,
> Your patience a vice
> Catching as a drug!
>
> ('Our Father').[21]

Like Boland's, Fiacc's mature work adopts a freer, more American, literary idiom and structures. A liberated form allows for liberated thought, both mediated by American experience. Montague's specific trauma was caused by being removed from his parents' care in Brooklyn to be raised by relatives in County Tyrone. Like the McCourt family in *Angela's Ashes*, the Montague family was caught up in and undermined by the cruel mechanics of the Great Depression.[22] As Batten points out, Montague's response to place, history, home and return has been influenced by his own childhood removal. Both Montague and Boland share histories of dislocation, though they are quite different in nature in important respects that underpin their work. These writers bring to Ireland wider and alternatively-tuned registers of thought, feeling and morality as legacies of the types of experiences that were just unavailable to people of their particular generations living in Ireland – in Boland's case, being a young woman in New York at the beginning of the women's movement, at its very epicentre, was hugely influential because it gave her something new and important to bring back to Ireland.

One reason why Boland is such an interesting writer is that she is difficult to categorize. In fact, a problem with her reception, influence and importance as a writer of poetry and prose has resulted from the fact that many scholars and critics have chosen to define her too narrowly, particularly in Ireland. Boland's years spent as an adolescent in New York combined with her many subsequent and continuing visits to America align her with the Irish diaspora in general and Irish America in particular, with ample evidence of both present in her work. To put this in context, we can contrast Boland and F. Scott Fitzgerald. The latter, who was born into an Irish American family in St Paul, Minnesota, wrote many great novels and short stories with barely a reference to Irish American experience whereas Boland, an Irish writer, has made this same experience that Fitzgerald ignores a recurring concern in her work. It is not the writer's place of birth that is important; instead, we must look at the kinds of experiences that authors embrace rather than the places where they were born. Wallace Stevens was neither of Irish background nor did he visit

Ireland though he engaged with it through his correspondence with Thomas McGreevy and wrote such memorable poems as 'Our Stars Come from Ireland' and 'The Irish Cliffs of Moher', both intense engagements with Irish time and space.[23] We are not accustomed to thinking of Marianne Moore as being Irish or Irish American until perhaps we come to the final stanza of 'Spenser's Ireland' and note:

> ... The Irish say your trouble is their
> trouble and your
> > joy their joy? I wish
> I could believe it;
> > I am troubled, I'm dissatisfied, I'm Irish[24]

Boland returned to Ireland in 1958 and remained there until 1996 when she took up her appointment as a professor of English at Stanford University. She currently divides her time between California and Dublin.[25] Of course, she made frequent and at times extended visits to the US between 1958 and 1996 that are reflected in some of her best poems, notably 'Love' and 'In a Bad Light', both published in *In a Time of Violence* (1994). Among the American universities where Boland served as a visiting professor, or held fellowships, are Bowdoin College, the University of Iowa, the University of Utah and Washington University in St Louis, as well as travelling to many other university campuses and cities to give readings. Today, outside of term-time at Stanford, Boland resides in Dublin. It should be noted that the chronology of composition and publication of Boland's American poems does not always match the experience described in the poem with 'Love' being a good example of this. The poem, first published in *The New Yorker*, appears in the middle section of *In a Time of Violence* (1994), though the events that gave rise to the poem occurred in Iowa City in 1979 where Boland and her husband Kevin Casey had travelled to serve as fellows of the University of Iowa's International Writing Program. While in Iowa, their second child was for a time 'gravely ill with meningitis'.[26] 'Love' is one of Boland's most memorable poems in which so many strands of life and literature are brought together. It is a poem that is set at the centre of things (Iowa) in the middle of America, in a city where the writer's life is honoured (Iowa City, a UNESCO City of Literature), and where a family of four away from Ireland had found deep ground:

> Dark falls on this mid-western town
> where we once lived when myths collided.
> Dusk has hidden the bridge in the river
> which slides and deepens
> to become the water
> the hero crossed on his way to hell.[27]

The illness and recovery of a child is a signal event in the life of a parent and this explains why the experience remained alive and why the poem was written many years later. Also, writers frequently take a long pause before transposing raw material into literary work. In Boland's case, it seems that America has always been a dynamic presence in her life (and hence her work) since she first experienced it first-hand as a teenager and that it has flown into and through her other lives, places and contexts. In addition to being a love poem to family, 'Love' is also a love poem to place – in this instance, Iowa City. Jody Allen Randolph categorizes Boland's connection to America as being organic and positive:

> For the first time Boland heard stories of Irish families who had left their country and come to the United States. Her mother took her to see the port where Irish immigrants arrived from Liverpool and Cobh. For the first time, also, Boland could open her mind to the idea that such migrations might not mean displacement but a new sense of place ... Later, as Boland's preface to *A Journey with Two Maps* reveals, she was able to use her American experience as a secondary

location, a widening of identity that allowed her to think of American poetry as well as Irish poetry: 'Long before I came to divide my time between California and Dublin I located myself on common ground: in American poetry as well as Irish'.[28]

To remain energetic, Irish literary culture has always required strong measures of influence imported from abroad. One great service that Boland has provided to Irish poetry is that she brought so much back to Ireland from the US. At times, such retrievals can be essentialized and gendered. It might be argued that Boland's interest in, and championing of, such poets as Adrienne Rich, Denise Levertov and Sylvia Plath serves a narrow agenda – that of promoting the work of women poets. To take this route is incorrect: Eavan Boland's practice and example benefits all Irish poets. All poets can learn from reading these three fine poets, as all poets can learn from reading James Wright, Charles Wright and W.S. Merwin. Certainly, the American poets that Boland has sought to promote are often women; however, they are always full of quality and interest. Many of these American poets, like Boland herself in her mature work, challenge the formalist conceits that have underlined Irish and American poetry and it is vital that such voices be heard and that orthodoxy be challenged. Recently, both Eavan Boland and Colm Tóibín have described themselves as writers who divide their time between the US and Ireland, or more precisely, and perhaps more tellingly, between Stanford and Ireland and New York and Ireland, respectively. Such constructions in no way indicate diminished levels of engagement with Ireland; today, as a result of how frequent and complex migration and travel have become, individuals develop deep and complex allegiances to places rather than to one singular place. As readers and critics in the field of Irish Studies, it is important that we allow clear spaces for such ranges of endeavours and attachments so that the work of writers like Boland, Tóibín and others is allowed to prosper and be understood for what it is. Given her various encounters with the United States from adolescence to the present and the nature of her American experience Boland is a unique figure in Irish American poetry.

From 'Migration' through 'Exile, Exile', the first poem from *New Territory* (1967) and the second from *Against Love Poetry* (2001) Boland has explored the experience of the Irish diaspora both directly and indirectly in America. Even in *Domestic Violence* (2007), 'Traveler' and 'How the Dance Came to the City' address aspects of the emigrant experience: the former is a New York poem and the latter a reading of Dublin as a city of departure and return. Some poems directly address Irish American experience while others, such as 'Migration', we can attribute to this subject matter. For the most part, Boland's work on diasporic themes is found in *In Her Own Image* (1980) and the books that follow it. Though 'Migration' is an exception, Boland's Irish American poems are written in the more open forms that she absorbed from contemporary American poetry while at the same time, when needed, retaining the formal patterns of her early work. A vital influence linking both aspects of Boland's career – work published before and after 1980, is that of Sylvia Plath. Both poets get to the point quickly in their work and honour precision and conciseness over elaboration and wordiness. As they achieve a simplicity of diction, image, line and voice, elegance and truthfulness builds. Trans-Atlantic migration is also an important and enabling aspect of Plath's own literary career. Among Boland's notable Irish American poems are 'After a Childhood Away from Ireland' (*Night Feed*, 1982); 'The Emigrant Irish' (*The Journey and Other Poems*, 1986); 'The River', 'In Exile', 'Ghost Stories' (*Outside History*, 1990); 'That the Science of Cartography is Limited', 'In a Bad Light', 'Love' (*In a Time of Violence*, 1994); 'Home'

(*The Lost Land*, 1998); 'Exile! Exile!', 'Emigrant Letters' (*Against Love Poetry*, 2001), and 'Traveler' (*Domestic Violence*, 2007). Although relatively few in number, these poems are high in quality and range across Boland's long and productive career. Boland's Irish American poems are among her most anthologized. Daniel Tobin includes four poems in *The Book of Irish American Poetry: From the Eighteenth Century to the Present*, his comprehensive anthology of Irish American poetry where Boland's work sits alongside Montague's, Mahon's, Fiacc's, Muldoon's, O'Donoghue's, Delanty's and other poets generally considered to be Irish rather than Irish American. Despite such evidence from both her work and its reception, Boland is not often cited as an Irish American poet. She has been categorized as a poet of suburbia, of Dublin, as an Irish and British poet, an Anglophone postcolonial poet, a woman poet associated with Adrienne Rich and Denise Levertov, a poet of place, a poet of revision, among other designations, but rarely as an Irish American poet. My own sense of Boland's work is that her great run of success as a poet begins with *In a Time of Violence* (1994) and extends to *Domestic Violence* (2007). As I have pointed out, the volumes that appeared during this time span include work dealing with the Irish American experience as both personal and diasporic history and can be counted among the best poems that Boland has written.

Boland's work belongs in and is central to the Irish American canon. A significant reason her poetry has not been spoken of more in this context, outside of Irish American academic circles, has been because the field itself, or designation, has just recently begun to emerge more fully into the light as a result of work undertaken by Charles Fanning and Daniel Tobin. In the first edition of his landmark scholarly work, *The Irish Voice in America* (1990), Charles Fanning explains why he has omitted a discussion of poetry from his study:

And yet, there have been few memorable Irish-American poems, especially before very recent times. The problem has been an endemic blight of programmatic melancholy or bravado that emerged from the experience and perception of forced exile. The stock-in-trade of Irish-American poetry has been the immigrant's lament for a lost, idealized homeland and the patriot's plea for Irish freedom from British oppression. Such materials make good songs but bad verse that exhibits simplistic strains of nostalgia or righteous indignation.[29]

Fanning's bleak summary neither entices the reader to read such work nor attracts poets who seek to be grouped under such a designation. In Fanning's view, Irish American poetry looked like a thematic and formal ruin. However, a decade later, in the revised and updated version of *The Irish Voice in America*, he reverses course and notes 'the coming of age of Irish-American poetry' as the result of the appearance of a younger generation of poets emerging both from Irish America and from first-generation immigrants from Ireland.[30] While both Fanning and Tobin acknowledge that there are great bolts of weak Irish American poetry, it can also be said that much of Irish American poetry is of great value, if our sense of what Irish American poetry is can be expanded. Daniel Tobin points out that:

Irish American poetry has not yet been sufficiently acknowledged or explored either for its continuities with the poetry of the homeland or for its own continuities and discontinuities or for its potent affinities with other diaspora literatures.[31]

What happens when we take Tobin's direction is quite startling; in addition to the abundance of bad verse that Fanning located, we also become aware of the work of important poets whose connections to Ireland are more oblique though in no way diminished by this fact: Robinson Jeffers, Marianne Moore, Wallace Stevens, Lola

Ridge and Robert Creeley, to provide but a few examples of poets whose work appears alongside Eavan Boland's in the *Book of Irish American Poetry*. It is easy to acknowledge that one's connection to place today is complicated by either forced or chosen mobility, but we learn from Tobin's research into the lives, backgrounds and work of American poets how this is hardly something new. By definition perhaps, given the necessity to assimilate into American cultural identity that is a condition of living in the United States, important connections to Ireland have been forced beneath the surface. It is just as easy – perhaps easier – for American writers than for their Irish equivalents to own various and complex allegiances to place, including Ireland. A feature of Tobin's work has been his recovery of hidden Irish American voices, such as Lola Ridge. Like Boland in 'That the Science of Cartography is Limited', Tobin seeks to show that how a discipline is mapped – openly or narrowly – determines our understanding of it:

> -and not simply by the fact that this shading of
> forest cannot show the fragrance of balsam,
> the gloom of cypresses
> is what I wish to prove.[32]

Cartography, emerging from China, had initially served as a function of military/colonial powers and as an aid to conquest. From maps much has been excluded. Literary anthologies, maps of another kind, have also operated in a similar manner, to which both Boland and Tobin stand in opposition. In Boland's case, the continuities and discontinuities that Tobin sees as being fundamental to our understanding of an expanded Irish American poetry are equally appropriate places to begin a discussion of her work in general.

Throughout Boland's Irish American poetry, one finds ebbs and flows and motions back and forth between human engagement with America and with the emigrant life as a personal and national experience, though both are often linked in her work. Of course, her Irish and American lives cannot be separated as they both inform her work, despite the theme or location of the poem. Furthermore, we should be careful not to overestimate either because, as Boland reminds us, she is, first and foremost, 'a voice'.[33] Both 'In a Bad Light' and 'Love' from her 1994 collection *In a Time of Violence*, capture the concerns that drive Boland's exploration of displacement. 'In a Bad Light' recalls a visit to a St Louis museum:

> I stand in a room in the Museum.
>> In one glass case a plastic figure
> represents a woman in a dress,
>> with crêpe sleeves and a satin apron.
> And feet laced neatly into suede.[34]

The speaker learns that while 'the silk is French' … the 'seamstresses are Irish': this knowledge sets off a chain of reflection, given that the women had emigrated from Ireland in the wake of the Famine and were now in St Louis near the outbreak of the Civil War. The museum's elegant display of this work by Irish women, the fact that their work is nowadays located in such a place and Boland's sensitivity to their lives and labours draws the speaker into their world:

> I see them in the oil-lit parlours.
>> I am in the gas-lit backrooms.
> We make in the apron front and from
>> the papery appearance and crushable
> look of crêpe, a sign. We are bent over
>
>> in a bad light. We are sewing a last
> sight of shore. We are sewing coffin ships.
>> And the salt of exile. And our own
> death in it. For history's abandonment
>> we are doing this. And this …[35]

For Boland, markers of these women's separation from Ireland is encoded in their work and visible to her because she has shared something of their experiences, albeit from another century and in different circumstances. By imaginatively involving herself in their tasks, Boland reminds herself that she too has been formed by exile. Like Seamus Heaney's famous 'Digging', Boland's 'In a Bad Light' is an example of an *ars poetica* in which the art of writing is aligned with manual craft. Both poets, in important democratic gestures, break down the barriers between high art and the art of the people.[36] In Boland's case, it is important to note that this gesture takes place in America before an exhibition of work by Irish American women. It is a poem written by an Irish American poet in a city of confluence, where things come together, 'This is St. Louis. Where the rivers meet./The Illinois. The Mississippi. The Missouri ...'[37]

'Love', as already mentioned, is set in Iowa City and recalls a period spent there when Boland was part of the University of Iowa's International Writing Program. It is a deeply personal poem recounting her daughter's illness with, and recovery from, meningitis. Here, the voice is that of mother, wife and poet and the allusions and tropes are not derived from, or pointed towards, exile but in the direction of classical literature, another important part of Boland's literary map. For the Irish person living abroad, many conditions of life are not the result of exile; rather, they occur because one has no choice and what transpires must be addressed out of love, necessity and fidelity.[38] Exile is not simple; in fact, sometimes exile is not even part of the equation when the process involves going back and forth to Ireland from other parts of the world. Boland understands the complexity of exile and her work gives elegant voice to its many-sidedness.

By choosing to use exile rather than emigration/ immigration as her term of reference, Eavan Boland reminds her readers that estrangement and separation from Ireland remain potent parts of people's lives, even if absences from Ireland may well be temporary now. Technology, one of Boland's other interests, allows individuals to remain in touch with friends and family at home in real time though in virtual rather than substantive modes of engagement. In Boland's wide and organic view, Irish exiles across generations are linked by common experiences. She does not argue in her work that the Ryanair-Irish are exact replicas of the coffin-ship Irish – to do so would be ludicrous – but what she does point us towards are the elements of shared experience that are the result of dislocation and loss. On another level, Irish women and men are energized, liberated and re-educated by absence from Ireland, and able, like Eavan Boland, to bring back to Ireland new ways of thinking and expanded notions of how to live in this world. To be Irish and Irish American is not only possible, but it is also desirable and it is no bad thing to be guided by multiple attachments to place that are as deep as they are resource building – both for individuals and for the communities they belong to and serve. If today's Irish emigrants are in Bolger's view 'commuters', they are also women and men whose links to Ireland and elsewhere are not slight. The lives of Irish emigrants belong in our literature. Eavan Boland gives them a dignified voice. Of course Eavan Boland is an Irish American poet though she is also simultaneously a poet of other places and other times and spaces.

NOTES

1   Eavan Boland, *Object Lessons: The Life of a Woman and the Poet in Our Time* (New York, Norton, 1995), p. 35.

2   Jody Allen Randolph, *Eavan Boland* (Bucknell, PA, Bucknell University Press, 2014), pp 1–11.

3   Boland, *Object Lessons*, p. 37.

4   Dominic Sandbrook, *Never Had it So Good: A History of Britain from the Suez to the Beatles* (London, Abacus, 2006), p. 48.

5   Allen Randolph, pp 18–19.

6   Eavan Boland, 'An Irish Childhood in England: 1951' in *New Collected Poems* (New York, Norton, 2008), p. 93.

7   Boland, *Object Lessons*, p. 37.

8   Boland, *New Collected Poems*, pp 231–32.

9   Colm Tóibín, *Brooklyn* (New York, Scribner, 2009), p. 46.

10 Tóibín, *Brooklyn*, pp 32–33.

11 Alistair Macleod, 'Vision' in *Island: The Collected Stories* (Toronto, Emblem Editions, 2001), p. 321.

12 Allen Randolph, p. xxi.

13 Boland, *Object Lessons*, p. 55.

14 Eavan Boland, *New Collected Poems*, p. 255.

15 Dermot Bolger (ed.) *Ireland in Exile: Irish Writers Abroad* (Dublin, New Island Books, 1993), p. 7.

16 Allen Randolph, p. xxi.

17 John Montague, *The Rough Field*, 5th edition (Winston-Salem, NC, Wake Forest University Press, 1989).

18 Padraic Fiacc (ed.), *The Wearing of the Black* (Belfast, Blackstaff Press, 1974).

19 Guinn Batten, '"Something Mourns": Wordsworth and the Landscape of Mourning in *The Rough Field* (1972)' in *Well Dreams: Essays on John Montague* edited by Thomas Dillon Redshaw (Omaha, NE, Creighton University Press, 2004), pp 167–193.

20 Gerald Dawe, 'Introduction' in *Ruined Pages: Selected Poems of Padraic Fiacc* edited by Gerald Dawe and Aodán Mac Póilin (Belfast, Blackstaff Press, 1994), p. 4.

21 Gerald Dawe and Aodán Mac Póilin (eds), *Ruined Pages: Selected Poems of Padraic Fiacc* (Belfast, Blackstaff Press, 1994), p. 93.

22 Frank McCourt, *Angela's Ashes* (New York, Scribner, 1996).

23 Daniel Tobin, *The Book of Irish American Poetry: From the Eighteenth Century to the Present* (Notre Dame, Indiana, University of Notre Dame Press, 2007), pp 87–89.

24 Grace Schulman (ed.), *The Poems of Marianne Moore* (New York, Viking, 2003), p. 246.

25 Allen Randolph, pp 1–11.

26 Allen Randolph, p. 55.

27   Eavan Boland, *In a Time of Violence* (Manchester, Carcanet, 1994), p. 18.

28   Allen Randolph, p. 21.

29   Charles Fanning, *The Irish Voice in America* (Lexington, University of Kentucky Press, 1990, 2000) p. 4.

30   Fanning, p. 368.

31   Daniel Tobin, *Awake in America: On Irish American Poetry* (Notre Dame, Indiana, University of Notre Dame Press, 2011), p. 11.

32   Boland, *New Collected Poems*, p. 204.

33   Boland, *New Collected Poems*, p. 235.

34   Boland, *New Collected Poems*, p. 207.

35   Boland, *New Collected Poems*, pp 207–08.

36   Seamus Heaney, 'Digging' in *Death of a Naturalist* (London, Faber and Faber, 1966), pp 1–2.

37   Boland, *New Collected Poems*, p. 207.

38   Boland, *Object Lessons*, p. 35.

REFERENCES

Guinn Batten, '"Something Mourns": Wordsworth and the Landscape of Mourning in *The Rough Field* (1972)' in *Well Dreams: Essays on John Montague* edited by Thomas Dillon Redshaw (Omaha, NE, Creighton University Press, 2004), pp 167–193.

Eavan Boland, *Domestic Violence* (New York, Norton, 2007).

   In a Time of Violence (New York, Norton, 1994).

   New Collected Poems (New York, Norton, 2008).

   Object Lessons: The Life of a Woman and the Poet in Our Time (New York, Norton, 1995).

   The Lost Land (Manchester, Carcanet, 1998).

Dermot Bolger (ed.), *Ireland in Exile: Irish Writers Abroad* (Dublin, New Island Books, 1993).

Gerald Dawe and Aodán Mac Póilin (eds), *Ruined Pages: Selected Poems of Padraic Fiacc* (Belfast, Blackstaff Press, 1994).

Charles Fanning, *The Irish Voice in America* (Lexington, University of Kentucky Press, 1990, 2000).

Padraic Fiacc (ed.), *The Wearing of the Black* (Belfast, Blackstaff Press, 1974).

Seamus Heaney, 'Digging' in *Death of a Naturalist* (London, Faber and Faber, 1966), pp 1–2.

Alistair Macleod, 'Vision' in *Island: The Collected Stories* (Toronto, Emblem Editions, 2001).

Frank McCourt, *Angela's Ashes* (New York, Scribner, 1996).

John Montague, *The Rough Field*, 5th edition (Winston-Salem, NC, Wake Forest University Press, 1989).

Marianne Moore, 'Spenser's Ireland' in *The Poems of Marianne Moore* edited by Grace Schulman (New York, Viking, 2003), pp 245–246.

Jody Allen Randolph, *Eavan Boland* (Bucknell, PA, Bucknell University Press, 2014).

Dominic Sandbrook, *Never Had it So Good: A History of Britain from the Suez to the Beatles* (London, Abacus, 2006).

Wallace Stevens, 'Our Stars Come from Ireland' and 'The Irish Cliffs of Moher' in *The Book of Irish American Poetry: From the Eighteenth Century to the Present* edited by Daniel Tobin (Notre Dame, Indiana, University of Notre Dame Press, 2007), pp 87–89.

Daniel Tobin, *Awake in America: On Irish American Poetry* (Notre Dame, Indiana, University of Notre Dame Press, 2011).

The Book of Irish American Poetry: From the Eighteenth Century to the Present (Notre Dame, Indiana, University of Notre Dame Press, 2007).

Colm Tóibín, *Brooklyn* (New York, Scribner, 2009).

Medbh McGuckian

THE EXTREMELY YOUNG AGE OF ALL SEAFLOOR

You can tell that the sky is from
Another day: apple and leaf are bringing
Gaudy colours out of the sunlight, so
Drawing out the Gospel marrow.

Of roses you are rose, though you did not
Watch for the last of me, but touched
One button of his twice after another
If only for the beauty of their flames.

That 'soon' turned out to be leafed into
Loops of full-blown, sunset-coloured roses
Wrapped in the shell of a church where often
I let myself in, so safe and dull.

What could make a goddess ever cool the world
Once a year, a sonnet in ivory, an ode
To desertification, a poem entered for
The marzipan prize, from there to Thankful

Where her name means midday? Sometimes
I chanted the Ordinary of the Mass,
Initial D with the Three Marys at the Tomb,
But never mourned for sins, as sins, before.

And why these gods and not others?
It's time for acts of completion,
For that green sometimes seen at the stem
End of a pineapple when the other end has faded:

For those nectar sippers, moonstone elderberries
That catch the cosmic shine like a breast
Ornament rubbed with silk and amberised
As if you were brought to bed, today, of a daughter.

FROM A WOMAN ON A TRAIN TO 'FORMAL FEELING': EAVAN BOLAND, FRANK O'CONNOR AND OUR TROUBLED IRISH JOURNEY[1]

Thomas McCarthy

Aengus and Etain lived for each other's pleasure,
With gold for the head of Aengus as a king
And gold so intricate in Etain's hair
No one could guess if the light scattering
Were a woman's beauty or a queen's treasure.[2]

These words are part of Eavan Boland's 'The Winning of Etain' published in *New Territory*, her very accomplished, and not in the least tentative, 1967 volume. This poem, a formal masterpiece of thirty eight stanzas, was a real attention grabber in the settled, formalised milieu of a settled and self-regarding Ireland.

By 1967, one year after the 1916 golden jubilee, two years after the Yeats centenary and four years after a Kennedy presidency, there were congratulations all round on the Emerald Isle. We were all living, even those of us born poor, on a plush Youghal carpet with Celtic designs. Even the literature was becoming a little unctuous: when the existential Thomas Kinsella told us that life was an ordeal and existence a misfortune we knew he didn't mean it. But even at that moment of national contentment before Ulster broke, comparable to the golden August in England of 1914, there were already many competing versions of Irishness. Every one of them was a distraction: Behan, Kavanagh, Frank O'Connor, Conradh na Gaeilge or the Legion of Mary, dragging us back into a dialogue of atavisms. The possibilities for public rhetoric were everywhere. Stitching the golden threads of Etain and Aengus into the deep pile of the translated Anglo-Irish tradition was one way of establishing a stall in this throbbing bazaar of Irish poetry. 'The Winning of Etain' was an announcement, if you like, of a serious new contender on the street, a street that ran imaginatively from the foyer of the Abbey Theatre, past the Garden of Remembrance, all the way up the other street to the portico of the Gate Theatre. Yes, *New Territory* would fit right in. Here, take a seat at the nation performing itself to itself.

Yet, in poetry what matters are achievements of personal imagination. It is not a matter of what is appropriate or what is inappropriate. The true rhythm is not in the sound of words but in the arrangement of an incident. All kinds of orthodoxies fetter the imagination; social expectations, political attachments of left and right, religious training, academic canons, those inevitable limitations set by commercial anthologists – all are sent to persecute us, to shackle or disrupt the stuff we're made of. As Louis MacNeice wrote in *Autumn Sequel*: 'Which some explain by reference to God/And others find an inexplicable fact,/But fact it is, as downright as a clod,//As unremitting as a cataract.'[3] Irishness can be a technical advantage in the wide world, as some novelists and poets have discovered since Moore's *Melodies*; but only in the context of the company we keep in the English language. It is only advantageous in terms of its relationship with Englishness – in any other context it is disastrously limiting, allowing the writer to make no great effort in order to create a literary effect. It offers an Irish writer the easy notoriety of rhetoric and bombast. Many have made good use of it, most especially those writing for the Anglophone theatre.

Frank O'Connor spent a lifetime trying to escape from narrow versions of Irishness. He lived at a time when the keys of the State had been handed over to the Catholic pieties, a situation that had been predicted a hundred years earlier, in 1836, by another Cork writer, Francis Sylvester Mahony, author of the *Reliques of Father Prout*. Writing as an invented clerical persona Father Prout, the wealthy and Jesuit-educated Rev Frank Mahony never relented in his journalistic campaign against Daniel O'Connell and his Repeal Movement. He could see the corrupt combination of O'Connell's 'placemen' and how second-rate ambition had made a deal with the Divine:

> This arch-lawyer's name was Dandeleone, of the old Carthaginian family of the Smuggleri, settled on the south-west coast, towards the Spanish port of Valencia. Always disaffected to the government in Turin, they were of course ineligible to posts of emolument in Sardinia, but they helped themselves to wealth in rather an off-hand manner. This is rather a delicate topic, which I would rather avoid, but the 'immaculate' party having adopted the bullying system in every minute matter, will insist on our not only reverencing a hero himself, but his grandfather and his grandchildren, his ox and his ass, and everything belonging to him. To drive a coach and four, or a 'six-oared gig,' through Sardinian law, was an exploit therefore to him of instinct and hereditary transmission.[4]

Mahony's campaign against the social and imaginative limitations of Catholic power (he also reported on the banning of stethoscopes in hospitals of the Vatican states), was understood by both Joyce and Beckett; and Mahony remains a vibrant, if un-named, presence in their work.

It is interesting that Frank O'Connor, another Corkman who would bang his head against the brick wall of a provincial Irish influence, could not comprehend Mahony/Prout's centrality. That he couldn't do so is a sure sign that clerical control not only of private morals but of public history was complete. The controlling narrative had been established; a narrative easily captured in a quick survey of any of those pietistic, unctuous anthologies of the nineteenth century, from Barter's *Gems of the Cork Poets* to Charles Gavan Duffy's *The Ballad Poetry of Ireland* (reprinted more than forty times by 1870), and a hundred other execrable collections of Thomas Davis inspired verse-craft. The controlling essence of Irish imagination has been in the provinces: County Cork, depraved, as Beckett's Murphy growls, thinking, no doubt, of Daniel Corkery's crowd at a Munster Hurling Final rather than Miss Counihan's lover upon the tomb of Father Prout in Murphy. Such provincial culture (think of the stories of Daniel Corkery, the plays of T.C. Murray or the paintings of Seán Keating) is male, sporting, homespun as a Connemara holiday and, sometimes, stupid with alcohol. It is what every Irishwoman has had to negotiate, that lethal conjunction of laddish politics and 'national feeling' – a feeling alarmingly identified by Yeats in his *Journal*, 14 March 1909:

> So long as all is ordered for attack, and that alone, leaders will instinctively increase the number of enemies that they may give their followers something to do, and Irish enemies rather than English because they are the more easily injured, and because the greater the enemy the greater the hatred and therefore the greater the power. They would give a nation the frenzy of a sect.[5]

And, all of this so aptly captured by an editorial in *An Camán*, 6 January 1934:

> We of the Irish-Ireland movement are wholeheartedly behind this anti-jazz campaign. In these columns we have never ceased to stress the dangers, morally and nationally, which

jazz music and jazz dance hold for our people, especially in rural areas. The false tolerance towards jazz, speciously advanced in argument by those who advocate freedom of choice in pastimes and recreations, has had its corrosive influence on all phases of national thought.[6]

Little over a year after this *An Camán* editorial, Frank O'Connor would write one of his great stories 'In The Train'. The central character, a woman who'd been found not guilty of her husband's murder, is placed at the periphery of the story.

It is also interesting to note, in the context of so much that Eavan Boland has written, how quickly 'freedom of choice' became something un-Irish, un-patriotic. The seeds of our Stasi-like republic that diminished women were sown long, long ago, and the trail of that national stain goes all the way back to the shrewd and ambitious 'place men' of Daniel O'Connell; the resurgence of Catholic power, that inertia so brilliantly captured by Joyce. It created a mind-set that dominates Irish commentary to this very day. If I linger too long in any Irish pub I meet Daniel Corkery-types thirty years younger than I, and their political and moral certainties frighten me. New media, digital media, that's all very well, but what if the hand pressing the edit button is stilled by the thoughts of Pius XI's *Vigilanti Cura* (1936) with its insistence on unceasing and eternal vigilance so that film narrative meets 'the requirements of the Christian conscience'. You must understand this: in Ireland the cowed and conventional still laugh loudest, for they are relieved from the burden of conscience. Developing and protecting the national conscience has been the major Irish project since the Act of Union. Guarding of the moral conscience was a shared anxiety in both the Republic and Northern Ireland, as anyone who reads Hubert Butler or John Hewitt will discover. We still act as if we were all either Repealers or Covenanters. It is the weather in this country.

The Ireland of what can best be described as the de Valera years, 1927–1967, was a land of established piety, legitimacy, conformity; a land of cowed intelligence. There were flashes of brilliance in this land, of course, from Kate O'Brien's *That Lady*, Máire Mhac an tSaoi's 'Ceathrúintí Mháire Ní Ógáin' in *Margadh na Saoire* to Edna O'Brien's *The Country Girls*. Such brilliance would be excluded from polite discourse or would be banned and rendered 'foreign'. As in all comfortably established tyrannies, what was immoral could not be considered 'national' or 'normal'. One of the most illuminating tropes or fictional constructs of that era is the invented suffering female as central character in the work of writers like Brian Moore, Austin Clarke, John Montague and Frank O'Connor. The hearts of these male writers were in the right place, I assume, but the effects they create reek of a sexist ventriloquism. No such ventriloquism was intended, I'm sure, but the assumption of authority over female victimhood, the audacity to speak for silenced experiences, to colonise a distinct territory of threatened Irish being – Moore's Judith Hearne, Clarke's Martha Blake, Montague's mother of Jimmy Drummond ('Her only revenge on her hasty lovers/Was to call each child after its father')[7] – was surely the clearest example of a masculine hegemony. Looking back now, as a male writer, such a pervasive literary presumption is simply breath-taking.

No female victim was ever so poignantly drawn by Frank O'Connor as the character of Helena Maguire in 'In the Train'; Helena who joins her fellow villagers for the terrifying return train journey to Farranchreesht after her acquittal. The villagers had perjured themselves in a collective effort to clear Helena's name – not because they loved or pitied her but only because they wanted to bring her home to punish her for the rest of her days:

> Then, just as the train was about to start, a young woman in a
> brown shawl rushed through the barrier. The shawl, which
> came low enough to hide her eyes, she held firmly across her
> mouth, leaving visible only a long thin nose with a hint of pale
> flesh at either side.[8]

Helena's destiny has a cinematic, Hitchcock-like quality; and in his story O'Connor creates an astonishing portrait of trapped and punished victimhood. This is fiction of such humanity and magnitude that it almost leaps across gender categories. High art such as 'In the Train' is very nearly genderless in its common humanity – except that it isn't. Our focus here is on O'Connor, the genius story-teller. The denouement is his, not Helena Maguire's. In the end, we will never know her voice, its quality or ambiguity, in the same way that we will never have but an elliptical knowledge of the life of a Judith Hearne or a Martha Blake. The true voice of any community literature has to wait for the arrival of the community itself. In Irish poetry this community arrived in 1980 with the publication of *In Her Own Image* and with *Night Feed* in 1982. The young everywoman, such an object of desire in the erotic work of Montague and Kennelly in the previous decade, now spoke of anorexia, menses, mastectomy and solitude. It was as if the love-object in Montague's 'Life Class' turned to the reader and spoke in her own voice, as in the poem 'Menses':

> Or when I moan,
> for him between the sheets,
> then I begin to know
> that I am bright and original
> and that my light's my own.[9]

In the chapter 'From Patria to Matria' (published in her Cork University Press study, *Eavan Boland*), Jody Allen Randolph maps both the political and sociological background to Boland's moment of insight:

In Her Own Image was written in the late 1970s, parallel to the emergence of feminist poststructuralist theory. The French feminist movement, as it was called at the time, began with the work of women theorists – Hélène Cixous, Julie Kristeva, Luce Irigary, Monique Wittig – who made bold restatements of theories linking sexuality to textuality. Their theories were gathered under the banner of écriture feminine, a term popularized by Hélène Cixous in 'The Laugh of the Medusa' (1975).[10]

In 1975, the year of the Cixous text, and just a few years before she created the founding texts of Irish feminist poetry, Boland published *The War Horse*. The collection contained poetry of real achievement which was structured brilliantly, being both robust and lyrical. I was with a group of young male poets when a copy of Boland's new collection came into the hands of John Montague, then our mentor and the uber-poet at UCC. The book was passed round in Montague's sitting room at Grattan Hill, Cork, and a male verdict was pronounced: this was terrific, unexpected stuff from Miss Boland. All agreed that it was as good as anything by Hartnett, who, at that very moment, in his *A Farewell to English*, had decided to stop writing in the English language, and who was then the undisputed leading poet of the south. Part of the shock of her subsequent 1980s texts was that embedded literary memory of her real achievement in conventional work between 1967 and 1975; and an inability in the male establishment to see how a poet could go outside history so irresponsibly. Her 1980s volumes were so unexpected that they were received and read as evidence of a technical breakdown rather than a break-out. In truth, Eavan Boland's first major achievement, born of innate character, was her ability to centre herself against a prevailing wind. As a poet, with the seas hostile and the deck heaving, she had an ability to balance in a storm of masculinities. Thomas Kinsella in his 1963 *Irish Press* review of her early *23 Poems* (1962) was among the first to spot this capacity for orientation: 'Eavan Boland has already the gift of setting the scene, as in 'Illusion at Shanganagh' or 'The Moon-Tree' or 'Dream of Cathleen', which begins:

> Here is the bridge; four swans inside
> The midnight, ovaled in stone
> And darkness, are asleep …

None of these reviewed poems would survive into *New Collected Poems*, though the Liffey, water and bridge, would be retained. Stones, water, flight, swans, fleeing lovers, Yeats, Etain, kings and earls: the poet might easily have settled into a narrow Austin Clarke-like mythology. A lesser imagination, so highly educated and socially placed, might have settled for the more settled, more worthy, discourse. But there was something more fearsome inside, some compelling discomfort, that is the basis of the original art in Boland's poetry. Her ability to centre the self, combined with a capacity to ignite the narrative outward, was what made her uniquely complete: 'I will be here/till midnight,/cross-legged in the dining room,/logging triangles and diamonds,/cutting and aligning,/finding greens in pinks/and burgundies in whites/until I finish it.//There's no reason in it.'[11] She has always written from the emotional place where the self is adamant. She is more than aware of the presumptions of our human knowing, as she states clearly in that same 'Patchwork or the Poet's Craft' –

> I have been thinking at random
> on the universe
> or rather, how nothing in the universe
> is random –[12]

It is best to see Eavan Boland's work as a singular, visual leap of conscience, away from those curators of national narrative, into a new studio, in order to act upon a fresh canvas. In this great leap of artistic conscience she was most like the visual artists, Norah McGuinness, Mainie Jellett and Evie Hone, who abandoned the dead dialogue of national representation in art and discovered a new conversation with modernism and with Cubism. But, as Paula McCarthy notes in *Irish Women: Image and Achievement: Women in Irish Culture from the Earliest Times* edited by Eileán Ní Chuilleanáin: 'Despite Mainie Jellett's enormous influence, Cubism was never fully accepted in Ireland'. A firm and powerfully-resourced nationalist viewpoint had its icy grip upon Irish imagination; it would be decades before that grip was even slightly eased. In a marvellous essay 'Evie Hone: Stained Glass Artist 1894–1955', first published in *Studies* (Summer 1955) and reprinted in *A Tribute to Evie Hone and Mainie Jellett*, edited by Stella Frost, C.P. Curran describes a turning point in the artistic life of Irishwomen, a first encounter between the Cubist Albert Gleizes and two Irishwomen in search of knowledge:

> Gleizes has left an entertaining account of this encounter from which I venture to quote. The date was 1921, when he was still immersed in his own technical problems with nothing further from his mind than the idea of teaching. The two friends said they wished to work along his lines and asked for lessons. Their quiet assurance and decided tone threw him into an agony of embarrassment. 'Give you lessons? But it is I who want lessons. What do you want me to teach you? I have the greatest trouble in clearing up my own difficulties. How do you think I can tackle yours? What have you done? Where have you come from?' They told him and went on to say that his work corresponded exactly with what they were looking for ... He pleaded his friendly relations with Lhote: he would not steal his pupils. 'But we are at perfect liberty to choose our own master.'[13]

In the weeks that followed, Gleizes' teaching and their powerful responses would transform both master and pupils. What the three worked towards was a fulsome repudiation of the idea of a single viewpoint. Art would not succumb to the given viewpoint, but would disturb it, rotate it, making inertia dynamic. Some years later Evie Hone would hold a joint exhibition at the Dublin Painters' Gallery with Mainie Jellett, but her innovative stained glass designs would still have to fight for their light until she met Wilhelmina Geddes in London.

What happens in visual art would also happen in literature. After ten years of Irish self-government the hegemony of one nation was complete. Even a cursory look at the lavish Saorstát Éireann *Official Handbook* (Dublin, 1932) will show that what was modern or modernist was not welcome:

> The Free State has not yet been established for a sufficient time to redeem the promise of those Irish artists who, in the eighth century, won for their country a pre-eminence in illuminated manuscripts and precious metal work over all other nations of Europe. The intervening dark years of turmoil and misery effectively prevented the development of a distinctly Irish School of Fine Art.[14]

The ignorance of this statement is simply astonishing; that it glosses over nearly three hundred years of landscape and portraiture of great beauty – but one can see why, politically. The ownership of studios and art in those centuries was mainly in the hands of Protestant Irishmen, persons seen in 1932 as a garrison population with alien interests. But that the fact of art can be denied shows the power of a political atmosphere. And as for literature, the same *Handbook* was adamant:

> Irish literature in English can scarcely be said to have become fully national til [sic] about the time of the Young Ireland in the 'forties of the nineteenth century. It has often been said that a new soul was born into Ireland at this time as a result of the inspiration of Thomas Davis and the 'Nation' group. It is equally certain that a new soul was born into Irish poetry.[15]

A new, modest orthodoxy, a national chauvinism, now ruled the public realm. With honourable exceptions, tiny pockets of bohemia created by *Ireland Today* or *The Bell*, a modest and quietly satisfied Catholic Ireland purred quietly for nearly half a century. Let us not forget that Boland's beginnings on paper were as orthodox and conventional as any other Irish poet of her era; a yen for history, a nod to the Celtic stuff, a go at gods or concepts scavenged from history or translations, that Irish naming of names that belong to the familiar:

> Son of Lir as lonely are you now
> As the leaf when lightning strikes the tree
> And the bird when thunder breaks his bough.
> Now is lost, as bird and leaf and tree
> Son of Lir, your humanity.
> – 'Malediction'[16]

Lir, bird, leaf, tree, even a broken bough. Here is someone who had heard Austin Clarke or Frank O'Connor speak. By the mid twentieth century, there had been an uncanny settling of orthodoxies in poetry: in Ireland it was a bird, a leaf, a Lir; and in, let's say, Russia, it was 'peace' 'commune', 'worker', 'pylon'. But there was always something slightly off-centre about the young Boland; an intensity and restlessness that gave her views of history more precision and much less sentimentality. Coming from a cradle of record-keepers, two generations back, who administered to over a thousand souls at Clonmel Workhouse, it was in Boland's inherited nature to keep records straight, to eschew what was easy, colloquial, congenial. She began very early to be a rapporteur for immortality. The love of precision always contains a dangerous political risk in a comfort zone like Ireland:

> maybe
> For those imprisoned here this was a small
> Consoling inland symbol – how could their way be
> Otherwise …
> – 'A Cynic at Kilmainham Gaol'[17]

From this beginning, she understood how to 'keep the or/of exile or arrival/And be at home in both.'[18] As early as *New Territory*, in 'Athene's Song' the poet lives within the pain of a secondary yearning, that yearning for pipe and music left behind in order to conform to a mythic purpose, a confirmation of art by men. The stillness of this beginning, a latent intelligence still waiting to declare its nature, is disrupted a few short years later by a sound now famous in the annals of Irish poetry – the sound of a straying Dundrum horse: 'clip, clop, casual//Iron of his shoes as he stamps death/Like a mint on the innocent coinage ...'[19] Something is broken by this sound, the winged horse of poesy is grounded, literally. In a very real sense that *The War Horse* is the harbinger of a major disintegration: the bond of authority that bound Eavan Boland to accepted Irish themes and lyric forms will collapse very quickly now – in the space of three or four years she will have migrated, emotionally and politically, from Ó Rathaille and Yeats to Lowell and Plath. It was an important leap into freedom: 'For the senses arise from the essences, they have their origin from the sting of desire, from the sourness; they are the bitterness, and run always in the mind' as Levertov wrote to Robert Duncan in 1959.[20] For Boland, Adrienne Rich and Denise Levertov were the Albert Gleizes and André Lhote of the new revelatory moment. Reviewing the correspondence of Duncan and Levertov years later, Boland wrote 'Duncan's way of becoming a poet was essentially – as was Pound's – collaborative. He needed witnesses, companions, an audience'.[21] The great irony of Boland's brave career is that the Irish audience, that crucial parish of rich women, needed her more than she needed them.

This audience yearned and Boland became. In becoming herself she created an entirely new field of poetic activity. I was an early witness to her profound effect upon a generation of new women writers. In Cork city in the bleak

1980s she was pivotal. The poets and fiction writers of the Cork Women's Poetry Circle found in her work, poems and commentary, an enabling, moral presence. And she responded to the responsibilities set up by the new expectations in her work; in the mid-1980s she encouraged women leaders like Máire Bradshaw in Cork by making the long journey south to give readings and preside over workshops. She carried other writers with her, from this land of Ireland to the better land of ideas. The act was gender-aware only because of exclusions based upon gender, for she has always understood, as Robert Graves wrote in his essay '-Ess,' that:

> poetry should not be an affair of sex any more than, for example, surgery. One says: 'Mary Smith is a surgeon,' not 'Mary Smith is a surgeoness,' or even 'Mary Smith is a lady surgeon.' Sex has no place in the operating theatre. Poetry is a sort of operating theatre.[22]

For poetry is where we dwell. It is a second country that requires the second map; or, to quote Graves again: 'This nobleman is at home anywhere/His castle being, the valet says, his title' ('The Cloak'). *Object Lessons* and *A Journey with Two Maps* are the double map of that title 'poet'. It is her attempt at integration, cultural and psychological integration, beginning at an estranged starting-point, that title 'Irish poet', and ending with political arrival, as described in her essay on Paula Meehan, 'The emergence of women has now made a new space in the Irish poem.'[23] It was Boland, working alone and constantly derided by the male of the species, who created that new space for poetry. She created a new masterpiece with her own name upon it. In these prose works, *A Journey with Two Maps* and *Object Lessons,* Eavan Boland is answering Yeats' command to the lyric poet; the command that the lyric poet should do everything to explain the life behind the lyrics. The motive of her autobiographical writing is not autobiographical.

There is no desperate effort of explanation or personal redress such as one finds in Frank O'Connor's *An Only Child* or Frank McCourt's *Angela's Ashes*. It is exploratory explication, an act of exemplary remembrance. Socially, Boland has no need to explain herself. In 1988, in a regular *Observer* review of Catherine Cookson's autobiography, Anita Brookner wrote:

> Autobiography is traditionally a genre peculiar to the upwardly mobile, the socially insecure, those who have no context to explain them. Its purpose is to expunge pain, but more than this, to create a life myth, an alternative support system. In rewriting history and establishing causation a measure of control over circumstances is achieved. It is a daring and agonising task which may not fulfil its intended purpose.

Boland's daring and agonising task has been to call back Irish life, that poor Free State of Austin Clarke living on lack, and to feed it retrospectively with insights of liberation; it is a prodigious effort not just to make the poem but to make the audience learn a little jazz. She has chosen to take on, in the hotly contested Irish field of literature, a society that has made boors of educated men and modest creatures of all women. If her mother was an artist then she is the prodigy, creating a vast studio of new work. Boland has been disciplined and determined, single-minded in a complex and elaborate manner. Her task has been work-centred, poem-centred. The later collections that followed the two founding texts of 1980 and 1982 are, in a very real sense, critiques of those early works. In the poem 'The Making of an Irish Goddess' from *Outside History* (1990) she writes:

But I need time –
my flesh and that history –
to make the same descent.

In my body,
neither young now nor fertile,

and with the marks of childbirth
still on it,

in my gestures'[24]

And, four years later, in *In a Time of Violence* she noted:

There is now
A woman in a doorway.

It has taken me
All my strength to do this.

Becoming a figure in a poem.

Usurping a name and a theme.[25]

I can't help thinking that her journey, I mean the supreme and insightful achievement of it, belongs with Mainie Jellett and Evie Hone as they scramble to put the last few centimes together for a second Paris latté. She belongs among such Irish women, the instinctive and the first-rate of every culture, really, who strive for a second kind of art, unrepresentative but exemplary. It's not that such a woman poet finds herself outside history but that history has detained her for re-training so that she may be able to create a new history out of the materials she had found once she'd escaped from the cultural beginnings of our Free State. She rewrites the *Handbook*. We can see that the social realism of O'Connor, hot-headed idealist, vituperative and incandescent critic of the petit bourgeois narrative of de Valera's Ireland, would be cooled into a counter-narrative by Boland, nocturnally walking the corridors of a life more complex and humane:

Eros look down.
See as a god sees
what a myth says: how a woman still
addresses the work of man in the dark of the night.

The power of form. The plain
evidence that strength descended here once.
And mortal pain. And even sexual glory.

And see the difference.
This time – and this you did not ordain –
I am changing the story.[26]

NOTES

1   A shorter version of this essay first appeared in Thomas McCarthy, 'Eavan Boland's Daring Integrity: A Quick Glance at the Poet's Context' in 'A Celebration of Eavan Boland', *PN Review*, 220 (Nov-Dec 2014), pp 64–5.

2   Eavan Boland, *New Collected Poems* (Manchester, Carcanet, 2005), p. 24.

3   Louis MacNeice, *Collected Poems* edited by Peter McDonald (London, Faber and Faber, 2007), p. 395.

4   'Don Jeremy Savonarola' in *Final Reliques of Father Prout*, 1876.

5   *The Collected Works of W.B. Yeats, Volume III, Autobiographies* (New York, Simon and Schuster, 1999), p. 369.

6   Quoted in Thomas McCarthy, 'Eavan Boland's Daring Integrity: A Quick Glance at the Poet's Context' in 'A Celebration of Eavan Boland', *PN Review*, 220 (Nov-Dec 2014), p. 64.

7   John Montague, 'Clear the Way' in *Selected Poems* (Toronto, Exile Editions, 1991), p. 53.

8   Frank O'Connor, *A Frank O'Connor Reader* edited by Michael Steinman (Syracuse, Syracuse University Press, 1994), p. 18.

9   Eavan Boland, *New Collected Poems*, p. 81.

10   Jody Allen Randolph, *Eavan Boland* (Cork, Cork University Press, 2014), pp 47–79.

11   Eavan Boland, 'Patchwork or the Poet's Craft', *New Collected Poems*, p. 105.

12   *New Collected Poems*, p. 105.

13   C.P. Curran, 'Evie Hone: Stained Glass Artist 1894–1955' first published in *Studies* (Summer 1955) and reprinted in Stella Frost (ed.), 'A Tribute to Evie Hone and Mainie Jellett', *The Irish Ecclesiastical Record*, Ser. 5, Vol. LXXXVIII (September, 1957), p. 215.

14   Saorstát Éireann: Irish Free State *Official Handbook*, Department of Industry and Commerce. E. Benn (Dublin, The Talbot Press, 1932), p. 239.

15   p. 283.

16   Boland, *New Collected Poems*, p. 13.

17   *New Collected Poems*, p. 16.

18   from 'Port of New York. 1956' in *A Poetic Celebration of the Hudson River*, with Michael Schmidt, John Ashbery, Eavan Boland, Jorie Graham, John Koethe, Yusef Komunyakaa, Paul Muldoon and Toon Tellegen (Manchester, Carcanet, 2009, limited edition).

19   Eavan Boland, 'The War Horse', *New Collected Poems*, p. 39.

20   Letter 141, Sept 1959 in *The Letters of Robert Duncan and Denise Levertov* by Robert J. Bertholf and Albert Gelpi (Stanford, Stanford University Press, 2003), p. 211.

21   Eavan Boland, 'Denise Levertov: Letters to a Broken World' in Boland, *A Journey With Two Maps: Becoming a Woman Poet* (Manchester, Carcanet, 2011), p. 189.

22   Quoted in McCarthy, *PN Review*, 220, p. 64.

23   Eavan Boland, 'Being an Irish Poet: The Communal Art of Paula Meehan', in *An Sionnach* 'Special Issue on Paula Meehan' edited by Jody Allen Randolph, and reprinted in Boland, *A Journey with Two Maps* (Manchester, Carcanet, 2011), p. 220.

24   Boland, *New Collected Poems*, p. 179.

25   from 'Anna Liffey', *In a Time of Violence* in *New Collected Poems*, p. 232.

26   'Formal Feeling', *The Lost Land* in *New Collected Poems*, p. 275.

Nuala Ní Dhomhnaill

TÁIMID DAMANTA, A DHEIRFÉARACHA

Táimid damanta, a dheirféaracha,
sinne a chuaigh ag snámh
ar thránna istoíche is na réalta
ag gáirl in aonacht linn,
an mhéarnáil inár dtimpeall
is sinn ag scréachaíl le haoibhneas
is le fionnuaire na toade,
gan gúnaí orainn ná léinte
ach sinn chomh naíonta le leanaí bliana,
táimid damanta, a dheirféaracha.

Táimid damanta, a dheirféaracha,
sinne a thug dúshlán na sagart
is na ngaolta, a d'ith as mias na cinniúna,
a fuair fios oilc is maitheasa
chun gur chuma linn anois mar gheall air.
Chaithheamair oícheanta ar bhántaibh Párthais
ag ithe úll is spíonán is róiseanna
laistiar dár gcluasa, ag rá amhrán
timpeall tinte cnámh na ngadaithe,
ag ól is ag rangás le mairnéalaigh agus robálaithe
is táimid damanta, a dheirféaracha,

Níor chuireamair cliath ar stoca
níor chíoramair, níor shlámamair,
níor thuigeamair de banlámhaibh
ach an ceann atá ins na Flaithis in airde.
B'fhearr linn ár mbróga a chaitheamh dínn ar bharra
taoide
is rince aonair a dhéanamh ar an ngaineamh fliuch
ar ghaotha fiala an Earraigh, ná bheith fanta

istich age baile ag déanamh tae láidir d'fearaibh,
is táimid damanta, a dheirféaracha,

Beidh ár súile ag na péisteanna
is ár mbéala ah na portáin,
is tabharfar fós ár n-aenna
le n-ithe do mhadraí na mbailte fearainn.
Stracfar an ghruaig dár gceannaibh
Is bainfear an fheoil dár gcnámha
Geofar síolta úll is craiceann spíonán
i measc rianta úr gcuid urlacan
nuair a bheimid damanta, a dheirféaracha.

Nuala Ní Dhomhnaill

WE ARE DAMNED, MY SISTERS
translated by Michael Hartnett

We are damned, my sisters,
we who swam at night
on beaches, with the stars
laughing with us
phosphorescence about us
we shrieking with delight
with the coldness of the tide
without shifts or dresses
as innocent as infants.
We are damned, my sisters.

We are damned, my sisters,
we who accepted the priests' challenge
our kindred's challenge: who ate from destiny's dish
who have knowledge of good and evil
who are no longer concerned.
We spent nights in Eden's fields
eating apples, gooseberries; roses
behind our ears, singing songs
around the gipsy bon-fires
drinking and romping with sailors and robbers:
and so we are damned, my sisters.

We didn't darn stockings
we didn't comb or tease
we knew nothing of handmaidens
except the one in high Heaven.
We preferred to be shoeless by the tide
dancing singly on the wet sand
the piper's tune coming to us

on the kind Spring wind, than to be
indoors making strong tea for the men –
and so we're damned, my sisters.

Our eyes will go to the worms
our lips to the clawed crabs
and our livers will be given
as food to the parish dogs.
The hair will be torn from our heads
the flesh flayed from our bones.
They'll find apple seeds and gooseberry skins
in the remains of our vomit
when we are damned, my sisters.

SUBVERSIVE IDENTITIES:
HISTORY, PLACE AND CULTURE
IN THE WORK OF EAVAN BOLAND

Gerard Smyth

In a perceptive essay on Patrick Pearse, first published in
that other commemorative year, 1966, Eavan Boland refers
to Pearse's St Enda's School for Boys as 'an experiment in
identity'.[1] Boland's own poetry of half a century has been,
if not an experiment in identity, certainly a very explicit
exploration of identity.

Her fellow Dublin poet, Thomas Kinsella, once
suggested that each individual writer has to make his or
her own 'imaginative grasp at identity' and if the means
were not there in the inherited conventions, would have to
start from scratch, perhaps to create what Boland in one
poem calls the 'fictions of my purpose'.[2]

Her material is drawn from a cabinet of identities that
sometimes stand alone, but frequently converge – her
identities as a woman, mother, wife, poet, daughter but
also as an Irishwoman and a Dubliner. It is often the

convergence of these various identities that provides the triggering moment in a Boland poem. Beyond the personal, there has been her engagement with the even less distinct, often trickier notions of national and cultural identity – a subject she explored with writers and political activists in a pioneering piece of journalism in *The Irish Times* in 1974.[3] In what Terence Brown described as a 'stimulating intervention'[4] Boland gathered a a group of writers (John Hewitt, Thomas Kinsella, James Plunkett and Francis Stuart) as well as representatives of Sinn Féin and the Ulster Defence Association to explore the meaning of identity and the complexities of heritage. Back then the young poet was already striking out and claiming the ground for what would be her poetic project: the questioning of shibboleths.

The title of her debut collection, *New Territory*, both prefigured and offered a clue to the poet's intentions – the creation of a different space, a space in which to assert identities she regarded as missing from the Irish poem, or having been blocked from view by the established orthodoxies; a space in which to register new terms of reference, but to do so in a very personal and consciously different idiom, to seek 'that gesture in the way you use language' (as she refers to predecessors in 'The Rooms of Other Women Poets').[5]

In an early ekphrastic poem, 'From the Painting *Back From Market* by Chardin', she voices some of her concerns:

… I think of what great art removes:
Hazard and death, the future and the past.
A woman's secret history and her loves –[6]

Boland herself, much later, in the preface to her *Collected Poems* declared that she 'began in a city and a poetic world where the choices and assumptions were near enough to those of a nineteenth century poet'.[7]

Yet, emerging as a young poet of high achievement, she did not initially – with her well-crafted, resounding apprentice poems – altogether reject the inheritance and the fruitfulness of tradition; in fact many of the poems either echoed, responded or alluded to iconic voices (Yeats, Aogán Ó Rathaille). Her strong sense of the historical past was not a mythologising one; there is no mimicking but rather a renovation of old familiar themes ('A Cynic at Kilmainham Gaol', 'The Flight of the Earls', the latter a far cry from the entrancement of Mangan's 'Lament for the Princes').[8] Boland resorted to myth and legend, too, in several of those first poems (often in her work stories out of myth and legend have been refashioned to striking effect in the devising of ways to deal with more personal subject matter).

However, the continuities ended there. For many poets, first collections act as a kind of clearing house, exercises in the shedding of assimilated influences and thematic fixations. In its range of subject matter, *New Territory* served that purpose; her second collection *The War Horse* fiercely signaled the poet's rejection of what she regarded as outmoded and outworn rhetoric; the 'broken images' she refers to in 'Child of Our Time', a poem in memory of one of the youngest of the victims of the 1974 Dublin bombings and in which she unequivocally declares the need for a 'new language'.

She knew that this 'new language' – and her solitary function as a poet – was to put flesh on what she called the 'mythic, emblematic' women in Irish poetry (constructed out of male concepts, fashioned to suit certain nationalistic incantations), find a new blueprint, unearth different imaginative processes that would alter the map and agenda of Irish poetry: a redress for the blighting effect of past omissions and inequities in the social, political and literary history of women. So, from early on, she was a poet of disaffection.

For Stephen Dedalus, history was the nightmare from which we try to escape. Boland's conviction – as woman and poet – was that history had in fact excluded her, so she confronted it and in doing so was a poet setting out to clear away that blocked view in the proscribed narratives; one who faced the challenge of having to write her way out of what she felt was a kind of isolation and devise the imaginative reconstruction of a poetic culture, make 'new art on old ground'.[9]

'Exile brings you overnight where it would normally take a lifetime to go':[10] that statement of Joseph Brodsky's comes to mind when considering Boland's early displacements out of Ireland; displacements that left an indelible effect and were formative experiences allowing her to find different and necessary routes to and through her 'country of the mind'.

Perhaps being the child of a diplomat had its advantages, providing the opportunity to have a distanced offshore view of Ireland and an off-centre viewpoint in formulating, through her own work, that reconstruction of a poetic culture.

She is particularly – and artfully – candid in the poems that recalled and released memories of a childhood that removed her from her roots, transformed her into 'a child in a north-facing bedroom/in a strange country' ('The Game').[11]

Of course Boland has never been an exile in the Brodsky manner, there has been no permanent re-rooting in another place; yet the loss of place and the strangeness of elsewhere can sometimes seem troubling in those poems in which she re-visits the out-of-Ireland episodes of her early life.

There is an intense breakthrough in poems such as 'An Irish Childhood in England, 1951' and 'Fond Memory', in the notes of tender remembrance in her vivid and exact snapshots:

At three o'clock I caught two buses home

where sometimes in the late afternoon
at a piano pushed into a corner of the playroom
my father would sit down and play the slow

lilts of Tom Moore while I stood there trying
not to weep ...[12]

Something essential in the making of Eavan Boland the poet grew out of those childhood years in England when Ireland was 'far away/and farther away/every year'[13] and where in a London convent – in response to her Irish argot – a teacher bluntly reminded that she was 'not in Ireland now'.[14] Perhaps what took root through those experiences were the critical judgements and self-assertion that led, not just to her understanding of her country, but her questioning of the imaginative perspectives through which generations of writers and artists had dealt with the subject.

Her adolescent years in New York appear to have further added to that sense of self as an 'outsider', of discovering that there are 'lost lands' and a lost language. It also sowed the seeds of the compassionate attitudes that have become commonplace in her poems; she became the journey-maker who, having 'sailed the long way home/on a coal-burning ship', steps on to:

the ground the emigrants

resistless, weeping,
laid their cheeks to ...

('After a Childhood Away from Ireland')[15]

Her empathy with 'emigrant grief', beautifully rendered in several poems, became a consistent theme; perhaps the insights that gave rise to that empathy first flickered on those outward journeys of childhood and adolescence; that close contact with the loss of belonging, her glimpses of the 'Long-suffering/in the bruise-coloured dusk of the New World'. The sentiment and graceful airs of 'all the old songs' is replaced by a much sterner outlook in Boland's poems, a shout of grievance on behalf of those put out 'the back, of our houses, of our minds'.

Images of departure frequently occur, 'the mailboat at twilight' ('The Lost Land') and those 'Daughters of Colony' who 'left for London from Kingstown harbour –/never certain which they belonged to' ('Daughters of Colony').

Her own departures have been significant not only in the shaping of attitude but in the perspectives she presents to us. Boland's editor and publisher at Carcanet, Michael Schmidt, once said about the English poet Donald Davie that although he had taken himself to America, his 'work, all of it, is beamed towards England. He is writing to us and of us'.[16]

'Writing to us and of us' is also what Boland has been doing through the various stages of her career; an ongoing meditation on Ireland and her relationship with the country – a relationship that seems to have intensified in the poems of her more recent collections and which she has written in the years of transatlantic commuting. Again the perspective of distance, the repetitive leave-taking and returning (a routine required by her academic duties in Stanford) may well be instrumental in her constantly refreshed stock-taking, the re-invigorated ways of looking at and thinking about her country and its fractured history, its evasions. It has been part, too, of her self-reckoning as a poet.

All in all, her country viewed in this way through her particular set of experiences and circumstance seems to have led to a place that often seems to lie somewhere between attachment and detachment.

'How do I know my country?' she asks in 'Unheroic'.

'Let me tell you it has been hard to do', is the answer she presents to herself and to us.[17]

Dublin, however, was a city that 'seemed made for poetry', she tells us in one of her *Object Lessons* essays; she was 'ready to record its contradictions'.

When the poet Roy Fisher, describing his *modus operandi* as a poet of his native city, stated that 'Birmingham is what I think with' he coined a wonderfully apt phrase applicable to many poets whose work is attentive to place.[18]

In many of her poems Ireland is what Eavan Boland *thinks with,* but more particularly Dublin is what she thinks with and does so with striking feeling for the particulars of place and with a sharply perceptive grasp of those 'contradictions'. As with Thomas Kinsella, the city is an emotional possession, a ready repository of memory and association that has been central to her work.

In this she belongs to the 'school of retentive memory' that is such a strong component of Irish poetry. Memory, including received memory (the early days of her parents' marriage, for example), has been a vital catalyst in her writing. As she says in one poem, 'Memory/is in two parts.//First, the re-visiting:'[19]

It is that first step, the act of 're-visiting' that retrieves so much from memory and gives it resonance in a Boland poem: the black lace fan her mother gave her, white hawthorn in the west of Ireland, the photograph on her father's desk, the recall of a Latin lesson or a child's illness and recovery in the poem 'Love', a moving and quite lovely homage to marriage.

In an interview with Paula Meehan (reproduced in this volume), Boland states that out of her reading of Yeats (who cared and wrote little about the city and then only obliquely or with an eye to its architecture and monuments and its role in the national dramas) she became interested in 'looking at a city as a place where the ghosts of power are remembered and tested'.[20] The players in those dramas of history are essentially those who are the 'ghosts of power' referred to by Boland.

In the same interview she expresses 'a distrust' of the idea of a poet of place (Kavanagh once disavowed the idea of the poetry of place but contradicted himself in his wonderful Monaghan pastorals and city sonnets). Yet her 'Dublin poems' possess not only a quite profound sense of connection but deep affection that is implied in the retrieval of evocative detail from her 'lost land of orators and pedestals and corners and street names and rivers'.

Boland has referred to 'the city that got into' her poems as the long-ago Dublin; these are, she says, poems that 'wander a bit more backwards'. Her re-imagining of this past is more than a backward glance; these poems of recollection, of reaching back to first curiosities and observations, might indeed be located in a city gone from view – one that existed between Joyce's Dublin of 1904 and Kinsella's of 1997 ('The Pen Shop') – but it is enshrined in memory and imagination and poem-making that penetrates into the spirit of a time and place. She evokes and records the moods and atmosphere of that 'long-ago Dublin', out of which came moments of personal significance, in vivid and factual detail and with characteristic and compelling exactness:

> The café had
> plastic chairs and lunch counters.
> […]
>
> I hunched my knees
> under the table. The vinegar bottle
> shifted its bitter yellows.
> ('Dublin, 1959')[21]

But then, in the same poem, she activates a subtle change of pitch, an arresting moment (such moments are frequent in her poems): 'Tell me a story about Ireland/I said as a child/to anyone in earshot …' Boland is a story-teller poet, an archivist of hidden histories (see poems like 'Quarantine', 'Code' and the poem to Hester Bateman); 'stories of Ireland' are used to brilliant effect to illustrate her themes as is the building-block construction of imagery in her multi-layered narratives. Beckoning opening lines ease us into these narratives:

> It was an Irish summer. It was wet.
> It was a job. I was seventeen.[22]

That bold simplicity and tone of voice and use of an emphatically plain diction comes with the full blast of an authoritative voice, one that is steadied by artistic confidence. The language is far move inventive and daring than the plain-spoken style quoted above might suggest. There are utterly marvellous moments of description and unexpected leaps of imagery – a coil of her mother's hair 'is the colour of corn harvested in darkness' ('The Source'); 'the camisole glow' of the white briar rose; or this from 'The Black Lace Fan My Mother Gave Me':

> The lace is overcast as if the weather
> it opened for and offset had entered it.

Her poems will quite often then shift into a rich and complex range of intimations and subtexts, or discursive digressions and expostulation. A visit to the Dolls Museum conjures images of the city where:

> The carriages are turning: they are turning back.
>
> Past children walking with governesses,
> Looking down, cosseting their dolls,
> then looking up as the carriage passes,
> the shadow chilling them. Twilight falls.
>
> ('The Dolls Museum in Dublin')[23]

These lines are an example of her ability to isolate a particular small moment before shifting to a larger-scale perspective.

Even in a poet as disciplined as Boland, the emotional ties with her 'old, torn and traded city' are strong and evident. The city that provided her younger self with certain experiences and insights is one she refers to as being 'dear to us and particular' ('The Huguenot Graveyard at the Heart of the City'). Her city landmarks are a powerful and often enabling presence, as they are, say, in the St Petersburg poems of Elena Shvarts.

In *A Poet's Dublin*, a mapping of her territories, old and new, we get a comprehensive and coherent sense of this deep relationship. The book's editors (Paula Meehan and Jody Allen Randolph) describe the poems as 'explorations of a very particular city, a city never exactly owned and never completely lost; a city imagined through absence and architecture; through women and colony'.

So much of what occurs in a Boland poem begins in the past, in that city of colony, wonderfully evoked as a place beguiled by a dance which came 'with the scarlet tunics and rowel-spurs/with the epaulettes and poisonous drizzles of gold' ('How The Dance Came to the City'). 'Poisonous drizzles of gold' is another example of the powerful impact and surprise her images can deliver, as is:

Her face flushed and wide-eyed in the mirror of his sword[24]

That face could belong to the mistress of the 'booted soldier' in another poem, or to a city itself, dazzled by its colonial masters. In the Boland lexicon, 'colony' has become a recurring and weighty word. Her 'City of Shadows' is also a 'momentary place' ('The Scar') and throughout so much of her work she has been attentive and responsive to the momentary place. When, in her mind's eye, she sees her 'father/buttoning his coat at Front Gate' ('City of Shadows') it is not simply a straightforward visualisation of a particular and intimate actuality but much more than that as the poem moves forward into the sweeping imagery suggesting a spectral place, a city of melancholy:

Grafton Street and Nassau Street were gone.
And the old parliament at College Green.
And the bronze arms and attitudes of orators
from Grattan to O'Connell. All gone.[25]

More tellingly, her Dublin is a city of home truths, one that holds the baggage of history, a city of hard contours, often represented in imagery of the city's statuary with its historical associations – the 'iron orators and granite patriots' – all of them representing only the patriarchal legacy in history and literature.

Her Dublin poems are vehicles for a discourse on that 'baggage', a critique of its falsehoods; but also for the telling of stories, as she does in so many poems, such as 'Making Money', a poem that uncovers a piece of local history from her home ground in Dundrum:

And the mill wheel turned so the mill
could make paper and the paper money.
And the cottage doors opened and the women
came out in the ugly first hour
after dawn and began

to cook the rags …[26]

In 'The Scar' (included in *A Poet's Dublin*), Boland acknowledges that 'Dublin rises out of the river reflecting it' and in one of her earliest poems, 'Liffeytown', a paean to the river as it passes through its mother city, she repeats the lovely and plaintive refrain:

O swan by swan my heart goes down
Through Dublin town, through Dublin town.[27]

In her essay 'Woman without a country: a detail',[28] she regards her city as one unfolding 'through surfaces of history, colony, survival'. A peeling back of the layers of concealment has been a fundamental and constant act in her work and perhaps no poem of hers has been as compelling in the way it presents this process as her sequence, *Anna Liffey*, a virtuoso centrepiece of her entire oeuvre.

It strikes a deeply personal note; the eponymous river acting as a metaphor for the self. Much in the way the river charts its course and through its choreography reveals itself, the poem charts a subjective journey of self-scrutiny. It is a poem of ringing declarations: *It is time to go back to where I came from.* And:

In the end
It will not matter
That I was a woman.[29]

If poets have moments of renewal 'Anna Liffey' reads like Boland's moment. Standing in her doorway with the hills where the Liffey originates in the background, the rumination involves no adjustment of her imperatives, the poem integrates a blend of complexities:

The city where I was born.
The river that runs through it.
The nation which eludes me.

Perhaps more critical to her work than the memory-journeys back to the 'long-ago Dublin', the city heartland of her youth, has been the Dublin of her married life and the 'close suburban night'. She took on the domestic mundane and elicited from it some of her finest work. Boland got into her stride as a poet in this new space out where 'town and country are at each other's throats'. There she found her 'new pastorals' and confirmed her own intuitions as a poet. There she became the beneficiary of 'the nourishment which springs from knowing and belonging to a certain place' (as Heaney described it in his essay 'The Sense of Place').[30]

If she saw one of her tasks as the revision of how the imaginative identity of women is represented in poetry, the suburb facilitated the setting in which this could be achieved through depictions of 'real' rather than 'idealised' lives. Which is not to say that she wasn't unaware that suburbia brought with it the possibilities of a new kind of exclusion and isolation, particularly for the 'suburban woman' who, among the lawnmowers and small talk across the privet hedge:

> … stares
> at her life falling with her flowers,
> like military tribute, or the tears
> of shell-shocked men, into arrears.[31]

But in her odes to suburbia she spoke for the value of these common, shared experiences, celebrated the joys of the quotidian and the small everyday events of the 'life unrecorded in the tradition', '… the hour of gathering', when:

> We call the children in.
> We stow the bikes and close the garage doors.[32]

Her disposition and instincts were on the side of those living their unseen lives among the 'Stove noises, kettle steam/And children's kisses'. The shared experiences on the new estates (Clarke in his own style had slightly touched on them, but as an observer of the city's social migrations) would fuel the imagery of these poems of suburban life in which, on occasion, the garden seems to suggest the possibility of a new Eden:

> I thought the garden looked so at ease.
> The roses were beginning on one side.
> The laurel hedge was nothing but itself.[33]

Or that electrifying image in 'Midnight Flowers' – 'I turn a switch and the garden grows./A whole summer's work in one instant!' or 'The poplars shifted their music in the garden'. Then there are 'the fruits of neighbourly gardens' stocked in her kitchen.[34]

She was an artist with an untested subject and that required her to 're-examine modes of expression and poetic organisation'. This unrecorded life was the reality on the inside of the suburban door. The opening of that door – or at least the drawing of the blinds – had its first revelatory moments in the poems of motherhood and domestic chores in *Night Feed*, hands-on poems, born out of the 'dailyness' and 'routine' of the woman who is:

> as round
> as the new ring
> ambering her finger.[35]

The situation demanded a new vocabulary and she created and developed it in those poems in which she defined that sphere behind the suburban door and, more vitally, the lives and experiences that animate the space. The minimalist and compact poems of the central sequence, 'Domestic Interior' introduce us to 'the way of life/that is its own witness'. She became the witness to the 'way of life' of the many; the act of 'local watchfulness' that Kinsella has referred to becomes central.[36]

That collection is also one in which Boland enters a new fluency and authority. The change in the design of the poems is a dramatic one: the sparseness of expression and the restraint are entirely appropriate to the themes the poems embody and the poet getting on with the job of putting 'the life I lived into the poems I wrote'. There is no equivocation, no reticence:

> Our way of life
> has hardly changed
> since a wheel first
> whetted a knife.
>
> ('It's A Woman's World')[37]

The daily factual life of the poet is the material. Boland sounds a more personal note dealing with married life and particularly its fledgling stages, the setting up of house and home, in poems of intimate disclosure:

A child
shifts in a cot.

No matter what happens now
I'll never fill one again.[38]

Just as intimate are Boland's love poems; poems that speak beautifully of the moments in a marriage (the bond that is brought to its ultimate gesture in the story of the famine couple told in 'Quarantine').

In 'A Ballad of Home', she concludes:

This house is built on our embrace
And there are worse foundations.[39]

Boland became a poet of the 'documentary lyric', poems which gave powerful expression not just to the life she was living – as mother, wife and poet in a particular setting – but, beyond her Dublin and its suburbs and hills, beyond her own contemporary time and issues, she confronts a disfigured history: the workhouse, the dispossessed victims of famine and emigration; the fate of those who came seeking refuge ('A Huguenot Graveyard') and the legacies of colonisation ('When the Dance Came to the City').

When Kinsella comes to the end of his contemplative journey in 'Nightwalker' he sees a 'Sea of Disappointment', in Boland we find a different but equally disturbing unease:

Beautiful land I whispered. But the roads
stayed put. Stars froze over the suburb.
Shadows iced up. Nothing moved.
Except my hand across the page. And these words.

('Whose?')[40]

As well as being chronicler and interrogator of the legacies of colonial disempowerment, Boland, in much of her work has been – as Terence Brown has noted – a poet 'responsive to the social and cultural shifts'[41] taking place in Ireland. She is well aware that at the end of her suburban road, 'They are making a new Ireland'. The question of nationhood and its complexities is frequently addressed:

> I won't go back to it –
>
> my nation displaced
> into old dactyls …
>
> ('Mise Eire')[42]

In 'Becoming the Hand of John Speed', (from *Domestic Violence*), there is a further declaration:

> I was born in a nation
> I had no part in making[43]

In an interesting and, no doubt, deliberate juxtaposition the following poem, 'Papers', reminds the reader about the role of her father and his generation:

> This is a new nation
> he has a hand in making.[44]

Somewhere in the dichotomy between these two statements Boland's focus has been to challenge the rigid, handed-down concepts of nationhood, to seek newer dispensations of that condition that would widen its boundaries, extend its definitions. She has, through her poetry and the expository essays (few poets have written, in prose form, so well and so intensely on the origins of their work) been a powerful advocate of the 'new Ireland' that she once recognised on her suburban horizon. Her forging of a revisionist perspective has fulfilled that original intention to put flesh on what she called the 'mythic, emblematic' women in Irish poetry; then there is the solemn matter of correcting what she perceived as the one-sidedness of the narratives of her gender, country and literary heritage.

The way in which her disaffections have found expression in her poetry are perhaps best seen in the binary effect of her lyrical and narrative gifts; her reinventions of classical material – myth and legend – and its enabling effect on her imagination have produced some of her most powerful poems.

The American poet and critic Richard Hugo believed that 'all good serious poems are born in obsession'.[45] Boland's readers can trace the obsessions – *passions* might be the better word – that have been the impulse behind her poems but it is the ways in which these passions spill into each other that creates the pattern that has shaped and given coherence to the work through various stages of development.

That coherence and continuity and, let it be said, the characteristic seriousness and passionate conviction of her work has been exemplary. If poetry is 'the subversive function of the imagination' – to borrow Adrienne Rich's phrase – Boland's subversion of a tradition has been both explicit and defiant.[46] As well as which she has conducted a fierce scrutiny of what she has called 'the fierce countenance of Irish history'.[47]

NOTES

1   In Eavan Boland, 'Aspects of Pearse', *Dublin Magazine* (Spring 1966).

2   Thomas Kinsella quoted in 'The poetry of an empty space' by Colm Tóibín, *The Irish Times*, 25 June 2011: 'In 1966 Kinsella had written an essay called "The Irish Writer", in which he ... asked himself a difficult and a liberating question, a question that haunts anyone who lives in this landscape now, or writes about it. "Is there", he asked, "any virtue, for literature, for poetry, in the simple continuity of a tradition? I believe there is not. A relatively steady tradition, like English or French, accumulates a distinctive quality and tends to impose this on each new member. Does this give him a deeper feeling for the experience gathered up in the tradition, or a better understanding of it? I

doubt it ... For the present – especially in this present – it seems that every writer has to make the imaginative grasp at identity for himself; and if he can find no means in his inheritance to suit him, he will have to start from scratch"'.

3   *The Irish Times*, 4 July 1974.
4   Terence Brown, *The Irish Times: 150 Years of Influence* (Gill and Macmillan, 2015), p. 291.
5   Eavan Boland, *New Collected Poems* (Manchester, Carcanet, 2005), p. 166.
6   Boland, 2005, p. 17.
7   *Collected Poems* (Manchester, Carcanet, 1995) p. ix.
8   James Clarence Mangan's 'A Lament for the Princes of Tyrone and Tyrconnel' appeared in Padraic Colum's *Anthology of Irish Verse*, 1922.
9   From 'How we made a new art on old ground', *New Collected Poems*, p. 296.
10   Joseph Brodsky, 'The Condition We Call Exile' in *On Grief and Reason* (New York, Farrar, Straus & Giroux, 1995), p. 32.
11   Boland, 2005, p. 169.
12   *Ibid.*, p. 156.
13   *Ibid.*, p. 222.
14   From 'An Irish Childhood in England', *Ibid.* p. 155.
15   Boland, 2005, p. 100.
16   Michael Schmidt, 'Time and Again: The Recent Poetry of Donald Davie', *Agenda*, 14 (Summer 1976), pp 33–44.
17   Boland, 2005, p. 251.
18   Roy Fisher quoted in *Contemporary British Poetry and the City* edited by Peter Barry (Manchester, Manchester University Press, 2000), p. 193.
19   From 'We are always too late', *New Collected Poems* (Manchester, Carcanet, 2005), p. 186.
20   'Two poets and a city' – a conversation between Paula Meehan and Eavan Boland in Paula Meehan and Jody Allen Randolph, (ds) *Eavan Boland: A Poet's Dublin* (Manchester, Carcanet, 2014), p. 98.
21   Boland, 2005, p. 267.
22   From 'Unheroic', Boland, 2005, p. 251.
23   Boland, 2005, p. 208.
24   'How the dance came to the city' in Paula Meehan and Jody Allen Randolph (eds), *Eavan Boland: A Poet's Dublin* (Manchester, Carcanet, 2014), p. 53.
25   Boland, 2005, p. 250.

26 *Ibid.*, p. 292.

27 *Ibid.*, p. 3.

28 PN Review 220, November-December edition, 2014.

29 *New Collected Poems* (Manchester, Carcanet, 2005). The 'Anna Liffey' sequence begins with the poem of that title and runs from pp 230–242.

30 Heaney, Seamus, 'The Sense of Place' [1977], *Preoccupations* (London, Faber, 1980), pp 131–49.

31 'Suburban Woman', Boland, 2005, p. 65.

32 Boland, 'Neighbours' in *Domestic Violence* (Manchester, Carcanet, 2007), p. 41.

33 From 'Daphne Heard with Horror the Addresses of the God', *New Collected Poems*, p. 181.

34 'Midnight Flowers', Boland, 2005, p. 193. Quotes from 'The Journey', p. 147 and 'Contingencies', p. 141.

35 'Domestic Interior', Boland, 2005, p. 91.

36 See Derval Tubridy, *Thomas Kinsella: The Peppercanister Poems* (Dublin, UCD Press, 2001), p. 192.

37 Boland, 2005, p. 110.

38 'Endings', Boland, 2005, p. 97.

39 *Ibid.*, p. 104.

40 *Ibid.*, p. 275.

41 Terence Brown, 'The Irish Times and a Modern Ireland', *The Irish Times: 150 Years of Influence* (Dublin, Gill and Macmillan, 2015), p. 387.

42 'Mise Éire', Boland, 2005, p. 128.

43 *Domestic Violence* (Manchester, Carcanet, 2007), p. 48.

44 *Ibid.*, p. 49.

45 Richard Hugo, *The Triggering Town: Lectures and Essays on Poetry and Writing* (New York, W.W. Norton, 1979) p. 7.

46 Adrienne Rich, *Arts of the Possible: Essays and Conversations* (New York, W.W. Norton, 2001), p. 174.

47 Boland, *Object Lessons* (Manchester, Carcanet, 1995), p. 96.

Jean O'Brien

RESONANCE
for Eavan Boland

Listening in the hushed auditorium
to her reasoning, this water carrier
of words speaking to our eager upturned faces,
tells us of histories lost and forgotten.
With her anew we mourn a past
irremediable.

No chronicle indexed in libraries,
this is the spoken story,
told by mothers to children
as they captain their kitchen's
scrubbed tables. Scattered
with mists of flour and her stories
mingling, baked into
a certainty of bread.

Relieved, I thought it is not lost.
Race-memory is carried
on the rim of reason;
or like a snail's history
small and carried on its back.
It only lacks – words.

'TELLING THE ISLAND TO MYSELF': IMAGES, HEROES

Jody Allen Randolph

Between the publication of *The Journey and Other Poems* in 1986 and *Outside History* in 1990 Eavan Boland wrote an essay called 'The Woman Poet in a National Tradition' and published it in the Jesuit journal *Studies* in 1987. There it remained, attracting little notice or comment until it reappeared, first in Attic Press's LIP pamphlet series in 1989 and then in the *American Poetry Review* in 1990.[1] Enabling critique and sometimes controversy, it became over the next two decades one of the most influential essays in both the history of Irish poetry and of women's poetry.

My subject here, however, is not the impact or reach of this essay, or how it framed the achievement of a diverse and talented generation of Irish women poets, or even how it changed the way we think and talk about images of women in Irish literature. My subject is the relation between 'The Woman Poet in a National Tradition' and two of Boland's most recent poems. The critique of image-making in this earlier essay, I will argue, both frames and anticipates a trajectory of imaginative growth in these later poems.

'The Woman Poet in a National Tradition' looked closely at image-making as a strategy of simplification. It formulated a view of patterns and devices in Irish poetry, which at one level seemed effective as symbolism but at another seemed reductive of the subject they were representing. Such practice presented women's lived experience through stylized motifs and patterns, or what Boland calls 'elements of design'.

The essay opens in a cottage in the west of Ireland, where a young Boland is studying for exams at Trinity College that she needs to retake. There she meets an old woman who speaks to her briefly about the suffering of local people during the famine and about Irish history. The encounter, brief as it is, gives the poet a sense of her own estrangement from the lived experience of Irish history.

As the essay progresses, Boland's encounter with the old woman prompts her toward a meditation on a circular movement of evasion and simplification. The encounter causes her to reflect on the use of women as emblems in Irish poetry:

> The majority of Irish male poets depended on women as motifs in their poetry. They moved easily, deftly, as if by right among images of women in which I did not believe and of which I could not approve. The women in their poems were often passive, decorative, raised to emblematic status. This was especially true where the woman and the idea of the nation were mixed: where the nation became a woman and the woman took on a national posture.[2]

Here Boland is referring to the history of figuration in Irish poetry of the nation as a young or old woman, or a mother for whom sacrifice is necessary: Dark Rosaleen, Kathleen Ni Houlihan, Sean Bhean Bhocht or Mother Ireland. 'Feminisation of the national', writes Angela Bourke, was 'consolidated by the Young Ireland movement in the 1840s and refined and elaborated by the Literary Revival in the two decades preceding the Easter 1916 Rising'.[3] It is this history of image-making, Boland suggests, that underlies even the contemporary use of women as a motif in Irish poetry.

Boland makes clear that she views this image-making as a maneuver, a deep-seated reflex within at least part of the project of Irish poetry. She argues that it points to a repetitious failure. The reflex she identifies is not just a failure of depicting women, it is a failure of imagining them:

> Women in such poems were frequently referred to approvingly as mythic, emblematic. But to me these passive and simplified women seemed a corruption. Moreover, the transaction they urged on the reader, to accept them as mere decoration, seemed to compound the corruption. For they were not decorations, they were not ornaments. However distorted these images, they had their roots in a suffered truth.[4]

Almost thirty years distant from that essay, it seems right to weigh its implications in the continuing work of Eavan Boland and indeed within the broader meaning of her argument. Has this interrogation of image-making, so central to her earlier work, continued in her later poems? Does she still associate that tendency with the powerful and even distorted expectations she felt were being put on Irish poetry by its historic association with the nation? These questions remain salient to her work and take on a new importance in this season of commemoration of 1916, with its powerful icons and symbols. Therefore it seems most useful to address them, at least at first, through a compelling theme that concentrates their meaning, a trope of central importance in Boland's work and one particularly relevant now.

The theme to be considered is a potent category within the broader story of image-making: the trope of hero-making.

From the start Boland had expressed her deep doubts about these almost routine transfigurations in Irish history. In *Object Lessons* (1995), Boland writes of her disillusion as a young woman with this by-product of the nation:

> The continuum between poet and patriot, between language and action, was not what I had thought. It was not a solid and useful bridge across which a history moved to safety. Instead, it was a soft and ugly connection, where words undid actions and actions could never be free of their own consequences in language. For every death there would be a ballad. In every ballad the broken-hearted transactions between drawing room and street corner, between English liberal and Irish rebel would be stated and re-stated.[5]

The history of these ideas is complex, leading both to biography and analysis. To trace them, some biography of Boland's first contacts with both images and heroic figures is necessary.

Boland's encounters with images came early. Her mother, Frances Kelly, was a working visual artist. When the family moved to London in the early 1950s, Kelly continued to paint in a room where the furniture was draped with sheets and the fog-laden light of London afternoons sometimes limited the painter's ability to continue. In her poem 'I Remember' from *The Journey* (1986) Boland describes one such session of portrait painting when she was the child observer, already noting violations in the relation of image to subject:

> I remember the way the big windows washed
> out the room and the winter darks tinted
> it and how, in the brute quiet and aftermath,
> an eyebrow waited helplessly to be composed[6]

The actual process of making images, together with their power to represent and distort, is already shown to be fraught in this poem. The artistic process is already deeply

ambiguous for the child observer and the poet looking
back on it:

> [...] my mother's portrait brushes
> spiked from the dirty turpentine and the face
> on the canvas was the scattered fractions
>
> of the face which had come up the stairs
> that morning and had taken up position in
> the big drawing-room and had been still
> and was now gone; and I remember, I remember
>
> I was the interloper who knows both love and fear,
> who comes near and draws back, who feels nothing
> beyond the need to touch, to handle, to dismantle it,
> the mystery ...[7]

An early fascination with and estrangement from the act of
image-making was Boland's response to watching her
mother at work, an experience she described in *A Journey
with Two Maps* (2011) as 'the first sign of expressive power
I saw as a child'.[8]

If her early experience of her mother's painting raised
issues of representation then her connection to her mother,
always a close one, occasionally generated conversations
which confirmed these doubts and insights. In an
unpublished page of memoir in the poet's papers, Boland
remembers one such conversation with her mother when
she was a teenager. Her mother recounted a story from
when she was a young painter. Seeking commissions, she
was visiting notable Irish figures to discuss painting their
portraits. One such meeting was with Maud Gonne
MacBride, the militant revolutionary and well-known
activist. In her memoir Boland notes that her mother's
recounting of this story came on the heels of Boland herself
reading Gonne MacBride's autobiography *A Servant of the
Queen*, first published in 1938.[9] The book, as the title
suggests, mapped out a visionary patriotism, an ecstatic
attachment to the cause of Irish freedom. The young

Frances Kelly met Gonne MacBride in her house in Dublin in the mid 1930s. There the young painter discovered the Irish revolutionary surrounded by many caged birds. W.B. Yeats had been struck by similar encounters with Gonne four decades earlier:

> I saw her always as she passed to and fro between Dublin and Paris, surrounded, no matter how rapid her journey and how brief her stay at either end of it, surrounded by cages, canaries, finches of all kinds … a parrot, and once a full-grown hawk from Donegal.[10]

In fact the keeping of birds in small domestic aviaries was not uncommon at that time. In *Answering to the Language* (1989), the New Zealand poet and writer C.K. Stead notes that Yeats too kept birds: 'Birds were important to Yeats. Like Maud Gonne he kept many in cages'.[11] At some point in the conversation, Frances Kelly mentioned the caged birds. She asked Gonne MacBride how she could advocate for freedom for so many and yet keep the birds away from theirs. Apparently the question chilled the conversation. The commission for a portrait was never given.

The fact that there could be an inconsistency in the life of a heroic figure like Maud Gonne MacBride remained with Boland as an insight gleaned from her mother's anecdote. Eventually these two threads – the violations of image-making itself and the dubious project of sustaining the heroic – would come to be braided together in Boland's later work. They are present in a new, as yet unpublished, poem, 'Statue'. Written as the 1916 commemoration approached, the poem provides not so much answers as a continuing spectrum of doubts and questions. Set in Stephen's Green, the poem is framed as an encounter between the speaker and the image of a heroine. This in itself takes some rich backlighting from an earlier poem 'Heroic' published in *The Lost Land* in 1998. There the teenage Boland, looking at a statue of a male figure, almost certainly of Robert Emmet in the same Stephen's Green, is bewildered and attracted by the very symbolism she would reject as a mature poet. She sees heroism as a possible model, even as a potential contagion. The speaker in the poem is looking back at the delusion and yearning of the moment:

> I looked up. And looked at him again.
> He stared past me without recognition.
>
> I moved my lips and wondered how the rain
> would taste if my tongue were made of stone.
> And wished it was. And whispered so that no one
> could hear it but him. *Make me a heroine.*[12]

The poem, as Helen Lojek notes, is constructed as a conversation between speaker and image: the mature poet looks at the younger poet who is looking at the statue. Insights gleaned from this conversation – about gender, about heroism, about the power of images – 'elicits reassessments of cultural images of heroism and encourages reinterpretation of public iconography'.[13]

The new poem, 'Statue', returns to cultural images of heroism. Only now the yearning and contagion have long been shaken off and it is the image of the heroine, not the hero, which is under scrutiny. In the iconic month of April in Stephen's Green, the mature speaker is weighing the past and present. But we are now in a contemporary and changed Ireland, with distracted people 'on their phones,/ tapping, frowning while two winter swans/sail down, up, down the minutes left to them for lunch'.[14]

The scene is ordinary but the sights, in their dailyness, prompt the speaker to remember being a younger woman. The fluidity and physicality of the memory will soon make a vivid contrast to the rest of the poem.

> I was young here. In those years night
> came quickly down on my neighborhood, my children slept,
> worn out by play. When I lit the lamp in the corner
> my hands were made of light.[15]

As the poem progresses this image of an ordinary woman, turning on a lamp in a domestic setting to offset evening, will be set against a static image of the heroic in the public statuary on the Green.

The encounter between image and speaker is not new in Boland's work. But here the poem moves quickly to irony. The statue she sees is of Constance Markievicz, a revolutionary leader of the Easter Rising, although she is not named in the poem and is exactly what the young subject of the earlier poem 'Heroic' yearned for. While the statue represents a real woman, she has been 'made' – like the statue of Robert Emmet in the earlier poem – into a heroine. It is not just the idea of a heroine Markievicz has been shaped into, but the physical moulding of one, with all the transformations of metal required by the process of statue-making.

The violence and subjugation of this identity – an apparent honouring which ends in an actual violation – is what the speaker in the poem 'Statue' weighs. As the language progresses, as the poem shifts from stanza to stanza, some of the large argument of the essay 'The Woman Poet in a National Tradition' returns, with all of its nuances and difficulties. Is it still possible that the history of women in Ireland is at risk of being displaced by a system that seems to shelter them in metaphor but at a deeper level continues to evade their reality?

These difficulties are immediately hinted at in the third stanza, in the description of the statue, in the way that the burnished surfaces of the metal casing show a woman released from decay, but also robbed of the natural life around her of which she once was a part:

> Her half-torso, her head and shoulders are rubbed
> to a glow; below her neck the frocked bronze
> and epaulettes she once wore
> are framed by the coarse flowers of the boxwood shrub.[16]

The transition between the static imagery of the statue and the dynamic imagery of nature gives force to the poem's developing argument about fixed images of the heroic.

The fourth stanza continues these sharp contrasts between the demands of iconography and the life of nature, showing how the observer must look to the side of the statue to see who made it:

> An Easter feel in the air. Wide
> hedgerows growing thicker and greener, miniature
> white flowers behind her and – if you look for it carefully –
> the sculptor's signature off to one side.[17]

Around the statue, the growth of the spring season continues, highlighting the arrested nature of the unchanging metal image.

But in the fifth stanza the poem makes a sharp swerve. The heroine represented here in stone and bronze, made into these because of her actions in this same month in 1916, is clearly deprived of her context by this attempt to honour her association with it. The poem – continuing the informal, conversational stanza and occasional end rhyme – shows the speaker intervening in an old argument:

> That reason and faith are at odds (and will always be) I accept,
> also that this turn of the year, this month,
> which is April, can never matter,
> ever, to the woman high above me on a stone plinth.[18]

The demands made by the existence and challenge of imagery, the conflict between reason and faith and the silencing of the subject all gesture towards the unresolved arguments of 'The Woman Poet in a National Tradition'.

Before discussing the remaining stanzas of 'Statue', it is helpful to refer to the title poem of Boland's most recent volume, *A Woman Without a Country*. The poem looks back to the engraving done of actual life figures during the famine of 1847. One of the source illustrations is very likely a drawing published a few years later in 1849 in the

Illustrated London News, titled 'Bridget O'Donnell and her Family'.[19] But the image of the engraver, central to the poem, is a separate fiction, if only because some engravings were done on wood as well as metal.

By the 1840s steel engraving was thriving in Dublin, was widely advertised and can be seen in portraits such as the 1844 engraving of Daniel O'Connell used in political biographies.[20] In fact Boland had long been familiar with the appearance – both harsh and eloquent – of steel engraving. When she was twelve years old, her mother had given her an original set of the two-volume edition of *The Scenery and Antiquities of Ireland*, whose authors were J. Sterling Coyne and N.P. Willis.[21] Published in 1842, the volumes are an invaluable if sanitized account of pre-famine Ireland with drawings by the celebrated illustrator, W.H. Bartlett. His drawings were taken from the engravings and his moody, romantic and often ominous representations of sheer cliffs and wild Irish rivers became famous.

Boland's engraver in the poem 'A Woman Without a Country' may owe something to her knowledge of Bartlett and her fascination with engraving, as well as her perception of its power to erase the identity it is representing. Certainly Bartlett's highly lyrical images of an afflicted country erased parts of its reality. She begins the poem, however, with a reference to the apparent neutrality of the craft:

As dawn breaks he enters
A room with the odor of acid.
He lays the copper plate on the table.
And reaches for the shaft of the burin.
Dublin wakes to horses and rain.
Street hawkers call.
All the news is famine and famine.
The flat graver, the round graver,
The angle tint tool wait for him.
He bends to his work and begins.[22]

But as the poem progresses we see this workaday engraver is in fact a hostage to the process and an agent, however unwitting, of violence:

> He starts with the head, cutting in
> To the line of the cheek, finding
> The slope of the skull, incising
> The shape of a face that becomes
> A foundry of shadows, rendering –
> With a deeper cut into copper –
> The whole woman as a skeleton,
> The rags of her skirt, her wrist
> In a bony line forever
>
>   severing
>
> Her body from its native air until
> She is ready for the page,
> For the street vendor, for
> A new inventory which now
> To loss and to laissez-faire adds
> The odor of acid and the little,
> Pitiless tragedy of being imagined.
> He puts his tools away,
> One by one; lays them out carefully
> On the deal table, his work done.[23]

It becomes apparent that the engraver, though he is a broker of a wide societal and even historical violence, is unaware of the moral implications of his own actions. This effect of his image-making on the actual subject is outlined with pessimistic power in 'A Woman Without a Country'.

In the unpublished poem 'Statue' the focus is sharper but comparable. The force of the casting, the bronze image-making, has not only constructed a hero, it has also – according to the figurative language of the poem – robbed the woman of the very origin and identity she is being honoured for: 'A scalding alloy of tin/and copper once rinsed everything out of this head'.[24] When the poem comes to its end, with a compelling irony, the statue, this icon of a history has lost, through the image-making process, her own place. She has become – by a different route but through the same process – a woman without a country:

> a molten bronze flowed out and poured away her name,
> emptying anything that might have been
>
> memory or action and in the end rinsed
> out even the fat apple blossoms of her native Magherlow,
> all flensed off to make this fixed look: to make it seem
> set, seem necessary. And I will never be convinced.[25]

The speaker's inability to be persuaded here returns us to the earlier essay. The fifth section of 'The Woman Poet in a National Tradition' ended with the poet's own need to locate her place in 'a powerful literary tradition' in which until then she had been 'an element of design rather than an agent of change'.[26]

To shift from design to change without availing of the symbolism she has contested has presented her with both a difficulty and a challenge. In *A Journey With Two Maps* she re-states these two aspects, suggesting how by scrutinizing patterns of image-making poets can find a way forward:

> Becoming a poet in the shadow and light of a powerful nationhood is not simple. I imagine a young poet in some other country, standing even now under another window. I imagine them transposing themselves, as I did, into wayward ideas of passion and conviction. It may be that they also will come to believe that challenging an inherited tradition – extricating a poetic identity from parts of it – is an essential part of growth.[27]

In another unpublished poem Boland revisits this theme directly. Called 'Margin', it is loosely grouped in a manuscript with 'Statue'. Its language and reference points indicate that like the previous poem it considers a time of national commemoration as a starting point. However as the poem progresses, it makes radical and deliberately self-limiting suggestions about the poet locating herself in a 'powerful literary tradition'. As such, it provides an important annotation not just of the earlier essay but of Boland's entire body of work.

When the poem begins the speaker is reading. The subject is a scientific anecdote, a reference to the remarkable properties of an insect, the hawk-moth, whose ability to see in the dark, and its purpose in doing so, is the subject of scrutiny. In fact the reference in the poem is not simply figurative; it is contemporary and accurate. A June 2015 BBC report conveys the remarkable ability of the hawk-moth to intensify what it can see in waning light. This adaptation of vision, however, often happens 'to the detriment of their other capabilities such as flight'. In this account the hawk-moth trades speed for vision:

> Scientists from the Georgia Institute of Technology and University of Washington in the US wanted to find out what sort of 'trade-off' makes this behaviour possible in the hawk-moth (*Manduca sexta*), an agile flyer that feeds on nectar at dawn, dusk and through the evening. They discovered that it was able to slow its brain to see better in dim light, while still being capable of hovering in mid-air and tracking the movement of its favourite flowers.[28]

This ability of the hawk-moth will become a figure for different kinds of vision in the poem 'Margin'.

As the poem opens, the speaker is considering these properties, weighing the kinds of sight attained by such a small creature. Here the poet has not yet started to apply these properties to the orders and definitions of vision required to see a national history in a time of commemoration, but she is almost certainly moving in that direction:

> Yesterday I read about the hawk-moth,
> common enough in the west and south
> of this island.

How it can slow down its brain at the end of the day
so as to see better
in failing light,
while evening lifts a flower to its mouth.[29]

The tone of the poem is conversational and, like 'Statue', open in the sense that it does not address any one person or entity. As in 'Statue' the position taken by the speaker is set between retrospect and statement.

But then the poem moves, as 'Statue' does, to a local place, a domestic neighbourhood. Both poems put the speaker firmly in the modest and regional locations of Dublin, in which so many of Boland's poems have been rooted. In so doing, they make a clear statement that this is the place from which the poet intends to make both claim and argument:

Today I waited for the last April cloudiness
to turn dark.
I walked out in our neighborhood as a drizzle
stung my lips and the hills slipped into a horizon[30]

Here the speaker is older. She no longer wonders, as did the young woman in 'Heroic', how the rain would taste if she were a statue, if her lips were made of stone. Her line of vision starts in a neighbourhood, as opposed to a heroic history. But the poem will make clear that the more modest location is also a site of poetry. Suddenly the poem opens into a broader reach, shifting without warning from the acts of reading and walking to a wider perspective in the following two lines, suggesting all of a sudden the moral and ethical responsibilities of history and memory:

How will we see inside our own dusk?
How will we look inside what is to come?

The flags rising. The memories failing.
No one to say who those men in the photograph are.
Old quarrels clothed in a hundred years of heat,
still shivering in the cold.[31]

The reach of these lines reflects a concern found also in 'The Statue', that the collective act of memory must always run the risk of turning into an iconography. That the symbols – 'the flags rising' – will persist even though human thoughts – 'the memories failing' – are not there to underwrite such symbolism. No one, the poem suggests, will be able to identify the actual people from the historical moments. No one can 'say who those men in the photograph are'. And yet the engine of icon, image, symbol, will drive on regardless.

Soon the poem shifts again, this time framing its progress as a small journey, a neighbourhood walk, but with the inference nevertheless of seeing, of pushing through the half-light as the hawk-moth does: 'I walk out past lighted windows, blinds down,/curtains drawn, trying to see what's ahead of me'.[32] The small scale is both important and deceptive. The questions that remain were those raised by Boland three decades earlier in 'The Woman Poet in a National Tradition': questions of representation, of authorship and, beyond that, of who could or should lay claim to a national literature, who could write their name in it.

As that essay came to an end, it seemed to be on the verge of defining a position away from the national collective, away from the general project. Yet the position is never actually defined. What it should *not* be, however, is strongly outlined in the final paragraph of the essay:

> Writers, if they are wise, do not make their home in any comfort within a national tradition. However vigilant the writer, however enlightened the climate, the dangers persist. So too do the obligations. There is a recurring temptation for any nation, and for any writer who operates within its field of force, to make an ornament of the past; to turn the losses to victories and to re-state humiliations as triumphs. In every age language holds out narcosis and amnesia for this purpose.[33]

While the poise Boland appears to be reaching for is not defined in the essay, it seems much closer to definition at the end of this new poem, 'Margin'.

The poem began with the marvellous, off-kilter image of the hawk-moth, a creature both familiar and overlooked, yet for all that capable of a true adventure of flight and perception. Now at the end of the poem, the woman walking in her neighbourhood, simply dressed for the cold – perhaps easy to overlook like the hawk-moth itself – is about to enact her own feat of vision: a narration of her place in this nation and its past which is at last of her own making:

> Dusk is colder now and the intimate unsettled colors
> show me up, a transient,
> a woman dressed for warmth
>
> telling the island to myself, as I always have:
> not the land of fevers and injuries
> we are about to remember.
>
> But the region
> I found for myself, carved out for myself,
> described to myself late at night in my own language.
>
> So I could stand,
> if only for one moment, on its margin.[34]

The context of one phrase is especially important here, in the frame of the earlier essay. It is the line 'telling the island to myself, as I always have'. For the young poet who stood outside a powerful national tradition scrutinizing its patterns of image-making, the narration described here had not seemed within reach.

In the earlier essay Boland describes how she came to an impasse. She could see the importance of the idea of a nation to poetry, but as a woman she felt she had no access to it:

At one point it even looked to me as if the whole thing might be made up of irreconcilable differences … that I was likely to remain an outsider in my own national literature, cut off from its archive, at a distance from its energy.[35]

But the essay also holds out as a possibility the idea that the nation can be repossessed. It is Boland's imagining of this repossession, and the vantage point from which it might be accomplished, that I wish to compare to these last lines of 'Margin', with their confident, assertive claim of narrating the island.

When set against the arguments of the essay, the trajectory of 'Margin' is particularly revealing. In the essay, Boland struggled with how to lay claim to the concept of an island that had been narrated for her, not one she could narrate for herself. But in a key moment in the essay she seems to anticipate the ending of this new poem, so many years away. She is prescient about her own future in considering that perhaps the margin will be the true vantage point for her as a poet:

Marginality within a tradition, however painful, confers certain advantages. It allows the writer clear eyes and a quick critical sense. Above all, the years of marginality suggest to such a writer – and I am speaking of myself now – the real potential of subversion.[36]

Many years later, the poem 'Margin' suggests that Boland has arrived at that relocation. The neighbourhood, the hawk-moth, the evening walk and the cold twilight are all parts of a story she is now able to tell to herself, in her own way and on her own terms.

Telling it on her own terms does not mean the nation is excluded from 'Margin'. The nation is present in the photograph whose subjects can no longer be named. The nation is present in the flags rising as the memories fail. But the location of the poem is no longer the national; instead it is a self-authored place, 'described to myself late at night in my own language'. And the result is an outcome of balance and location: 'So I could stand/if only for one moment, on its margin'.[37]

Speaking at the Abbey Theatre in 2014, President Michael D. Higgins observed of the season of national introspection: 'We need new myths that not only carry the burden of history but fly from it, making something new'.[38] In 'Margin' Boland raises the burden of history not as the land of 'injuries we are about to remember', but as the ethical obligation to find new ways of seeing. As a figure for the poet, the hawk-moth slips from the national harness of hero-making into an image both native and transient. It is this vantage point on the margin that allows the poet to narrate her island.

NOTES

1   It was revised, with title changes along the way, appearing in the LIP pamphlet series as *A Kind of Scar: The Woman Poet in a National Tradition* (Dublin, Attic Press, 1989), and in final form as 'Outside History' in *Object Lessons: The Life of the Woman and the Poet in Our Times* (Manchester, Carcanet, 1995), pp 123–153.

2   Eavan Boland, 1995, p. 134.

3   Angela Bourke, 'Ireland/Herland: Women and Literary Nationalism, 1845–1916', in *The Field Day Anthology of Irish Writing: Volumes IV and V: Irish Women's Writing and Traditions*, edited by Angela Bourke *et al* (New York, New York University UP, 2002), p. 895.

4   Boland, 1995, p. 134.

5   Boland, 1995, p. 61.

6   Eavan Boland, *New Collected Poems* (Manchester, Carcanet, 2005), p. 127.

7   Boland, 2005, p. 127.

8   Eavan Boland, *A Journey With Two Maps: Becoming a Woman Poet* (Manchester, Carcanet, 2011), p. 13.

9   Maud Gonne MacBride, *A Servant of the Queen* (London, Gollancz, 1938).

10 W.B. Yeats, *Autobiographies: The Collected Works of W.B. Yeats Volume III* (New York, Simon and Schuster, 2010), p. 120.

11 C.K. Stead, 'Stendhal's Mirror and Yeats' Looking Glass: A Reconsideration of *The Tower*', in *Answering to the Language: Essays on Modern Writers* (Auckland, Auckland University Press, 1989), pp 29–46 (p. 20).

12 Boland, 2005, p. 269.

13 Helen Lojeck, 'Man, Woman, Soldier: Heaney's "In Memoriam Francis Ledwidge" and Boland's "Heroic"', *New Hibernia Review*, 10.1 (2006), pp 123–38. Reprinted in *Eavan Boland: A Critical Companion*, edited by Jody Allen Randolph (New York, Norton, 2008), pp 179–80.

14 Eavan Boland, 'Statue', November 2015, TS, private papers.

15 *Ibid.*

16 *Ibid.*

17 *Ibid.*

18 *Ibid.*

19 James Mahony, 'Sketches Made in the West of Ireland', *The Illustrated London News*, 22 December 1849, p. 37.

20 'This day is published, price Half-a-Crown, a new and faithful likeness, engraved on steel, of Daniel O'Connell', *The Illustrated London News*, 7 September 1844, p. 159.

21 J. Sterling Coyne and N.P. Willis, *The Scenery and Antiquities of Ireland*, illustrated by W.H. Bartlett (London, James S. Virtue, 1842).

22 Eavan Boland, *A Woman Without a Country* (Manchester, Carcanet, 2014), p. 39.

23 Boland, 2014, pp 39–40.

24 'Statue'.

25 *Ibid.*

26 Boland, 1995, p. 138.

27 Boland, 2014, p. 56.

28 Zoe Gough, 'How a moth slows its brain to see in the dark', *BBC Earth*, 11 June 2015, <http://www.bbc.com/earth/story/20150 610-hawkmoth-slows-brain-to-hover-and-see-in-the-dark> [Accessed 31 October 2015].

29 Eavan Boland, 'Margin', November 2015, TS, private papers.

30 *Ibid.*

31 *Ibid.*

32 *Ibid.*

33 *Object Lessons*, p. 153.

34 'Margin'.

35 *Object Lessons*, p. 128.

36   *Object Lessons*, p. 145.
37   'Margin'.
38   Michael D. Higgins, 'Of Myth-making and Ethical Remembering', keynote address at the Theatre of Memory Symposium, Abbey Theatre, 16 January 2014.

BIBLIOGRAPHY
Boland, Eavan, *A Journey With Two Maps: Becoming a Woman Poet* (Manchester, Carcanet, 2012)
   A Kind of Scar: The Woman Poet in a National Tradition (Dublin, Attic Press, 1989, LIP pamphlet).
   'Margin', November 2015, TS, private papers.
   New Collected Poems (Manchester, Carcanet, 2005).
   'Outside History', *American Poetry Review*, 19.2 (March/April 1990), pp 32–36.
   'Outside History', *Object Lessons: The Life of the Woman and the Poet in Our Times* (Manchester, Carcanet, 1995), pp 123–153.
   'Statue', November 2015, TS, private papers.
   'The Woman Poet in a National Tradition', *Studies*, 76 (Summer 1987), pp 148–58.
   A Woman Without a Country (Manchester, Carcanet, 2014).
Bourke, Angela, 'Ireland/Herland: Women and Literary Nationalism, 1845–1916', in *The Field Day Anthology of Irish Writing Volumes IV and V: Irish Women's Writing and Traditions*, edited by Angela Bourke *et al* (New York, New York University UP, 2002), pp 895–900.
Coyne, J. Sterling and N.P. Willis, *The Scenery and Antiquities of Ireland*, illustrated by W.H. Bartlett, 2 volumes (London, James S. Virtue, 1842).
Gonne MacBride, Maud, *A Servant of the Queen* (London, Gollancz, 1938).
Gough, Zoe, 'How a moth slows its brain to see in the dark', *BBC Earth*, 11 June 2015, <http://www.bbc.com/earth/story/20150610-hawkmoth-slows-brain-to-hover-and-see-in-the-dark> [Accessed 31 October 2015]
Higgins, Michael D., 'Of Myth-making and Ethical Remembering', keynote address by President Michael D. Higgins at the Theatre of Memory Symposium, Abbey Theatre, *President of Ireland: Speeches*, 16 January 2014, <http://www.president.ie/en/media-library/speeches/keynote-address-by-president-michael-d.-

higgins-at-the-theatre-of-memory-sy> [Accessed 1 November 2015]

Lojeck, Helen, 'Man, Woman, Soldier: Heaney's "In Memoriam Francis Ledwidge" and Boland's "Heroic"', *New Hibernia Review*, 10.1 (2006), pp 123–38. Reprinted in *Eavan Boland: A Critical Companion*, edited by Jody Allen Randolph (New York, Norton, 2008), pp 179–80.

Mahony, James, 'Sketches Made in the West of Ireland', *The Illustrated London News*, 22 December 1849, p. 37.

Stead, C.K., 'Stendhal's Mirror and Yeats' Looking Glass: A Reconsideration of *The Tower'*, in *Answering to the Language: Essays on Modern Writers* (Auckland, Auckland University Press, 1989), pp 29–46.

'This day is published, price Half-a-Crown, a new and faithful likeness, engraved on steel, of Daniel O'Connell', *The Illustrated London News*, 7 September 1844, p. 159.

Yeats. W.B., *Autobiographies: The Collected Works of W.B. Yeats Volume 3* (New York, Simon and Schuster, 2010).

Nessa O'Mahony

ROLE REVERSAL
after Eavan Boland

There will come a time, mother,
when the transformed spring opens up
and the charioteer holds out a hand;
he might have my father's face, might not;
his gestures might be gentle or rough
as he eases you into a space made ready
and shows you the pomegranate.
And you will take the seed and eat,
willingly perhaps, not caring
that every bargain has its cost,
or will your hand be stayed
by the sun's ray on your face?
I will not have time to catch up,
to forestall the nine long days,
the nine long nights of wandering.
And I'll have no deal to strike;
no backward glance, no waiting
for the seasons to turn back to me.

TWO POETS AND A CITY:
A CONVERSATION

Eavan Boland and Paula Meehan

Eavan Boland: A Poet's Dublin, edited by Paula Meehan and Jody Allen Randolph, is a collection of Boland's poems concerned with Dublin, selected from her entire published work, alongside her own black and white photographs taken over a three week period in August 2013. It was published by Carcanet Press in 2014, with an introduction by Jody Allen Randolph, her biographer, to celebrate Eavan Boland's seventieth birthday. This conversation between Eavan Boland and Paula Meehan, which took place on the Peacock Stage of the Abbey Theatre in June 2014, is reprinted here with the publisher's permission.

PAULA MEEHAN: You have been going about Dublin with your camera these past few weeks, gathering images to accompany the poems we've chosen. The poems were written at different stages of your life, when you were mapping and negotiating a very particular Dublin; they span something like fifty years. In a way each poem is also a time capsule. So, this August you've been revisiting the places against which the life happened, and in which the life happened – that must be opening emotional channels in memory. How have you found that? What have been the erosions? What has been the most loaded photograph you've taken?

EAVAN BOLAND: It's a good question – to look at what a camera does to and with memory. I have mixed emotions about it. Taking the photos of the city in the last few weeks has made me think about this more carefully. A camera is a heavy-handed editor. The long-ago Dublin that got into my poems is the instinctively discovered city of my late teens and early twenties. As a city, it had some peculiar features. I didn't have an Irish childhood. I was out of the country from the age of five until I was thirteen. I never found those streets as a child. I never met my friends on a certain corner. I didn't take the same bus for years at a time. So there I was walking around Stephen's Green as a student, or going back to Morehampton Road where I had a flat. There was no archive and no name-hoard to help me track what I was doing. All the same I knew it was a place of origin. In fact I was tracking that sense of origin in a more intense, emotional way than I knew at the time. That nameless city is the one in my poems. I wish it could reliably be the one in the photographs. But I don't think it's as easy to find with the lens, the way I found it with language. But now and then something quirky – like the shape of a pepper pot in one of the photos – reminds me that fragments can point at something accurately. Which brings me to a question for you. Both of us are, in our own way, Dublin poets – or at least poets with strong ties to the city. But unlike me, you did have an Irish childhood. In your powerful poem 'The Pattern' you write about 'fitting each surprising/city street to city square to diamond'. Did having that original childhood connection reveal the city to you or hide it from you?

PAULA MEEHAN: My childhood city was the north inner city – Sean MacDermott Street where we lived in one of the corporation tenement flats, the Gloucester Diamond, Mountjoy Square. My parents were back and forth to London throughout the fifties, migrant workers. I was left with my grandparents a good deal: a great blessing. My grandfather taught me to read and write quite early, so I was somewhat equipped to decode the messages I was getting from the city and from the education system. These messages were clear: the poor were corralled into poor housing, the city was divided along class lines, and you stayed in your box. As young girls myself and my classmates were being prepared for work in the sweatshops or in service: modes of being that were already nearly extinct even as we were given the last vestiges of a Victorian education. I was aware quite early that there were vastly different Dublins, depending on your address. I could be in a neighbour's flat with an old woman asleep on straw on the floor covered in old coats or walk with my father to Merrion Square to the Gallery, to the museums, or be brought to Slowey's on Henry Street by my grandmother for a new coat.

I think why I understood your city very well as I began to encounter it in your poems was because I realized that an accent is not a politics.

To all intents and purposes, our maps shouldn't overlap. What I love about poetry is that it makes sectarian or sectional stances redundant. Once, in the eighties, I was in a friend's flat when you came on the radio, reading poetry, talking about poetry, and I said: 'I want to hear this'. One of the women there, an activist, said, 'No you don't, listen to that accent!' There was an argument – about class, about solidarity, about women finding common ground. I was having this argument everywhere, and seeing this argument everywhere. And then it was, suddenly, both a political and a literary argument. About who writes the city. I began to see that the city you were writing into your poems was not a scenic backdrop for the working out of the drama of the self, that, in fact, your relationship was with the *polis*, with the power structures of the state as manifest in architecture, in statuary, in the suffered histories of the excluded as much as in the commemorated and sanctioned official histories. That was very attractive to the combative young woman I was then.

EAVAN BOLAND: The city you describe in this moving way wasn't visible to me. My father was a civil servant. Compared to other people we were secure. Where I could read something different was in the life of my mother. She was a fifth child, her mother dying at thirty-one in Holles Street and her father drowning later in the Bay of Biscay. Much of my childhood was lived out of Ireland. When I came back at fourteen I was just a foggy, displaced teenager with little understanding of my surroundings and even less consciousness of its inequities. So the city you describe wasn't my city. In fact the more I think about a poet in the city – which is what we're talking about – the more it seems to me they build one another out of the materials they already have. In my father's background were British military men, a workhouse master, a Tipperary sergeant. In other words people who could operate the colonial levers in Ireland. Maybe for that reason when I looked at Dublin as a young poet I saw the city through that lens: as a place where colony – the layering of power over people – had happened in a very intense way. When I began to read Yeats something stirred in me about a sensibility that participates in a city's history, and doesn't just witness it. Yeats isn't a Dublin poet. But there's a fraction of his work that hovers above the city all the same. There are his angers in 'September 1913' and his bitterness in 'The Death of Synge'. From reading him and others, I was interested in looking at a city as a place where the ghosts of power are remembered and tested. For me these ghosts are often colonial. But sometimes they're just spirits of place. For all that, I distrust – at least for myself – the idea of being a poet of place. It seems too pastoral, too remote for what I felt when I first thought of myself as a Dubliner. Yet in poems of yours – I'm thinking of 'My Father Perceived as a Vision of St Francis' – place names like Dubber Cross are braided into the lines. Would you call yourself a poet of place?

PAULA MEEHAN: I always puzzled at being told Irish poets have a great *sense of place*. I suspected that underneath was an unstated *and you should stay in your place.* It felt like a simplification: like old-fashioned amateur landscape painting. It has become such a cliché that it masks, possibly drains of power, one of the most vital and crucial acts of the poet, the compact between the non-human and the human. Between the locale and its creatures, what waters and nourishes, as well as what threatens, what grows there. You mention *spirit of place* and this rings truer to me than *sense of place.* We can trace this aspect of our work back to the Dinnseanchas, the responsibility we once had to enshrine, possibly encode, in language the lore and etymology of place. As aboriginals sing Immrama to provide actual maps that can be journeyed on in the here and now, we, underneath all the layers of contemporaneity, real and illusory, still provide a mapping. As one might, should they frack Leitrim, reconstruct from John McGahern's stories an actual mile of hedgerow, as if he had archived it in amber. In the same way we can, from your suburban poems, say, reconstruct or conjure up out of time the forward movement of the city out to the mountains, and learn what it was like to be a woman in a kitchen in those churned-up acres with the smell of new concrete and newly mown grass under the constellations and the shadow of the mountain. I know when I read *Night Feed* and especially *In Her Own Image*, I was inspired to look more intensely at where I actually was, rather than to the unreal place I was told, in subtle and not so subtle ways, I lived in. It encouraged a generation of women, I believe, and their male contemporaries, those who were tuned in to the zeitgeist at least, to go hunt the real poems of their lives in the places where they actually lived. Do you have any sense of how you shifted the ground in this way, for those who came after?

EAVAN BOLAND: I'm not sure I had sense of shifting ground, either for myself or other people. But I know I felt when I came to Dundrum, and began to live a life so many other people lived, that it was largely unrecorded. Why? I think there were odd snobberies and exclusions attached to living in a suburb. When I was a student at Trinity I picked up this sense of two cities. One city gave a distinct feel of being the centre of the earth: that is, the bars, the theatres, the library, the conversations, the events. The Dublin of writers, journalists, artists. I won't say that it was smug. But it was definitely insular. And I picked up something that was almost disdain for this other Dublin, the place where I would end up living in a few years. Where meals were put on the table, and children had to go to school, and people had to catch the last bus, and pay their rates. It was deemed to be anti-intellectual. And I want to be fair here. Ireland, in the sixties, was only beginning to shake off the grip of small-minded conventions and over-religious influence. Writers and intellectuals in the forties – I'm thinking particularly of *The Bell* and Seán Ó Faoláin – had done their best to open out a conversation about Irish life. So there was some honest tension between this vibrant urban centre and this more orthodox perimeter where people lived so-called conventional lives. The danger was that the first would try to ordain what was a fit subject for literature, for poetry, and assume it could never come from this conventional world. So when I migrated from one world to the other, and from one part of Dublin to the other – from being a student to being a family woman – my sense of a divided city was very sharp. I learned to write poetry in one. But I lived the poems I wanted to write in the other. Now in 'The Pattern' the voice of the mother at the end says 'One of these days I must/teach you to follow a pattern'. Did you feel any conflict in terms of living the poem, or selecting its subject matter between the life you came from and the city where you began to be a poet?

PAULA MEEHAN: We moved from the north inner city out to Finglas, to the edge of a new estate, as I came into my teens. It was the end of the sixties and free education saw me in the local convent school, constantly in trouble, and having a great time in the new, or what felt like a new, youth culture. There was a vibrancy in music, folk and rock; in poetry, the Beats and the Liverpool poets were very influential and there were counter cultural energies. This was a culture of the streets so far removed from what we were getting in school that something had to give. I was expelled by the nuns, which in retrospect was the best thing that ever happened to me: I learned the habit of self direction and independent study. And I started writing song lyrics, which connected to my readings in the tradition especially the Romantics, Shelley and Keats and Coleridge, and of course Yeats who seemed a natural inheritor of their energies. From my inner city childhood I had begun to experience the city as a palimpsest – Brendan Behan's Dublin I knew well from the tenements; and he was the first actual writer I saw – my father pointed him out to me. He was staggering from Murray's public house in Sean MacDermott Street. 'A great writer, but a terrible messer', was my father's verdict. The tenement plays of Sean O'Casey were wonderfully affirmative as I had lived amongst the children and grandchildren of his characters and I never agreed with the notion that he wrote caricatures – if people have nothing except their personalities then there is an art to their being in the world which might come across as larger than life. And James Joyce, when I came to his work, had another map, more difficult but a model for an endless dance in words with the city. You can see from the names that I had no female models as writers when I was young. The only woman on the Leaving Certificate syllabus was Emily Dickinson. One might argue that her specific gravity is so intense that it would be sufficient. And of course you could sing *her* lyrics if you had a tune. But *your* mapping of Dublin in your poems, which I came across in my mid-twenties, was really the start of believing that what I might make of the inherited patternings of my mother and grandmother, their wisdom and their silences, would be as important to me as the yang side of the legacy. And quite simply I just loved the city. Though sometimes it was very hard to live here – I had left home by the time I was seventeen and was a student at Trinity College, staying just one step ahead of the posse, always on the brink of homelessness or living in some terrible kips.

'Ireland as distinct from her people, is nothing to me', said James Connolly, another persuasive writer when I was beginning to make poems. I wanted to honour the lives I saw, lives of deprivation but also of great courage and, of course, great humour, which is the signature mode of the city – as I'm sure you've found yourself. I think there was a moment when I began to take the city personally. I was emotionally and psychically bound up in making a poem that would somehow resonate with the timbre of the Dublin accent itself, with the remnants of a powerful oral tradition that came to me in songs and stories and daily ramblings about the streets. Whenever I'm away and I come back it hits me, that accent which should probably have a preservation order slapped on it, it hits me in the gut. And, we live in a kind of wonderful Babel now: so many languages snagging at the ear as we walk about the city. As if *Finnegans Wake* has come home to us. I would prophesy that the new poetries of the city will come from out of the struggle of the new Irish to tell of their lives, their fluencies and their hesitations, with all the ghosts of their ancestors' song and poetry traditions. Do you ever get that sense that we will have new versions of Dublin beyond our wildest imaginings in the coming generations?

EAVAN BOLAND: Cities certainly have a way of reinventing themselves. And usually from the margins, not the centre. So I'm absolutely ready to believe that some great redefining energies will come from the new Irish. It's a matter, to use your phrase, of 'taking the city personally'. I did at one point. But I didn't have, and didn't look for, what you describe as 'the remnants of a powerful oral tradition'. I didn't have access to it. My first real connection to the city came in the years after I left boarding school. Especially when I was a student. What I remember most is walking down from Trinity on those pre-winter evenings when there seemed to be a kind of violet-coloured, cloudy sky overhead. I would walk down Grafton Street and past Stephen's Green and on down Merrion Row towards Morehampton Road where I lived. And it wasn't a city of voices to me. It was a city of ideas, and the ideas were inside my head. Some of them were just the sparks flown off from a kind of displacement. I'd spent a good part of my childhood, in London and New York, knowing I didn't come from the places I lived in. Now, here was a place I lived in that I also came from. And yet I didn't have a history with it. I didn't have a childhood I could map onto it. So I found some comfort in making my own map back then. Printing that part of my life, in the most fractional way, on the railings, the roads, the buildings, the bus stops. It was as if I'd been dropped into a story with no chapter headings. All of this is by way of saying that my city wasn't communal as I think yours was – at least not at that point. I didn't seek to be a communal poet, which I think has been such a strength in your work. It was a solitary enough encounter for me. At least at first. And it didn't really prepare me for that extension of the city, and that disruption of it I would find later. My life in the suburb proved to be such a contrast. Suddenly – well not suddenly, I suppose, but it felt like it – I was in a communal situation. The city all around me then, which had crept out to the Dublin foothills, was a city of houses, families, all those tentacles of important, delicate connections. I knew perfectly well that the people I first met, that I considered 'literary', would disdain that city. But I wanted to include it. It was now the location of my life. So that makes me curious. Did you feel there were several cities for you as you wrote Dublin poems? Or one coherent space?

PAULA MEEHAN: Yes – cities within cities, nestled like Russian Matryoshka dolls, and the myriad cities all internalised, a kind of inner city within the boundary of the skin. The poem might integrate the inner and the outer cities into a kind of *ur*-city. For instance, I think of a poem I wrote in 1982, 'Buying Winkles': it comes from a note in a journal of 1979, remembering a scene from when I was a child of eight; it's set on Gardiner Street, not far from

Mountjoy Square where I lived in the mid-seventies as a student. There are layers of memory in this poem, people dead and alive, all looking for attention. The neighbours of my childhood would have been invisible to my student friends living on the very same street. I feel now I was constantly negotiating across the lines, translating, almost, one community to another. The poem, as it happens, found its final form in the nineties, in some quiet garden or in a coffee shop, I don't quite remember which.

The process of making the poem is not usually happening at the same speed as is your life. Just now, I counted up the addresses I have had in the city and it comes in at around thirty. If there is a rootedness it is probably wishful thinking, or perhaps a willed and quite likely simplified narrative.

And now consider the other games that are being played, when you sit down to work with a poem: with the language itself, English and its imperial nature, our resistant version of it, the beautiful words with their own histories, their ghosts; the play with the shape of the poem, which might rhyme or use some demented and obsessive syllabic structure (maybe just to keep from getting bored?). The way a poem lets you hold so much in mind. That excites me. It's the hit I get from making a poem. Why I go back again and again, craving the making.

Aren't we always making the city up? The cities?

EAVAN BOLAND: Talking about inventing cities brings me to something else I'm curious about. Who do you think wrote well about Dublin? Was there some piece about it that seemed instructive to you as a poet? For myself, I can think of two examples. That is, leaving aside James Joyce who plainly owned the city in a defining way. But apart from Joyce here are two of the writings I think of. The first is Beckett's 'Dante and the Lobster'. That main character is so inward, fussy, a wonderful anti-hero of micro thoughts and obsessions. He ponders his lunch within an inch of its life. He seems remote from anything practical. But all the same, late in the story he visits the house of his Aunt. 'Let us call it Winter, that dusk may fall now', he writes. And then lists the sights he sees on the way. A horse lying down, with a man sitting on its head. About which he puts in a wonderful Beckett observation: 'I know, thought Belacqua, that that is considered the right thing to do. But why?' Then there's a lamplighter 'who flew by on his bike', and a couple standing in 'the bay of a pretentious gateway'. The story only names fractions of the city that identify it – like Mountjoy Gaol and *The Evening Herald*. But it evokes the atmosphere. Then the second example for me is Louis MacNeice's 'Dublin' where he says almost at the outset 'This was never my town'. And the wry catalogue of objects and aspects that follows that – it's so eloquent, and moving: 'She is not an Irish town/And she is not English,/Historic with guns and vermin/And the cold renown/Of a fragment of Church Latin'. And of course there were lines in the poem that especially spoke to me: 'But yet she holds my mind/With her seedy elegance,/With her gentle veils of rain/And all her ghosts that walk/And all that hide behind/Her Georgian façades'. Obviously I couldn't see MacNeice's Dublin in the way he saw it. He was a sophisticated migrant and an ironist. Two things I was never going to be. But when I felt like an outsider myself, having come back to the city late, and without the language of a childhood lived there, I particularly liked this passage. Were there writings on Dublin that you turned to when you thought about being a poet in and of the city?

PAULA MEEHAN: 'Micro thoughts and obsessions' – the city moving through consciousness. Beckett said his favourite view in Dublin was up on Feltrim Hill in Kinsealy, from where he could look east and north to Portrane Lunatic Asylum – I read him with a Dublin accent, it doubles the humour. *At Swim Two Birds,* Flann O'Brien's meta romp, had cowboys and codders, general mayhem all over Dublin, a shaggy dog story writ large. A curious short novel by James Stephens was a set text in school and deeply affected the way I read the city: *The Charwoman's Daughter,* the chronicle of Mrs Makebelieve's grooming of her daughter, Mary, for the better things in life. The gulf between the brutal reality of her life and her dreaming aspirations for the girl struck home. Even though the novel was published in 1912 it felt like an accurate template for a kind of sad Dublin, of the thwarted yearnings that I saw around me when I was a girl.

I found Anna Akhmatova's Leningrad or Allen Ginsberg's New York most useful as guides for making poems about Dublin. The ferocious and loving attention they brought to their cities was an inspiration to me. Gary Snyder's Kyoto, ancient city of Buddhist temples and modern site of Beat satori, made me determined to write a city of parks and ecstatic delight as well as tenements and the suffered histories. I loved the way he saw a skyscraper as a gravel streambed set on edge. The way the city was also part of nature, as we are, and subject to the same forces and processes. How he saw the raw materiality of the made world, very like the way indeed your daughter of colony wears a straw bonnet made from an Irish field. Or how in your poems water is the undersong everywhere in the city and its hinterlands, an insistent reminder of source and resource.

I know you've said you are not a nature poet, or rather, that you're an indoor nature poet; and you rightly distrust the dead hand of the pastoral tradition, or its modern derivative, the mannered set-pieces of something called 'nature' as a mere backdrop to some anthropocentric, even separatist stance.

One of the most powerful elements in the *A Poet's Dublin* selection of your city poems is the appearance, the manifestation even, of those two ghost wolves at the very edge of the city in the poem 'Once'. As if they had strolled out of aboriginal mind, which I believe to be the antithesis and possibly salvific antidote to the institutionalized mind. As if they had urgent news for us. They break my heart.

> Irish wolves. A silvery man and wife.
> Yellow-eyed. Edged in dateless moonlight.
> They are mated for life. They are legendary. They are safe.

The way they come out of the ghost forest that was once your suburb of Dundrum, how you recreate the thrushes that sang in the ghost tree where your house now stands. The coming together of these histories in place, histories human and creaturely, amplifies our vulnerability, intimates our own threatened survival.

EAVAN BOLAND: 'Threatened survival' is such an interesting phrase. And together with it, you mention a name there that belongs with that idea, a poet we both admire: Anna Akhmatova. In her great poem 'Epilogue to the Requiem' she writes about St Petersburg, although of course at the time of the poem, in the early 1940s, it was Leningrad. She describes the Stalinist Terror, the endless lining up at the prison gates, where her son was, the sounds of anguish in the prison queue. She ends by saying that if they ever want to make a statue of her, it should be placed near the prison gates where she shared that ordeal with others. One translation reads: 'Lest in blessed death I should ever forget/The grinding scream of the Black Marias'. I think of that because it's a gesture that radicalizes a poet's relation with a city. That makes the reader see a different reality. And it shows Akhmatova's willingness to see a city within a city. After all, as a young woman and a young poet in the Stray Dog Cabaret she lived in an entirely different place: bohemian, welcoming, exuberant. I'm interested in that idea of a city within a city. Sometimes in Dublin I see traces of a colony within a colony. For instance, it's striking to me that the statues of male writers and orators in Dublin are official, named and legible. Kavanagh by the canal. Oscar Wilde. Grattan. Burke. O'Connell. Parnell. But the women statues are women out of a song, like Molly Malone, or out of a place myth like Anna Liffey, or anonymous like the two women chatting on the bench. I think that my original uneasiness when I went from being a student to living in a suburb had something to do with my sense that the bias against the dailyness of an ordinary neighbourhood, in terms of art or ideas, was a sort of extension of a colonial attitude. In Akhmatova's case, speaking of a city within a city, there's a clear fracture between her first graceful, bohemian city and the dark prison of Leningrad during the war. Here in Dublin I can connect the historic city with the present day one. When you think of your relation to Dublin, the city you write about, is it always in the present? I think of you as staying in that zone a little bit more than I do. My poems wander a bit more backwards. But I know you've been acutely aware of the history of the city in your poems both as art and architecture.

PAULA MEEHAN: There's a fine bust of Constance Markievicz by the Cork sculptor Seamus Murphy in St Stephen's Green, but you're right, there's a paucity of memorials to actual women. I love Rachel Joynt's sculpture on the southern side of O'Connell Bridge. Its foot prints, paw prints, shoe prints, heel prints, high-heel prints, bird tracks, cat tracks, in various metals laid flush to the concrete of the traffic island. I love it because its not an erection – you have to be crossing the road to actually see it and you see it best by walking over it. And it captures perfectly the random contacts and passings that one makes in the city. And, remarkably, we will have the Rosie Hackett Bridge, our newest bridge over the Liffey connecting Abbey Street to Hawkins Street and named for a lifelong trade unionist and member of the Irish Citizen Army.

I'm very interested in what you say about the traces of colony you found and find – a hurt or wounded city within the quotidian city. There's a sense always in Dublin of the traumatised city: it hovers in a name change perhaps, New Brunswick Street becomes Pearse Street, Rutland Square becomes Parnell Square, it shimmers around erosions and accretions both. James Joyce Street now where we had Montgomery Street, in the heart of the old red-light district.

I have a family connection there – my great grandmother Anna Meehan was a madame at the turn of the nineteenth century when Monto was the biggest red-light district in Europe. A hidden history in our family; I came to it late when Terry Fagan of the Inner City Folklore Project walked up to me one day and said 'I've great stuff on your great-granny'.

I know I've been accused (and accused is the accurate word) of something called identity politics in my poetry and I know you have too. Poems of yours like 'Making Money', a true act of empathy with the paper mill workers of turn-of-the-nineteenth-century Dundrum, a poem wonderfully rich in the detail of the toxic process and drudgery of making paper for the printing of banknotes, for an empire gearing up for a war that would render the banknotes themselves redundant. I was astonished at the negative reaction to that poem. You were accused (that word again!), bizarrely, of appropriating the sufferings of those women. Why do you think an act of compassion would so annoy a critic?

I remember a girl in my class in The Central Model Girls' School, a beautiful child called Clare, who died of diphtheria in the early sixties. Diptheria! She lived in a two-room flat with her parents and twelve siblings in corporation buildings. That experience and many others like it haunted, and I believe formed, my imagination. Why shouldn't I remember Clare in a poem?

The seven tower blocks of Ballymun, named for the executed leaders of the 1916 Rising, became a byword for disastrous urban planning within one generation. Ill-conceived, ill-managed and eventually demolished. We played as young teenagers in the foundations, having walked across the back fields from Finglas. Am I supposed not to remember this, to speak of this?

Then there were the inner-city flat complexes named for Marian shrines and Catholic saints: Lourdes House, Fatima Mansions (where I lived for a few years in the eighties), St Mary's Mansions: communities in crisis as traditional sources of work in the city disappeared. You'd need a miracle to get housed out of them was the joke. I remember attending funeral after funeral, burying the brightest and the best of the kids as heroin swept like a juggernaut through the poor communities. Should I not speak of this?

I had to believe that there was a home in poetry for the lives I saw about me. I had to believe I could find a language to honour the courage I saw everywhere.

And to loop back to your question – I saw the historic city as something you could read like a text, that would, through close study, yield up its mysteries, and make sense of the sociology, if you like, of the lives I witnessed. The deeper I dug into the past of the city, the more sense I could make of what I was seeing lived out in the present moment.

To walk the streets of the city was, is, to stroll at will through the layers of its making and its peopling, to learn to place a particular building within its era, to see the lineaments of the Viking city, the Christian settlements, the Norman castle, the Georgian mansions, and then the famine cabins of the backstreets, the stables and abattoirs down the mews lanes. All that, and always the lives lived there.

But, I have a sense also of something else at work – a kind of dream city or dreaming city. It doesn't exactly map on to any known verifiable place. It's the private sonic Dublin each poet makes – the individuated song of the self in place, the free self in the given place. Maybe that's our true city?

EAVAN BOLAND: In her book of essays, *Blood, Bread and Poetry*, Adrienne Rich has a powerful statement about poetry and politics. And it touches on 'appropriation'. Here's what she says:

> There were many voices then, as there are now, warning the North American artist against 'mixing politics with art'. I have been trying to retrace, to delineate, these arguments, which carry no weight for me now because I recognize them as the political declarations of privilege. Perhaps many fear an overtly political art because it might persuade us emotionally of what we think we are 'rationally' against; it might get us to a level we have lost touch with, undermine the safety we have built for ourselves, remind us of what is better left forgotten.

I agree with Rich. Critics who attach the word 'appropriation' to subjects that make them uncomfortable tend to be white, academic, and they usually aim the argument at women. And that simply isn't a sophisticated or textually sound approach to a poem. The truth is that any poet should have whatever license he or she needs to broaden the poem in a political or public way. Some of the most powerful poems of the century come from that broadening – Ginsberg's 'Howl', 'North American Time' by Rich, 'Sunday Morning' by Lowell.

Of course, it's ridiculous to think a poet like yourself could be open to those censorships. But let's not forget that one noted critic wrote at the time of publication about 'Howl': 'It is only fair to Allen Ginsberg ... to remark on the utter lack of decorum of any kind in his dreadful little volume'. And this was in the *Partisan Review*. So critics about to launch criticisms at political or public poetry should read that line and pause. Ginsberg's 'dreadful little volume' went on to define the innovative, committed public poem for our time. The critic did not.

I think for any poet writing about a city, the balance between public and private becomes key. That's why I'm so interested in your comment about a city that 'doesn't exactly map on to any known verifiable place'. I think any poet can have that dream city. Some of *Ulysses* gets its great texture and sweetness from the dream city at the beginning. And when Stephen Dedalus begins his great walk through the city in *A Portrait of the Artist as a Young Man* it seems to be half a dream. Then again in 'The Dead' the real city of music, posture, conversation, food and conviviality gives way to that dreaming, snowy Dublin in which revelation happens. I'm curious. Is Joyce's evocation of Dublin one you found instructive?

PAULA MEEHAN: I loved *Dubliners*. To walk the named fictional streets and the real streets as I was reading it, so many of the buildings extant before my eyes, was really exciting, quite apart from the characters, types easily translatable to the characters I saw around me. Joyce's north cityscapes themselves were intact if you squinted past Busarus and Liberty Hall and didn't stray too far beyond Glasnevin.

But there's a strange thing: I heard *Ulysses* first before I read it. One long winter with no money, no television, no phone, before mobiles or internet, it was read to me; sure what else would you be doing? The perfect virtual experience. What abundance now to remember! When I came to the text I found it a hard read, harder to read than to listen to. Joyce must have heard them very clearly, the voices of the city, his remembered city: such prodigious recall and invention. But *Finnegans Wake* is of a different order of challenge. It demands a huge amount of surrender. Surrender just to the heft of it as sound; as text it can sometimes feel more like the experience of doing a cryptic crossword.

Olwen Fouéré has made a theatre piece of a section of the novel – and in a sense it will always be a work in progress for its readers. I think it will be mined and retrieved and deconstructed and reconstructed and retrofitted for generations to come. I felt that *Finnegans Wake* was making me up as I read it.

Here's a question for you: Would you have written very different poems if Joyce had not so exhaustively written the city? And perhaps a second question: did you ever find yourself writing, or find you had written, in counterpoint to Joyce? Is he a ghost you'd tangle with in the way, say, you so obviously tangle with Yeats?

EAVAN BOLAND: I first came on Joyce in a roundabout way. I was back in Ireland, at boarding school in Killiney. My godparents lived in Sandycove, and I visited their house often because I was a friend of their daughter. The owner of the house, my godfather, the architect Michael Scott, had bought and built on that land in the 1940s – right there in Sandycove – and the Martello Tower went with the purchase. So there I was at about fifteen, lucky enough to be able to go up to the top of the tower often, and in different seasons, and look out at the view Stephen Dedalus sees in the first chapter of *Ulysses*. It was one of my first panoramas of the city. The long view of

Sandymount Strand in the distance, the harbour and, of course, Stephen's 'bowl of bitter waters'. A little later, as a teenager, trying to read *Ulysses,* a fair amount of it defeated me. But the first part was always crystal clear, maybe because I could visualize it from those times standing at the top of the tower. It was the first time I had the experience that gradually led to me realising that a city could be mapped, not just by cartography or history, but by instinct, memory, passion. That certainly had an influence on me. But to answer the question, I don't think I ever wrote in counterpoint to Joyce. Nor was he a ghost I tangled with. I thought of him as a writer who had lent extraordinary dignity to the city we all lived in by mapping it with his losses and his feelings. But I saw a different city. Because I was a young woman, when I started, very unsure where my name could be found, or – to put it more exactly – fairly sure it couldn't be found, I saw a city where inscriptions of authority and power, of colony and history, were everywhere. It made me think. Who writes a city? When I was seventeen I had a summer job at the Gresham Hotel. It comes into one of the poems, 'Unheroic'. When I came out at the end of the day I sometimes looked at Parnell's statue with the inscription 'No man has a right to fix the boundary to the march of a nation'. I came to feel very resistant to that rhetoric. The city I began to build for myself was seen through that resistance. So no, Joyce was a gift and a grace but not in any way a Jacob's angel.

PAULA MEEHAN: I'm sitting in the back bedroom of the house with a rough version of this book [*A Poet's Dublin*] printed off (*plain paper, fast, black and white*). Your poems and photographs cover the floor. I have spent the last while arranging and rearranging the running order. Soon I will talk to Jody who is in New York and we will no doubt shift and rearrange again as we have all been doing over the last while. There's the statuary – Emmet, O'Connell. There are the made images – Anna Liffey's river head wired up for illumination, a portrait your mother Frances Kelly painted, of you with one of the dolls from a collection she later gave to The Dolls Museum. The dramas of the poems are set against these peaceful, composed photographs, distanced in black and white. Text ironizes some of the images. You may not be an ironist in poetry but the photographs are loaded: '*Ailesbury*' carved in granite in a suburb, Dundrum, which translates as The Fort of the Ridge, the ghost of colony spilling out into the suburbs laying a pretentious naming over green field sites. '*Meadowbrook*' how far from Cluainabhainn or any native under-naming? Was there a meadow? Was there a brook? The mother tongue displaced in the Pale by the step-mother tongue of empire. And then the image of the text of '*Dundrum Town Centre*', signage that surely signifies late-century capitalism, mall culture. And the quote from Damien Dempsey's song lyric painted along the docks in retro Dublin lettering, a homage to the signwriters of our childhoods from the artist Maser.

And those two heartbreaking monuments to lost children: the plaque of your poem 'Tree of Life' in Merrion Square (Archbishop Ryan Park, to give it its official name) that commemorates the babies who died in the nearby National Maternity Hospital. And the monument to the victims of the 1974 Dublin and Monaghan Bombings that accompanies your poem 'Child of Our Time'. That sad roll call of names whose families still haven't had justice, still no proper calling to account of the perpetrators of those murders and their enablers.

And here, as elsewhere, the monument speaks to the living memory. I remember that bombing as a huge trauma for the city. Everyone was connected to somebody who was affected either directly or indirectly. I narrowly missed walking into the Lincoln Gate explosion and I finally understood what it must be like to live in a city during a war. It made a lifelong pacifist of me. And though you may not be aware of this, many people took ownership of your poem; I saw it torn from the newspaper and thumbtacked or sellotaped up on many walls. Some years ago when I was involved in a commemoration for the victims, it was still on the lips of the bereaved families. It meant such a great deal to them, and still does.

I have always sensed that poetry is public speech. A communal art. You spoke once of the journey being one from self-expression to art. I experience poetry as public speech. It pre-dates literature. It's not the same thing as literature, though since moveable type was invented it has a long and fascinating relationship with the book. What it carries over from its oral days can sometimes be mere ornament or mannerism. But even where on the surface it deals with private narratives, or coded, secret narratives, even where the poet pushes the language itself to the edge of glossolalia or, as Beckett might put it, *divine aphasia*, the poem still desires another human consciousness to resonate with or through.

EAVAN BOLAND: I admire that definition of a communal poet and it seems in keeping with it how you see poetry as public speech. I hesitate around those issues, although I think the conversation about a communal art is important. It all depends how you think about the word, even the concept behind it. That adjective 'communal' has a related verb – an old fashioned one – which is communing. A word I've always loved. And one, when you look at it, that's quite a bit removed from the adjective that seems close to it. For me, even when a poem is not apparently communal, even when it seems to be private, it can still commune. In fact it may make a particularly strong community with a reader, and still not be communal, just by speaking to and of solitude, their own inwardness. That communion seems to me valuable: truly one of the great possibilities for the poem. But I don't think of it as public speech. So do we differ on that? We probably do. And that seems a very good moment to approach the end of this conversation on the city, which I've so enjoyed. Because if we differ, it only proves again what we already know: that Dublin is a chameleon city – one that's always generated different writing, different perspectives, different poems, different poets. Which is as it should be.

EAVAN BOLAND:
SHORT BIBLIOGRAPHY

Books:

23 Poems (Dublin, Gallagher, 1962)

Autumn Essay (Dublin, Gallagher, 1963)

New Territory (Dublin, Allen Figgis, 1967)

The War Horse (London, Gollancz, 1975; Dublin, Arlen House, 1980)

In Her Own Image (Dublin, Arlen House, 1980)

Introducing Eavan Boland (New York, Ontario Review Press, 1981)

Night Feed (Dublin, Arlen House, 1982)

The Journey (Deerfield, Deerfield Press and Dublin, Gallery Press, 1983)

The Journey and Other Poems (Dublin, Arlen House, 1986; Manchester, Carcanet Press, 1987)

Selected Poems (Manchester, Carcanet Press in association with WEB [Women's Educational Bureau], 1989)

Outside History: Selected Poems, 1980–1990 (New York, Norton, 1990)

Outside History (Manchester, Carcanet Press, 1990)

In a Time of Violence (New York, Norton, 1994)

A Christmas Chalice (Buffalo, State University of New York, 1994)

Collected Poems (Manchester, Carcanet Press, 1995) published as *An Origin Like Water: Collected Poems, 1967–1987* (New York, Norton, 1996)

Object Lessons: The Life of the Woman and the Poet in Our Time (Manchester, Carcanet Press, 1995); published (New York, Norton, 1995); republished (London, Vintage, 1996)

Anna Liffey (Dublin, Poetry Ireland, 1997)

The Lost Land (New York, Norton, 1998)

Limitations (New York, Center for the Book Arts, 2000)

Against Love Poetry (New York, Norton, 2001); published as *Code* (Manchester, Carcanet Press, 2001)

New Collected Poems (Manchester, Carcanet Press, 2005)

Domestic Violence (New York, Norton, 2007)

New Collected Poems (New York, Norton, 2008)

A Journey with Two Maps (New York, Norton, 2011)

New Selected Poems (Manchester, Carcanet Press, 2013)

A Woman Without a Country (Manchester, Carcanet Press, 2014)

Eavan Boland: A Poet's Dublin edited by Paula Meehan and Jody Allen Randolph (Manchester, Carcanet Press, 2014)

Other:

W. B. Yeats and His World, Boland with Micheál MacLiammóir (London, Thames and Hudson, 1971); republished (New York: Thames and Hudson, 1986)

A Kind of Scar: The Woman Poet in a National Tradition, LIP pamphlet (Dublin, Attic Press, 1989); republished in *A Dozen Lips* (Dublin, Attic Press, 1994)

Gods Make Their Own Importance: The Authority of the Poet in Our Time (London, Poetry Book Society Productions, 1994)

Introduction, *Adrienne Rich, Selected Poems 1950–1995* (Co. Clare, Salmon Poetry, 1996)

Committed to Memory: 100 Best Poems to Memorize, edited by Eavan Boland with John Hollander (New York, Riverhead Books, 1997)

The Making of a Poem: A Norton Anthology of Poetic Forms, co-edited by Eavan Boland with Mark Strand (New York, Norton, 2000)

Journey with Two Maps: An Anthology, edited by Eavan Boland (Manchester, Carcanet Press, 2002)

Three Irish Poets: An Anthology: Eavan Boland, Paula Meehan, Mary O'Malley, edited by Boland (Manchester, Carcanet Press 2003)

After Every War: Twentieth-Century Women Poets, compiled and translated by Eavan Boland (Princeton, Princeton University Press, 2006)

Irish Writers on Writing (The Writer's World) edited by Eavan Boland (San Antonio, Trinity University Press, 2007)

The Selected Poems of Charlotte Mew, edited by Eavan Boland (Manchester, Carcanet Press, 2008)
The Making of a Sonnet: A Norton Anthology, co-edited by Eavan Boland with Ed Hirsch (New York, Norton, 2008)

Interviews (selected):

Deborah Tall, 'Question and Answer with Eavan Boland', *Irish Literary Supplement* (Fall 1988), p. 39.

Marilyn Reizbaum, 'An Interview with Eavan Boland', *Contemporary Literature* 30.4 (1989), pp 471–479.

Deborah McWilliams Consalvo, 'Between Rhetoric and Reality: An Interview with Eavan Boland', *Studies: An Irish Quarterly Review* 81.321 (1992), pp 89–100.

Jody Allen Randolph, 'An Interview with Eavan Boland', *PN Review*, 20.1 (1993), pp 52–57.

Neil Sammells, 'An Underground Poet: Eavan Boland talks to Neil Sammells', *Irish Studies Review* 4 (1993), pp 12–13.

Eileen Battersby, 'The Beauty of Ordinary Things: An Interview with Eavan Boland', *The Irish Times*, 22 September 1998, pp 1–5.

Vicki Bertram, 'Defining Circumstances: An Interview with Eavan Boland', *PN Review*, 25.2 (1998).

Jody Allen Randolph, 'A Backward Look: An Interview with Eavan Boland', *PN Review*, 26.5 (2000), pp 43–48.

Elizabeth Schmidt, 'Where Poetry Begins: An Interview with Eavan Boland', www.poets.org/viewmedia.php/prmMID/15939>, 2001.

Anne Fogarty, 'Imagination Unbound: Eavan Boland interviewed', *The Irish Book Review* 1.3 (2005), pp 32–33.

Pilar Villar-Argáiz, 'The Text of It: A Conversation with Eavan Boland', *New Hibernia Review* 10.2 (2006), pp 52–67.

Pilar Villar-Argáiz, 'Poetry as a Humane Enterprise: Interview with Eavan Boland on the Occasion of the 50th Anniversary of her Literary Career', *Estudios Irlandeses* 7 (2012), pp 113–120.

Bibliographies:

Jody Allen Randolph, *Eavan Boland: A Sourcebook* (Manchester, Carcanet Press, 2007; New York, Norton 2008)

Jody Allen Randolph, 'Eavan Boland Checklist: A Selected Bibliography', *Irish University Review: Special Issue Eavan Boland* 23.1 (1993), pp 5–22.

JODY ALLEN RANDOLPH is currently a research fellow at the Centre for Gender, Culture and Identities at the Humanities Institute at University College Dublin. Previously she lectured in the graduate program in the School of English, Drama & Film at University College Dublin, and served as Assistant Dean of the British Studies at Oxford Programme at St. John's College, Oxford. During her graduate studies at the University of California, Santa Barbara she held research fellowships from the Andrew Mellon/Woodrow Wilson National Fellowship Foundation, the Interdisciplinary Humanities Center and University of California Regents. Jody's research and teaching specialties are Irish literature and culture and Anglophone literatures. Her most recent books are *A Poet's Dublin*, co-edited with Paula Meehan (Carcanet, 2014), *Eavan Boland* (Cork University Press, 2014), and *Close to the Next Moment: Interviews from a Changing Ireland* (Carcanet, 2010).

Born in Dublin in 1959, the poet, playwright and novelist DERMOT BOLGER has also worked as a factory hand, library assistant and publisher. In 2012 he published his ninth poetry collection, *The Venice Suite: A Voyage Through Loss*, which commemorated his late wife, Bernie, who died in 2010. He also published his first ever novella that year, entitled *The Fall of Ireland*. He has published nine novels, and numerous stage plays.

PATRICIA BOYLE HABERSTROH, Professor Emerita of Art History and of English at La Salle University in Philadelphia, received her Ph.D. from Bryn Mawr and has been a Fulbright Fellow at University College Dublin. She serves on the Editorial Board of the *New Hibernia Review* and has published four books: *Women Creating Women* (1996), *My Self, My Muse, Irish Women Poets Reflect on Life and Art* (2001), *Opening the*

Field, co-edited with Christine St Peter (2007), and *The Female Figure in the Poetry of Eiléan Ní Chuilleanáin* (2013).

SIOBHAN CAMPBELL's collections include *Cross-Talk* and *That Water Speaks in Tongues*. Her fourth, *Heat Signature,* will be published by Seren in 2017. She has won awards in the National and the Troubadour International Competition and recently was awarded the Oxford Brookes International Poetry Prize. She is on faculty at The Open University, Department of English. Her work is anthologised widely including in *The Field Day Anthology of Irish Literature* (NYU Press), *Identity Parade* (Bloodaxe) and *The Golden Shovel Anthology* for Gwendolyn Brooks (University of Arkansas Press). Her criticism appears in *Poetry London* and *Poetry Ireland* as well as in *The Portable Poetry Workshop* (Palgrave) and *Making Integral: Critical Essays on Richard Murphy* (CUP).

MOYA CANNON has published five collections of poetry, her most recent being *Keats Lives* (Carcanet Press, 2015). Her poems reflect preoccupations with landscape and seascape, with archaeology, with music, with language itself and with our visceral attachment to the beauty of the earth. The work sings of deep connections – the impulse to ritual and pattern that, across centuries, defines us as human, a web of interdependences that continue to sustain the 'gratuitous beauty' of our endangered earth. Her previous collection, *Hands* (Carcanet Press, 2011) was nominated for the 2012 *Irish Times*/Poetry Now Award.

LUCY COLLINS joined UCD in 2008 after previously teaching at Trinity College Dublin and in the UK at the University of Cumbria. A graduate of Trinity College Dublin, where she completed both her BA and PhD degrees, she spent a year at Harvard University on a Fulbright Postdoctoral Fellowship. Her research interests are in poetry and poetics; recent publications include *Contemporary Irish Women Poets: Memory and Estrangement* (2015), *Poetry by Women in Ireland 1870-1970: A Critical Anthology* (2012) and a co-edited collection of essays

Aberration in Modern Poetry (2011). She has published widely on individual poets from Ireland, Britain and America and has a particular interest in gender issues and in ecocriticism. A co-edited anthology, *The Irish Poet and the Natural World: An Anthology of Verse in English from the Tudors to the Romantics*, was published by Cork University Press in 2014.

GERALD DAWE was educated at the University of Ulster, Coleraine, and the National University of Ireland, Galway. He is the author of nine collections of poetry, most recently, *Selected Poems* (2012) and *Mickey Finn's Air* (2014). His other publications include *The Proper Word: Collected Criticism, Ireland, Poetry, Politics* (2007) and *Of War and War's Alarms: Reflections on Modern Irish Writing* (2015). He has edited several anthologies of Irish poetry and criticism, including *Earth Voices Whispering: Irish War Poetry 1914–1945* (2008) and is currently working on *Elbow Room: Selected Prose* and editing *The Cambridge Companion to Irish Poets*. He is Professor of English and fellow of Trinity College Dublin.

PÉTER DOLMÁNYOS is associate professor at the Department of English Studies of Eszterházy Károly University, Eger, Hungary. He earned his Ph.D. at Eötvös Loránd University in Budapest in 2007. His research interests focus on a variety of aspects of contemporary Irish literature, including on Seamus Heaney, Derek Mahon, John Montague and Roddy Doyle, publishing work in *The Eger Journal of English Studies* and other forums in Hungary and abroad.

KATIE DONOVAN was born in 1962 and spent her youth on a farm near Camolin in Co. Wexford. She studied at Trinity College Dublin and at the University of California at Berkeley. She worked for *The Irish Times* for 13 years as a journalist. She was Writer-in-Residence for Dun Laoghaire/Rathdown 2006–8 and has taught many courses (in Media and Contemporary Irish Literature as well as Creative Writing) in IADT Dun Laoghaire (2006–13) and she currently teaches Creative Writing at NUI Maynooth. She has published four books of poetry, including *Entering the Mare* and *The Day of the Dead*, all with Bloodaxe Books. Her fifth, *Off-Duty*, was published by Bloodaxe in September 2016.

THOMAS KINSELLA was born in Dublin in 1928. His many collections of poems include: *Another September* (Dolmen, 1958); *Butcher's Dozen* (Dublin, Peppercanister, 1972); *Fifteen Dead* (Dolmen, Peppercanister, 1979); *Nightwalker and Other Poems* (Dolmen, Oxford, New York, Oxford University Press, 1968; New York, Knopf, 1969); *Peppercanister Poems 1972-1978* (Dolmen 1979; Winston Salem NC, Wake Forest University Press, 1979); *St Catherine's Clock* (Oxford University Press, 1987); *Poems From City Centre* (Oxford University Press, 1990); *Madonna and Other Poems* (Peppercanister, 1991); *Love Joy Peace* (Peppercanister, 2012); and *Fat Master* (Peppercanister, 2012). His awards and honours include Guggenheim Fellowships, the Denis Devlin Memorial Award, the Irish Arts Council Triennial Book Award and honorary doctorates from the University of Turin and the National University of Ireland. In 2007 Thomas Kinsella was awarded the Freedom of the City of Dublin. He lived and worked in the USA for many years and currently lives in Philadelphia.

MICHAEL LONGLEY (b. 1939, Belfast) is a central figure in contemporary Irish poetry. A forceful figure within the Arts Council of Northern Ireland, where he founded the literary programme, he is one of the 200 distinguished artists who are members of Aosdána. He is also a Fellow of the Royal Society of Literature and a recipient of the Queen's Gold Medal for Poetry and the Wilfred Owen Award. In addition, he has won the Whitbread Prize, the T.S. Eliot Prize, the Hawthornden Prize, the Irish Times Irish Literature Prize for Poetry and the Librex Montale Prize. He was made a CBE in the Queen's Birthday honours 2010.

PAULA MEEHAN was born in Dublin where she still lives. Besides six award-winning poetry collections she has also written plays for both adults and children. She has conducted residencies in universities, in prisons, in the wider community, and her poems and plays have been translated into many languages, including Irish. Recent collections are *Dharmakaya* and *Painting Rain*, from Carcanet Press, Manchester and from Wake Forest University Press, North Carolina. *Music for Dogs*, a collection of award-winning radio plays is available from Dedalus Press who have also reissued *Mysteries of the Home*, a selection of seminal work from the 1980s and 1990s.

JOHN MONTAGUE was born in Brooklyn in 1929 and educated in Northern Ireland, Dublin and the US. His major poetry publications include *The Rough Field, The Great Cloak, Mount Eagle* and *Smashing the Piano*. His *New Collected Poems* were published by Gallery Press in 2012. He is a winner of the Marten Toonder Award in 1977, a Guggenheim fellowship in 1980, and the Ireland Funds Literary Award in 1995. In 1998 John Montague became the first Ireland Professor of Poetry, and in 2010 the French State honoured him as a Chevalier de la Légion d'Honneur. He is also the author of the story collections *An Occasion of Sin* (1992) and *Death of a Chieftain* (1964), as well as the novella *The Lost Notebook* (1987), the essay collection *The Figure in the Cave* (1989), and the memoirs *Company* (2001) and *Born in Brooklyn* (1991). John Montague is a member of Aosdána and shares his time between homes in Cork and Nice.

SINEAD MORRISSEY was born in 1972 in Co. Armagh and grew up in Belfast. She is the author of five poetry collections: *There Was Fire in Vancouver, Between Here and There, The State of the Prisons, Through the Square Window* and *Parallax*. She has won the Irish Times Poetry Prize twice, and was the recipient of the T S Eliot Prize in 2013. Her other awards include a Lannan Literary Fellowship, First Prize in the UK National Poetry Competition and the E M Forster Award from the American Academy of Arts and Letters. She is Professor of Creative Writing at the Seamus Heaney Centre, Queen's University, Belfast.

PAUL MULDOON was born in County Armagh in 1951. He now lives in New York. A former radio and television producer for the BBC in Belfast, he has taught at Princeton University for almost thirty years. He is the author of twelve collections of poetry including *Moy Sand and Gravel*, for which he won the 2003 Pulitzer Prize. His most recent book is *Selected Poems 1968–2014*.

THOMAS McCARTHY is from County Waterford. He studied in UCC under John Montague, received the Patrick Kavanagh Award in 1977 for his first collection, and is a recipient of the Lannan Foundation's Literary Award. He has published nine volumes of poetry, and several books of non-fiction and criticism. He lives in Cork.

MEDBH McGUCKIAN was born in 1950 in Belfast where she continues to live. She has been Writer-in-Residence at Queen's University, Belfast, the University of Ulster, Coleraine, and Trinity College, Dublin, and was Visiting Fellow at the University of California, Berkeley. She has won The Cheltenham Award, The Rooney Prize, the Bass Ireland Award for Literature, the Denis Devlin Award, the Alice Hunt Bartlett Prize, and, in 2002, The Forward Prize for Best Poem. Her poetry collections include *Captain Lavender*, *The Currach Requires No Harbours* and *Blaris Moor*. She is a member of Aosdána.

NIGEL McLOUGHLIN was born in Enniskillen in 1968. In 2005 he moved to take up post at the University of Gloucestershire where he is now Professor of Creativity & Poetics. He has published five poetry collections and written many contributions to creative writing pedagogy. As well as guest editing and reviewing for a number of literary journals, McLoughlin is Editor of *Iota* magazine. He co-edited *Breaking the Skin: Twenty-First Century Irish Writing* (Black Mountain Press, 2002).

CHRISTINE MURRAY lives in Dublin. She has published a number of volumes, including a small collection of 'Cycles' and interdependent poems *Cycles* (Lapwing Press, 2013), *She,* a book-length single poem (Oneiros Books, March 2014) and *The Blind* (Oneiros Books, 2013). She has published two chapbooks *Three Red Things* (Smithereens Press, 2013) and *Signature* (Bone Orchard Press, 2014). She is curator of the Poethead poetry blog.

EILÉAN NÍ CHUILLEANÁIN was born in Cork City in 1942, educated there and at Oxford before spending her working life as an academic in Trinity College, Dublin. She was a founder member of *Cyphers* literary journal. She has won the Patrick Kavanagh Award, the *Irish Times* Award for Poetry, the O'Shaughnessy Award of the Irish-American Cultural Institute which called her 'among the very best poets of her generation', and the International Griffin Poetry Prize. Her most recent collection is *The Boys of Bluehill* (Gallery Press, 2015). Eiléan Ní Chuilleanáin is a Fellow and Professor of English (Emerita) at Trinity College, Dublin and a member of Aosdána. In 2016 she was appointed as the new Professor of Irish Poetry.

NUALA NÍ DHOMHNAILL was born in 1952 and grew up in the Irish-speaking areas of West Kerry and in Tipperary. She studied English and Irish at University College, Cork in 1969 and became part of a group of Irish language poets who were published in the literary magazine *Innti.* She now lives in Dublin. She has published four collections of poems in Irish, *An Dealg Droighin* (1981), *Féar Suaithinseach* (1984), *Feis* (1991) and *Cead Aighnis* (1998). The Gallery Press has published four collections of her poems, with translations into English, *Pharaoh's Daughter* (1990, translations by 13 writers), *The Astrakhan Cloak* (1992, translations by Paul Muldoon), *The Water Horse* (1999, translations by Medbh McGuckian and Eiléan Ní Chuilleanáin) and *The Fifty Minute Mermaid* (2007, translations by Paul Muldoon). She held the Heimbold Chair in Irish Studies at Villanova University in 2001 and has taught at Boston College and New York University. She has received many scholarships, prizes, and bursaries and has also won numerous international awards for works which have been translated into French, German, Polish, Italian, Norwegian, Estonian, Turkish, Japanese and English. She is a member of Aosdána and was Ireland Professor of Poetry (2001–2004) and the first Professor of Irish (language) Poetry.

JEAN O'BRIEN has published four poetry collections including *Dangerous Dresses*. Her fifth and latest is *New & Selected: Fish on a Bicycle* (Salmon, 2016). She was a founder member of the Dublin Writers' Workshop. She holds a MPhil in Creative Writing from Trinity College, Dublin and has taught widely including at the Dublin Writers' Centre. She was also Writer in Residence for Laois in 2005. Among her awards are the Fish International Poetry Prize 2008 and The Arvon International Poetry award, which she won for her poem 'Merman'. She has citations in many other competitions, including the Forward Prize 2014. She currently lives in Dublin after an eight year stint in the Irish Midlands.

NESSA O'MAHONY was born in Dublin in 1964. She completed a PhD in Creative Writing at Bangor University, North Wales, in 2006. She has published four volumes of poetry, the most recent being *Her Father's Daughter* (Salmon Poetry, 2014). She is the recipient of two artists' bursaries from The Arts Council.

MARY ROBINSON is the first woman President of Ireland (1990–1997), a former United Nations High Commissioner for Human Rights (1997–2002), and founder and President of Realizing Rights: The Ethical Globalization Initiative (2002–2010. As an academic (Trinity College Law Faculty 1968–90), legislator (Member of the Irish Senate 1969–89) and barrister (Irish Bar 1967–90, Senior Counsel 1980; called to the English Bar 1973) she sought to use law as an instrument for social change, arguing landmark cases before the European Court of Human Rights and the European Court in Luxembourg as well as in the Irish courts. A committed European, she also served on expert European Community and Irish parliamentary committees. The recipient of numerous honours and awards throughout the world including the Presidential Medal of Freedom from President Obama, Mary Robinson is a member of the Elders, former Chair of the Council of Women World Leaders and a member of the Club of Madrid. She serves on several boards including the European Climate Foundation, the Mo Ibrahim Foundation, and is a member of the Royal Irish Academy and the American Philosophical Society.

GERARD SMYTH was born in Dublin in 1951. His first volume of poems, *The Flags Are Quiet*, was published in 1969. His most recent volume, *A Song of Elsewhere*, was published by Dedalus in 2015. He worked as a journalist with *The Irish Times*, and on his retirement took on the role of that newspaper's poetry editor. He was elected a member of Aosdána in 2009 and in 2011 he received the O'Shaughnessy Poetry Award. He co-edited the anthology *If Ever You Go* in 2014.

COLM TÓIBÍN was born in Enniscorthy, County Wexford in 1955. He is a novelist, short story writer, essayist, playwright, journalist, critic and poet. He is the current Irene and Sidney B. Silverman Professor of the Humanities at Columbia University and professor of creative writing at the University of Manchester. He has received numerous awards, including the Dublin IMPAC Prize, the LA Times Novel of the Year, the Prix du Meilleur Livre and the Costa Novel of the Year.

EAMONN WALL teaches at the University of Missouri-St. Louis. He is a past-president of the American Conference of Irish Studies and author of *From the Sin-e Cafe to the Black Hills*, winner of the Michael J. Durkan Prize. He is the author of seven collections of poetry: *Junction City: New and Selected Poems 1990-2015* (2015); *Sailing Lake Mareotis* (2011); *A Tour of Your Country* (2008); *Refuge at De Soto Bend* (2004); *The*

Crosses (2000); *Iron Mountain Road* (1997); *Dyckman-200th Street* (1994), all published by Salmon Poetry.

This volume would not have happened were it not for the assistance of a number of people. Thanks first to Alan Hayes of Arlen House, for his imaginative embracing of the project in the first place and for all his help with its production.

We would like to thank Michael Schmidt for his generous permission to include quotations from Eavan Boland's poetry and prose published in various Carcanet publications including: *Outside History* (1990); *In a Time of Violence* (1994); *Object Lessons: The Life of the Woman and the Poet in Our Times* (1995); *The Lost Land* (1998); *New Collected Poems* (2005); *Domestic Violence* (2007); *Eavan Boland: A Sourcebook* (2007); *A Journey With Two Maps: Becoming a Woman Poet* (2011); *Eavan Boland: A Poet's Dublin* (2014); *A Woman Without a Country* (2014). We are also grateful for his permission to publish Colm Toibín's essay, an earlier version of which was published in *The PN Review*, 220, Vol 41, No. 2 (Nov-Dec 2014).

We would like to thank the following publishers for permission to publish quotations from Eavan Boland's poetry from the following collections: *New Territory* (Dublin, Alan Figgis, 1967); *The War Horse* (London, Victor Gollancz, 1975); *In Her Own Image* (Dublin, Arlen House, 1980); *Night Feed* (Dublin, Arlen House, 1982); *The Journey and Other Poems* (Dublin, Arlen House, 1986, Manchester, Carcanet, 1987); *New Collected Poems* (New York, Norton, 2008).

We are particularly grateful to Jody Allen Randolph and Paula Meehan for their advice and assistance throughout the project.

We are also grateful to Diana Copperwhite for her permission to use *Fake New World* as the cover image for this volume.

Our deep appreciation is due to each of the contributors for their swift and generous response to our request for essays and poems. We would like to acknowledge the following permissions granted:

'Wedded' is taken from *That Which is Suddenly Precious: New & Selected Poems* by Dermot Bolger, reproduced by permission of the author.

Moya Cannon's poem 'Finger-fluting in Moon Milk', reproduced by permission of the author, first appeared in 'The Goose' – an online journal for the association for literature, environment and culture in Canada (ALECC).

'Doors', by Katie Donovan, reproduced with the permission of the author. This poem also appears in *Off Duty* (Bloodaxe, 2016).

This version of 'The Hebrides', by Michael Longley, is taken from the Belfast Group website http://belfastgroup.digitalsch olarship.emory.edu/groupsheets/longley1_10316/#longley1_1 0315 and appears with the permission of the author.

'The Extremely Young Age of all Sea Floor', by Medbh McGuckian is reproduced by permission of the author.

'It is all I ever wanted', by Paula Meehan, is reproduced by permission of the author. It appears in *Dharmakaya* (Carcanet Press, 2000).

'Táimid Damanta, a Dheirféaracha', by Nuala Ní Dhomhnaill and its translation 'We are Damned, My Sisters' by Michael Hartnett are taken from *Rógha Dánta* (New Island) by Nuala Ní Dhomhnaill, are reproduced by permission of the author and publisher.

'Resonance', by Jean O'Brien, is published with permission from the author.

'Sibyl's Morning' by John Montague, first published in *Mount*

Eagle and appearing in *New Collected Poems*, Oldcastle, Co. Meath, Gallery Books, 2012, is published with permission from the author.

'Putsch' by Paul Muldoon, is published with permission from the author.

'The Mayfly' by Sinead Morrissey, is published with permission from the author.

'Westland Row' by Thomas Kinsella, in *Collected Poems*, Manchester, Carcanet, 2001, is published with permission from the author.

'Role Reversal' by Nessa O'Mahony, is published with permission from Salmon Poetry.

We are also grateful to the editors of the following journals and websites for permission to reproduce quotations. *College English, Icarus, Irish University Review, New Hibernia Review, Poetic Orphanage, The Poetry Foundation.*

INDEX